graphis annual 82|83

82|83

graphis annual

The International Annual of Advertising and
Editorial Graphics

Das internationale Jahrbuch der Werbe-
graphik und der redaktionellen Graphik

Le répertoire international de l'art graphique
publicitaire et rédactionnel

Edited by / Herausgegeben von / Réalisé par:

Walter Herdeg

Graphis Press Corp., Zurich (Switzerland)

GRAPHIS PUBLICATIONS

GRAPHIS, International bi-monthly journal of graphic art and applied art
PHOTOGRAPHIS, The international annual of advertising and editorial photography
GRAPHIS POSTERS, The international annual of poster art
GRAPHIS PACKAGING VOL. 3, An international survey of package design
CHILDREN'S BOOK ILLUSTRATION VOL. 3, VOL. 4, An international survey of children's book illustration
GRAPHIS DIAGRAMS, The graphic visualization of abstract data
FILM + TV GRAPHICS 2, An international survey of the art of film animation
ARCHIGRAPHIA, Architectural and environmental graphics
GRAPHIS EPHEMERA, Artists' Self-Promotion

GRAPHIS-PUBLIKATIONEN

GRAPHIS, Die internationale Zweimonatsschrift für Graphik und angewandte Kunst
PHOTOGRAPHIS, Das internationale Jahrbuch der Werbephotographie und der redaktionellen Photographie
GRAPHIS POSTERS, Das internationale Jahrbuch der Plakatkunst
GRAPHIS PACKUNGEN BAND 3, Internationales Handbuch der Packungsgestaltung
KINDERBUCH-ILLUSTRATION BAND 3, BAND 4, Eine internationale Übersicht über die Kinderbuch-Illustration
GRAPHIS DIAGRAMS, Die graphische Visualisierung abstrakter Gegebenheiten
FILM + TV GRAPHICS 2, Ein internationaler Überblick über die Kunst des Animationsfilms
ARCHIGRAPHIA, Architektur- und Umweltgraphik
GRAPHIS EPHEMERA, Künstler-Eigenwerbung

PUBLICATIONS GRAPHIS

GRAPHIS, La revue bimestrielle internationale d'arts graphiques et d'arts appliqués
PHOTOGRAPHIS, Le répertoire international de la photographie publicitaire et rédactionnelle
GRAPHIS POSTERS, Le répertoire international de l'art de l'affiche
GRAPHIS EMBALLAGES VOL. 3, Répertoire international des formes de l'emballage
ILLUSTRATIONS DE LIVRES D'ENFANTS VOL. 3, VOL. 4, Un aperçu international des illustrations de livres d'enfants
GRAPHIS DIAGRAMS, La visualisation graphique de données abstraites
FILM + TV GRAPHICS 2, Un panorama international de l'art du film d'animation
ARCHIGRAPHIA, La création graphique appliquée à l'architecture et à l'environnement
GRAPHIS EPHEMERA, Autopromotion des artistes

Distributors / Auslieferung / Distribution:

USA: HASTINGS HOUSE, PUBLISHERS, INC., 10 E. 40th St., New York, N.Y. 10016 – **(ISBN: 8038-2720-2)**
CANADA: HURTIG PUBLISHERS, 10560-105 Street, Edmonton, Alberta T5H 2W7, tel. (403) 426-2469
FRANCE: GRAPHIS DISTRIBUTION, Milon-la-Chapelle, F-78470 St-Rémy-lès-Chevreuse, tél. 052-13-26
ITALIA: INTER-ORBIS, Via Lorenteggio, 31/1, I-20146 Milano, tel. 422 57 46
SPAIN: COMERCIAL ATHENEUM, S.A., Consejo de Ciento, 130-136, Barcelona 15, tel. 223 14 51-3
AMERICA LATINA, AUSTRALIA, JAPAN AND OTHER ASIAN COUNTRIES, AFRICA:
FLEETBOOKS S.A., c/o Feffer & Simons, Inc., 100 Park Avenue, New York, N.Y. 10017, tel. (212) 686-0888

All other countries / Alle anderen Länder / Tout autres pays:

GRAPHIS PRESS CORP., 107 Dufourstrasse, CH-8008 Zurich (Switzerland)

PUBLICATION No. 168 (ISBN 3-85709-182-7)

Contents   Inhalt   Sommaire

Abbreviations   Abkürzungen   Abréviations

English		German		French	
Argentina	ARG	Argentinien	ARG	Afrique du Sud	SAF
Australia	AUS	Australien	AUS	Allemagne occidentale	GER
Austria	AUT	Belgien	BEL	Argentine	ARG
Belgium	BEL	Brasilien	BRA	Australie	AUS
Brazil	BRA	Bulgarien	BUL	Autriche	AUT
Bulgaria	BUL	Dänemark	DEN	Belgique	BEL
Canada	CAN	Deutschland (BRD)	GER	Brésil	BRA
Columbia	COL	Finnland	FIN	Bulgarie	BUL
Cuba	CUB	Frankreich	FRA	Canada	CAN
Czechoslovakia	CSR	Grossbritannien	GBR	Colombie	COL
Denmark	DEN	Hongkong	HKG	Cuba	CUB
Finland	FIN	Indien	IND	Danemark	DEN
France	FRA	Iran	IRN	Espagne	SPA
Germany (West)	GER	Irland	IRL	Etats-Unis	USA
Great Britain	GBR	Israel	ISR	Finlande	FIN
Hong Kong	HKG	Italien	ITA	France	FRA
India	IND	Japan	JPN	Grande-Bretagne	GBR
Iran	IRN	Kanada	CAN	Hongkong	HKG
Ireland	IRL	Kolumbien	COL	Inde	IND
Israel	ISR	Kuba	CUB	Iran	IRN
Italy	ITA	Kuweit	KUW	Irlande	IRL
Japan	JPN	Mexiko	MEX	Israël	ISR
Kuwait	KUW	Niederlande	NLD	Italie	ITA
Mexico	MEX	Norwegen	NOR	Japon	JPN
Netherlands	NLD	Österreich	AUT	Koweit	KUW
Norway	NOR	Polen	POL	Mexique	MEX
Poland	POL	Schweden	SWE	Norvège	NOR
South Africa	SAF	Schweiz	SWI	Pays-Bas	NLD
Spain	SPA	Spanien	SPA	Pologne	POL
Sweden	SWE	Südafrika	SAF	Suède	SWE
Switzerland	SWI	Tschechoslowakei	CSR	Suisse	SWI
USA	USA	USA	USA	Tchécoslovaquie	CSR
Venezuela	VEN	Venezuela	VEN	Venezuela	VEN

Cover Design/Umschlag/Couverture: André François

In the introduction to this volume Stanley Mason praises the continuity of graphic design, the steady development and constantly high quality of the best work since the first issue of this annual appeared thirty years ago. We too would like to extend our thanks for constancy in a slightly different connection – that with which our contributors have continued to send in their best work year by year.

Im Vorwort zu diesem Band lobt Stanley Mason die Kontinuität in der Leistung der Graphik-Designer, die konstante Entwicklung und gleichbleibend hohe Qualität der Arbeiten seit dem Erscheinen der ersten Ausgabe dieses Jahrbuches vor dreissig Jahren. Wir möchten allen an dieser Stelle unseren herzlichen Dank für die Beständigkeit aussprechen, mit der sie Jahr für Jahr ihre Arbeiten für GRAPHIS ANNUAL eingeschickt haben.

Dans la préface qu'il a écrite pour cet ouvrage, Stanley Mason souligne la continuité et le niveau élevé de la création graphique de qualité depuis la première édition de notre annuel il y a 30 ans. Nous aimerions remercier ici vivement tous les artistes publicitaires qui ont bien voulu, avec une constance qui leur fait honneur, nous faire parvenir régulièrement leurs travaux pour que nous puissions les inclure dans GRAPHIS ANNUAL.

ANDRÉ FRANÇOIS, who designed our dust jacket, is well known to readers of GRAPHIS (see Nos. 106 and 205). His covers for *The New Yorker*, his campaigns for the *Nouvel Observateur* and Air France, his posters for the town of Evry, French Railways, UNESCO, ICOGRADA and so forth, his illustrations for the poems of Raymond Queneau and the exhibitions of his paintings and sculptures have demonstrated his versatility to a wide and appreciative public. Today he devotes himself chiefly to his painting, though he continues to carry out occasional graphic design commissions.

ANDRÉ FRANÇOIS, von dem der Umschlag zu diesem Buch stammt, wird nicht nur jedem GRAPHIS-Leser (s. Nr. 106 und 205) wohlbekannt sein. Seien es Umschläge für den *New Yorker*, Kampagnen für den *Nouvel Observateur*, die Air France, Plakate für die Stadt Evry, die französischen Staatsbahnen, UNESCO und ICOGRADA (um nur einige zu nennen), ein Gedichtband von Raymond Queneau oder Ausstellungen seiner Bilder und Plastiken – überall begegnet man den Werken dieses vielseitigen Künstlers. Heute widmet er sich fast ausschliesslich der Malerei und arbeitet nur noch gelegentlich als Gebrauchsgraphiker.

ANDRÉ FRANÇOIS, qui a réalisé la couverture du présent ouvrage, n'est pas connu que des lecteurs de GRAPHIS (voir les nos 106, 205). Qu'il s'agisse de couvertures du *New Yorker*, de campagnes pour le *Nouvel Observateur*, pour Air France, d'affiches pour la ville d'Evry, la S.N.C.F., l'UNESCO ou l'ICOGRADA, d'un recueil de poésies de Raymond Queneau ou d'expositions de ses tableaux et sculptures – les œuvres de cet artiste polyvalent s'imposent à nous un peu partout. Il se consacre aujourd'hui presque exclusivement à la peinture et ne revient qu'occasionnellement à la création publicitaire.

Stanley Mason

STANLEY MASON was born in Alberta, Canada, in 1917,
studied English at Oxford and later moved to Switzerland,
where he has worked as a teacher, translator and magazine
editor. A long-standing member of the GRAPHIS staff, he has
also translated many books on art and cultural subjects and
has published an English course and a book of verse.

Preface

This publication has now appeared regularly for thirty years. To many readers the difference
from one volume to the next may seem minimal, as though hardly anything were changing in
the field of graphic design. This impression is misleading, for change is continuous and the
small steps it takes in a year are not always very conspicuous. It is the same with the people
around us: if we see them almost daily, they do not seem to alter much; but a comparison of a
ten-year-old photograph with the present reality at once unmasks the transformation of time.
Archaeologists know the same phenomenon in a different setting: if you walk across a corn-
field, there is nothing to see but a uniform expanse; take a helicopter and fly over it, and it may
well reveal quite clearly the outlines of an ancient Roman fortress.

Those who take the trouble to look back at the first volume of GRAPHIS ANNUAL, which
appeared in 1952, are probably in for a surprise. They will see that the work of graphic designers
even in those far-off days was already skilled and sophisticated; but the surprise is more likely
to be triggered by a decorative grace, a light-fingered and poetical playfulness that we had
not really associated with those dour post-war years. The work in the present volume is by
comparison stronger, more dynamic, and full of a greater variety of approaches.

But the point that deserves making lies less in the changes that have come about in thirty
years than in the continuity that underlies them. Graphic design has progressed steadily in our
own age, its best exponents maintaining a constant standard of excellence, so that many
works produced thirty years ago, even if we see them through a faint veil of nostalgic antiqua-
tion, still appear good and adapted to their purpose and worthy of admiration.

Just how astonishing this constancy is comes out when we consider what has happened to
fine art in the same period. Around 1950 Abstract Expressionism, a proof in itself that traditional art had lost its bearings, was in its last throes in the works of de Kooning. The way
beyond was not clear. Clifford Still and Barnett Newman put their hope in a new simplicity, a
movement that culminated in the Rothko Chapel of Rice University, where subjectless and
formless panels invite transcendental meditation and seem to imply art's final apotheosis. A
branch of the same line led to the Minimalists, of whom it has been whispered that "rarely has
anyone who had nothing to say said it with such force and clarity", to the targets and washed-
out flags of Jasper Johns. Op Art withdrew from the scene into the decorative world of patterns, Pop Art tried to get back into life by accepting the daily bric-à-brac of a consumer
society, with an apogee in Warhol's picture of 200 identical soup cans. While Robert Rauschenberg and Claes Oldenburg were trying out three-dimensional whimsies, Roy Lichtenstein
looked for salvation in glorified comic strips. Other people tried to get things moving by
building objects that were stirred by the wind or driven by electric motors. Before long a heap
of bricks strewn over the ground could be declared art—provided that it appeared in a
museum, since in a builder's yard it would only have been taken as evidence of disorderliness
on the part of some bricklayer. To escape from the dominion of the museum, other artists
began to formulate their concepts in the environment, as with Robert Smithson's *Spiral Jetty*
in the Great Salt Lake, since swallowed without comment by the rising waters.

All this is not quoted to make fun of fine art today, which is obviously at the end of an era, and
a pretty dead end at that; but to show that change has here been headlong and incessant. The
despairing attempts to say something meaningful have become a rout, and we seem not far
removed from the time when isms will be wasms almost before they can be recognized, and
when, as Andy Warhol has so nicely put it, everybody will be famous for fifteen minutes.

What a contrast to all this is the continuity of graphic design! Many fine artists, and many
believers in fine art, still continue to sneer at graphic design on the grounds that it is merely
commercial, or merely utilitarian. It might be retorted that most of the art of the past was
utilitarian, commissioned for definite purposes in days when there was no photography and
pictures were widely needed. As for commercialism, fine art today has become if anything
more commercialized than graphic design, with art dealers building up their stables of artists
and contriving markets in which astronomic sums of money change hands.

It must of course be admitted that much work that comes under the heading of graphic design has few artistic pretensions. It is merely the sober tool of those who have something to communicate or something to sell. Even so, there is a good deal of design that is of artistic value, and that is also a valid and serious expression of our age in a way in which Smithson's jetty or Oldenburg's *Clothespin* cannot really be said to be serious. What is more, the productions of graphic design are not directed to a museum-going elite but are getting over daily to the general public of the second half of the twentieth century.

It may well be that in fifty years' time the distinction between fine and applied art will already have become a historical or at least an academic one. There are already artists who move happily in both spheres, and Roman Cieslewicz, for instance, can say: "I cannot remember a single moment at which my work has been influenced by the requirements of a client to the detriment of my personal researches. I make no distinction between my studio work and my so-called commercial graphic work."

The arguments set forth here would therefore be pointless except as a plea for more generous recognition of the achievements of graphic design. The arrows and anonymous figures of Jean Michel Folon, the vegetables of Tadashi Ohashi, the strange but memorable beasts of André François – to take only three examples, all of them once more represented in the pages of the present volume – have given more people more pleasure over the years than the products of most fine artists, and they surely deserve an accolade for it.

Certain changes can be gathered merely from the distribution of work in this annual without looking at individual styles, and one of the most encouraging is the recent increase in the number of illustrations, especially those from American newspapers. Illustration has always been a step-sister of the fine arts, and the growing acceptance by the press of a visual – and often highly imaginative – complement to the word inspires the hope that before long fine art will come down off its crumbling pedestal and commissioned art will come up from its basement, and both will become one voice speaking to the people – and to all of the people.

A similar dichotomy of course exists, or has existed, in other fields. In sport, for example, it is now becoming more and more difficult to separate the amateur from the professional. Among soldiers a difference used also to be made between those who fought for their lord or their country and those who were only mercenaries; and mention of the latter recalls the lines – perhaps not wholly irrelevant here – from A. E. Housman's epitaph on an army of them:

> Their shoulders held the sky suspended;
> They stood, and earth's foundations stay;
> What God abandoned, these defended,
> And saved the sum of things for pay.

Stanley Mason

STANLEY MASON wurde 1917 in Alberta, Kanada, geboren.
Er studierte Englisch in Oxford und zog später in die Schweiz,
wo er als Lehrer, Übersetzer und Redakteur von Zeitschriften
arbeitete. Er ist seit langem Mitglied der GRAPHIS-Redaktion
und hat ebenfalls zahlreiche Bücher über Kunst und Kultur
übersetzt, sowie einen Englisch-Lehrgang und einen
Gedichtband veröffentlicht.

Vorwort

Dieses Jahrbuch erscheint nun seit dreissig Jahren. Vielen Lesern wird der Unterschied
zwischen zwei aufeinanderfolgenden Ausgaben minimal erscheinen, als wenn sich auf dem
Gebiet des Graphik-Design kaum etwas ändern würde. Dieser Eindruck ist irreführend, denn
es gibt einen fortwährenden Wandel, aber die kleinen Schritte, in denen er sich während eines
Jahres vollzieht, sind nicht sehr spektakulär. Es ist wie mit den Menschen unserer Umgebung:
wenn wir sie fast täglich sehen, scheinen sie sich kaum zu verändern; aber ein Vergleich einer
zehn Jahre alten Photographie mit der gegenwärtigen Realität macht den Wandel durch die
Zeit sofort sichtbar. Archäologen kennen dieses Phänomen in einem anderen Zusammenhang:
wenn man durch ein Kornfeld geht, sieht man nichts als die ebenmässige Weite des Feldes;
überfliegt man es aber mit einem Hubschrauber, lassen sich möglicherweise sehr deutlich
die Umrisse einer alten römischen Festung erkennen.

Wer sich die Mühe macht, die 1952 erschienene erste Ausgabe von GRAPHIS ANNUAL wieder
einmal durchzuschauen, wird wahrscheinlich eine Überraschung erleben. Man wird feststellen,
dass die Arbeiten der Graphik-Designer sogar zu jener Zeit bereits gekonnt und anspruchsvoll
waren; die eigentliche Überraschung aber liegt in der dekorativen Anmut, einer leichthändigen,
poetischen Verspieltheit, die wir in jenen schweren Nachkriegsjahren wohl nicht vermutet
hätten. Im Vergleich dazu sind die Arbeiten im vorliegenden Band stärker, dynamischer
und vielseitiger von der Idee her.

Es sind aber weniger die Veränderungen während der letzten dreissig Jahre, die unsere
Aufmerksamkeit verdienen, als vielmehr die Kontinuität, die sich durch diese Periode verfolgen
lässt. Die Entwicklung im Graphik-Design ist beständig, seine besten Vertreter haben einen
gleichbleibend hervorragenden Standard beibehalten, so dass viele Arbeiten, die vor dreissig
Jahren entstanden – auch wenn wir sie durch einen Schleier der Nostalgie sehen – noch
immer gut sind, ihrem Zweck entsprechen und hohe Anerkennung verdienen.

Wie erstaunlich diese Kontinuität eigentlich ist, wird deutlich, wenn man sich vergegenwärtigt,
was sich in der bildenden Kunst im gleichen Zeitraum abspielte. Um 1950 lag der abstrakte
Expressionismus – der an sich ein Beweis ist, dass die traditionelle Kunst ihre Richtung
verloren hat – in den Bildern De Koonings in den letzten Zügen. Der Weg heraus war nicht
klar. Clifford Still und Barnett Newman setzten ihre Hoffnung in eine neue Einfachheit, eine
Richtung, die in der Rothko-Kapelle der Rice-Universität ihren Höhepunkt findet, wo Flächen
ohne Inhalt und Form zur transzendentalen Meditation einladen, als scheinbar endgültige
Apotheose der Kunst. Aus der gleichen Richtung kamen die Minimalisten, von denen jemand
meinte, dass «kaum jemand, der nichts zu sagen hat, es je mit soviel Kraft und Klarheit gesagt
hat», sowie auch die Zielscheiben und ausgewaschenen Flaggen von Jasper Johns. Op Art
zog sich zurück in die dekorative Welt des Gemusterten. Pop Art versuchte es mit den alltäg-
lichen Gebrauchsgegenständen der Konsumgesellschaft, was in Warhols Bild von 200 iden-
tischen Suppendosen gipfelte. Während Robert Rauschenberg und Claes Oldenburg sich in
dreidimensionalen Fantasiegebilden versuchten, sah Roy Lichtenstein die Lösung in glori-
fizierten Comics. Andere versuchten es mit der Konstruktion von Objekten, die vom Wind oder
von elektrischen Motoren bewegt wurden. Ein Haufen Ziegelsteine, auf dem Boden verstreut,
konnte vor kurzem noch als Kunst bezeichnet werden – vorausgesetzt, dass der Ort des
Geschehens ein Museum war, denn im Hof einer Baufirma hätte man dies wohl eher als die
Unordnung eines Maurers gedeutet. Um der Macht der Museen zu entkommen, begannen
andere Künstler ihre Konzepte in die Landschaft zu tragen, wie z. B. Robert Smithson mit
seiner *Spiral Jetty* (Spiral-Pier) im Great Salt Lake, der inzwischen kommentarlos von den
Wellen verschlungen wurde.

Dies alles wird nicht angeführt, um sich über die heutige Kunst lustig zu machen – sie ist
offenbar am Ende einer Ära angelangt – es soll vielmehr gezeigt werden, dass die Veränderungen manchmal abrupt und unablässig stattfanden. Die verzweifelten Versuche, etwas
Bedeutendes zu sagen, wurden zu einer wilden Flucht, und wir scheinen nicht weit entfernt
von einer Zeit zu sein, in der Richtungen, sobald sie erkennbar werden, bereits der Ver-

gangenheit angehören, einer Zeit, in der, wie Andy Warhol so schön gesagt hat, jeder für 15 Minuten berühmt sein wird.

Was für ein Kontrast zu all diesem ist die Kontinuität des Graphik-Design! Viele Künstler und viele Liebhaber der Kunst betrachten das Graphik-Design immer noch abfällig, weil es aus rein kommerziellen oder aus Gründen der Nützlichkeit entstanden ist. Man kann dem entgegnen, dass der grösste Teil der Kunst in der Vergangenheit ebenfalls utilitarisch war, für bestimmte Zwecke in Auftrag gegeben, als es noch keine Photographie gab und Bilder gebraucht wurden. Was die Kommerzialisierung angeht, so ist die Kunst heute kommerzieller als Graphik-Design, ziehen sich doch allerorts Kunsthändler einen Rennstall von Künstlern heran und tun Märkte auf, in denen astronomische Summen Geldes den Besitzer wechseln.

Natürlich muss man zugeben, dass viele Arbeiten, die unter dem Namen Graphik-Design laufen, wenig Künstlerisches aufweisen. Sie sind das nüchterne Werkzeug jener, die etwas mitteilen oder verkaufen müssen. Dennoch ist ein grosser Teil des Graphik-Design und der Illustrationen künstlerisch wertvoll, und diese Graphik ist zudem ein gültiger und seriöser Ausdruck unserer Zeit, was sich von Smithsons Pier oder Oldenburgs *Clothespin* (Wäscheklammer) nicht mit der gleichen Überzeugung sagen lässt. Hinzu kommt, dass Graphik-Design nicht an eine elitäre Gruppe von Museumsbesuchern gerichtet ist, sondern täglich mit den gewöhnlichen Menschen der zweiten Hälfte des zwanzigsten Jahrhunderts in Berührung kommt.

Es ist gut möglich, dass in fünfzig Jahren die Unterscheidung zwischen freier und angewandter Kunst bereits zu einer historischen oder wenigstens akademischen Frage geworden ist. Es gibt bereits Künstler, die sich in beiden Sphären zu Hause fühlen, und Roman Cieslewicz z. B. sagt: «Ich kann mich nicht an einen einzigen Moment erinnern, in dem meine Arbeit durch die Aufgabenstellung des Kunden zum Nachteil meiner persönlichen Experimente beeinflusst wurde. Ich mache zwischen meiner freien Atelier-Arbeit und meiner sogenannten kommerziellen Graphik keinen Unterschied.»

Die hier vorgetragenen Argumente wären sinnlos, würden sie nicht als Aufruf zu einer grosszügigeren Anerkennung der Leistungen auf dem Gebiet des Graphik-Design verstanden. Die Pfeile und anonymen Figuren von Jean Michel Folon, die Gemüse von Tadashi Ohashi, die seltsamen, denkwürdigen Geschöpfe von André François – um nur drei Künstler zu nennen, die wiederum auf den Seiten des vorliegenden Bandes vertreten sind – haben über Jahre mehr Leuten mehr Freude bereitet, als die Werke der meisten freien Künstler, und sie verdienen dafür Anerkennung.

Änderungen kann man allenfalls an der Aufteilung der Arbeiten in diesem Jahrbuch erkennen, ohne auf einen bestimmten Stil zu achten, und eine der erfreulichsten davon ist die seit kurzem steigende Anzahl von Illustrationen, besonders aus amerikanischen Zeitungen. Die Illustration war schon immer die Stiefschwester der Kunst, und die wachsende Anerkennung durch die Presse für diese visuelle – und oft äusserst einfallsreiche – Ergänzung zum Wort lässt hoffen, dass die freie Kunst über kurz oder lang von ihrem bröckelnden Sockel herabsteigen und die angewandte Kunst aus dem Untergeschoss aufsteigen wird, und dass beide zu einer Stimme werden, die zu den Menschen spricht – und zwar zu allen Menschen.

Stanley Mason

STANLEY MASON, né à Alberta (Canada) en 1917, a étudié
l'anglais à Oxford, puis s'est établi en Suisse, où il a été
professeur, traducteur et rédacteur de magazines. Membre de
longue date de l'équipe de GRAPHIS, ce fin lettré a traduit un
grand nombre d'ouvrages d'art et de civilisation et est l'auteur
d'un manuel d'anglais. Poète, il a publié un recueil de vers.

Préface

GRAPHIS ANNUAL paraît sans interruption depuis maintenant trente ans. D'une année à
l'autre, le lecteur peut avoir l'impression que les volumes se ressemblent à quelques dif-
férences près, comme si l'art publicitaire ne connaissait qu'un rythme de changement très lent.
C'est là une impression erronée, car ce rythme est continu, et les petits pas en lesquels il se
décompose chaque année n'apparaissent pas toujours évidents. Il en est de même des personnes qui composent notre entourage: en les rencontrant tous les jours, les transformations
qui s'opèrent en elles restent imperceptibles; pourtant, une photo vieille de dix ans nous
permet de voir l'ampleur du changement. Les archéologues connaissent le même phénomène
à une échelle différente: traversez un champ de blé, vous ne verrez qu'une marée ondulante
uniforme; mais survolez le même champ en hélicoptère, et les contours d'une ancienne forte-
resse romaine s'y dessineront.

De la même manière, celui ou celle qui entreprend de consulter l'annuel de 1952, le premier
volume de GRAPHIS ANNUAL paru, ira d'étonnement en étonnement. Les réalisations des
artistes publicitaires de l'époque étaient déjà soignées et sophistiquées; et surtout, elles
étaient investies d'une grâce décorative, d'un sens ludique fait d'affleurements et de poésie
qu'il nous est difficile d'associer aux austères années de l'immédiat après-guerre. En compa-
raison, les travaux réunis dans le présent volume respirent une vigueur accrue, davantage de
dynamisme, et une bien plus grande diversité des approches créatrices.

Toutefois, la continuité de l'évolution s'impose encore plus à notre attention que la somme
des changements intervenus. L'art publicitaire a connu une progression constante à notre
époque, et les meilleurs graphistes ont su maintenir un niveau de qualité inchangé, de sorte
que nombre de travaux réalisés il y a trente ans, une fois dissipé le voile de nostalgie rétro qui
nous en sépare, nous paraissent de bonne facture, parfaitement adaptés au but recherché et
dignes d'admiration.

Cette constance est d'autant plus admirable lorsqu'on la met en relief avec l'évolution qu'ont
connue les beaux-arts durant la même période. Vers 1950, l'expressionnisme abstrait, preuve
de la désorientation de l'art traditionnel, était lui-même en agonie dans les œuvres de Willem
de Kooning. Ce qui allait suivre était encore dans les limbes. Clifford Still et Barnett Newman
optèrent pour une nouvelle simplicité, mouvement qui devait culminer dans la Rothko Chapel
de l'Université Rice, où des panneaux sans sujet et sans forme invitent à la méditation trans-
cendantale et semblent signifier l'apothéose finale de l'art. Une autre branche de la même
tendance aboutit aux minimalistes, dont on a affirmé sous le manteau que «rarement quel-
qu'un qui n'avait rien à dire l'a dit avec tant de vigueur et de clarté», aux cibles et drapeaux
délavés de Jasper Johns. L'op art a quitté la scène pour le monde décoratif des patterns. Le
pop art tenta de rejoindre la vie réelle en incorporant tout le bric-à-brac quotidien de la société
de consommation, culminant dans le tableau de 200 boîtes de consommé identiques par
Warhol. Tandis que Robert Rauschenberg et Claes Oldenburg s'essayaient à des fantaisies
bizarroïdes en trois dimensions, Roy Lichtenstein cherchait le salut dans la bande dessinée
survoltée. D'autres artistes s'employèrent à créer le mouvement en construisant des objets
mus par le vent ou un moteur électrique. Bientôt, il fut possible de déclarer œuvre d'art un tas
de briques éparpillées à même le sol, à condition de procéder à l'opération dans un musée et
non pas sur un chantier, où l'artiste aurait été confondu avec un maçon négligent. Pour
échapper à l'emprise des musées, d'autres artistes formulèrent leur conception de l'art dans un
environnement naturel, d'où la *Spiral Jetty* (la Jetée spirale) du Grand Lac Salé par Robert
Smithson, disparue depuis, inglorieusement, lors de crues.

Toutes ces indications ne doivent pas porter à croire que les beaux-arts contemporains
s'épuisent en loufoqueries, mais à faire comprendre que leur progression est arrivée en fin de
course au terme de changements constants et importants. On s'évertue à formuler quelque
chose de significatif, mais la déroute est générale, et plus d'une œuvre artistique appartient
déjà au passé avant même que d'être reconnue comme telle. Le temps est proche où, pour
employer la jolie formule d'Andy Warhol, chacun sera célèbre pendant quinze minutes.

Quel contraste frappant nous offre alors la continuité qui caractérise la progression de l'art publicitaire! Un grand nombre d'adeptes des beaux-arts et une bonne partie de leur public continuent de regarder de haut l'art graphique au service de la publicité sous prétexte qu'il s'agit d'un art purement commercial, purement utilitaire. A quoi il est facile de répliquer que la majeure partie du grand art du passé a été réalisé pour des raisons utilitaires à une époque où la photographie n'existait pas encore, mais où le besoin d'images était aussi impérieux. Pour ce qui est du caractère commercial de l'art publicitaire, il faut bien constater que les beaux-arts ont totalement dérapé dans le circuit commercial, les marchands d'art composant des écuries de fringants poulains qui rapportent cher, et la structure ingénieuse du marché permettant à des sommes astronomiques de s'investir au gré de chaque transaction.

Admettons néanmoins que nombre de travaux publicitaires ont peu de prétentions artistiques. Le design graphique n'est que le sobre outil de ceux qui ont quelque chose à communiquer ou à vendre. Et pourtant, une bonne partie des travaux réalisés à cet effet présentent une valeur artistique, ce qui constitue une expression valable et sérieuse de notre époque, dans un sens où ni la jetée de Smithson ni le *Clothespin* d'Oldenburg ne peuvent être considérés comme des œuvres sérieuses. Qui plus est, les productions de l'art publicitaire ne sont pas destinées à une élite fréquentant les musées, mais atteignent quotidiennement le grand public de cette seconde moitié du XXe siècle.

Il est possible que dans cinquante ans la distinction entre les beaux-arts et les arts appliqués se sera effacée au point de ne plus constituer qu'un problème historique ou du moins académique. Certains artistes œuvrent déjà avec beaucoup de bonheur dans les deux domaines, de sorte qu'un Roman Cieslewicz peut affirmer: «Je ne me souviens pas d'un seul moment où mon travail a pu être conditionné par les exigences d'un client au détriment de mes recherches personnelles. Je ne fais pas de différence entre mon travail dit d'atelier et mon travail graphique dit commercial.»

On peut en déduire que le design graphique mérite une reconnaissance plus généreuse pour ce qui est de ses réalisations de pointe. Les flèches et les figures anonymes de Jean-Michel Folon, les légumes de Tadashi Ohashi, le bestiaire insolite et pourtant si mémorable d'André François – pour ne prendre que ces trois artistes que l'on trouvera une fois de plus représentés dans cet annuel – ont apporté plus de plaisir à plus de gens au cours des années que les produits de la plupart des «grands» artistes. A ce titre, ils méritent toute notre gratitude.

Les changements intervenus depuis quelques années se constatent rien qu'en observant la répartition des travaux réunis au sein du présent ouvrage, sans même considérer les styles individuels. Parmi les plus encourageants de ces changements, notons la récente augmentation du nombre des illustrations notamment en provenance de journaux américains. L'illustration a toujours été la demi-sœur des beaux-arts, et l'acceptation grandissante d'un complément visuel souvent fort imaginatif du mot écrit dans la presse fait espérer que le «grand» art finira bien par descendre de son piédestal vacillant et que l'art sur commande viendra à sa rencontre pour unir sa voix à la sienne et en faire une seule voix pour un seul public.

Index to Artists
Verzeichnis der Künstler
Index des Artistes

Index to Designers
Verzeichnis der Gestalter
Index des Maquettistes

Index to Art Directors
Verzeichnis der künstlerischen Leiter
Index des Directeurs Artistiques

Index to Agencies and Studios
Verzeichnis der Agenturen und Studios
Index des Agences et Studios

Index to Publishers
Verzeichnis der Verleger
Index des Editeurs

Index to Advertisers
Verzeichnis der Auftraggeber
Index des Clients

■ Entry instructions may be requested by anyone interested in submitting samples of exceptional graphics or photography for possible inclusion in our annuals. No fees involved. Closing dates for entries:
GRAPHIS ANNUAL (advertising and editorial art and design): 31 January
PHOTOGRAPHIS (advertising and editorial photography): 30 June
GRAPHIS POSTERS (an annual of poster art): 30 June
Write to: Graphis Press Corp., Dufourstrasse 107, 8008 Zurich, Switzerland

■ Einsendebedingungen können von jedermann angefordert werden, der uns Beispiele hervorragender Photographie oder Graphik zur Auswahl für unsere Jahrbücher unterbreiten möchte. Es werden keine Gebühren erhoben.
Einsendetermine:
GRAPHIS ANNUAL (Werbe- und redaktionelle Graphik): 31. Januar
PHOTOGRAPHIS (Werbe- und redaktionelle Photographie): 30. Juni
GRAPHIS POSTERS (ein Jahrbuch der Plakatkunst): 30. Juni
Adresse: Graphis Verlag AG, Dufourstrasse 107, 8008 Zürich, Schweiz

■ Tout intéressé à la soumission de travaux photographiques et graphiques recevra les informations nécessaires sur demande. Sans charge de participation.
Dates limites:
GRAPHIS ANNUAL (art graphique publicitaire et rédactionnel): 31 janvier
PHOTOGRAPHIS (photographie publicitaire et rédactionnelle): 30 juin
GRAPHIS POSTERS (annuaire sur l'art de l'affiche): 30 juin
S'adresser à: Editions Graphis SA, Dufourstrasse 107, 8008 Zurich, Suisse

Editor and Art Director: Walter Herdeg
Assistant Editors: Stanley Mason
Project Manager: Heinke Jenssen
Designers: Martin Byland, Ulrich Kemmner
Art Assistants: Marino Bianchera, Willy Müller, Peter Wittwer

1

Magazine Advertisements

Newspaper Advertisements

Zeitschriften-Inserate

Zeitungs-Inserate

Annonces de revues

Annonces de presse

1

2

1 Full-colour advertisement from an advertising campaign of the Swiss Cheese Union using a slogan comprised of the first letters of the following words in Swiss German: "Fondue isch guet und git e gueti Luune" (fondue is good and makes for a good mood). (SWI)
2 Full-page advertisement for an orange drink. In shades of orange and yellow. (ITA)
3 From a series of full-colour advertisements for fresh milk products, by the Central Marketing Association of the German agrarian economy, with motifs from fairy-tales. (GER)
4 Magazine advertisement in the form of a puzzle for *Robinson's* barley water. (GBR)
5 Full-page advertisement for *Bahlsen* biscuits, with coupons for raffled sample packets. Golden-brown biscuit with a blue, white and red trademark. (GER)
6 Double-spread advertisement for *Milka* chocolate. A purple cow is employed as an allusion to the standard colour of the wrapping, a theme used for many years. (GER)

1 Mehrfarbige Anzeige aus einer Werbekampagne der Schweizerischen Käseunion, deren geheimnisvoller Slogan sich aus den Anfangsbuchstaben der folgenden Worte (im Originaltext schweizerdeutsch) zusammensetzt: «Fondue ist gut und gibt eine gute Laune.» (SWI)
2 Ganzseitige Anzeige für ein Orangengetränk. Vorwiegend in Orange- und Gelbtönen. (ITA)
3 Aus einer Serie von mehrfarbigen Anzeigen für Milchfrischprodukte der Centralen Marketinggesellschaft der deutschen Agrarwirtschaft, mit Motiven aus der Märchenwelt. (GER)
4 Zeitschrifteninserat in Form eines Ratespiels, für ein gerstehaltiges Getränk. (GBR)
5 Ganzseitiges Inserat für *Bahlsen*-Kekse, mit Coupon für eine Verlosung von Probierpäckchen. Goldbrauner Keks mit blau-weiss-rotem Markenzeichen. (GER)
6 Doppelseitige Anzeige für *Milka*-Schokolade, mit einer violetten Kuh als Anspielung auf die violette Verpackung, ein Grundthema, das schon seit Jahren verwendet wird. (GER)

1 Annonce polychrome figurant dans la campagne de l'Union suisse pour le commerce du fromage placée sous le slogan énigmatique de «figugegl», abréviation d'un dicton suisse allemand qui veut dire: «La fondue est bonne et procure la bonne humeur.» (SWI)
2 Annonce pleine page pour une orangeade. Tons orange et jaunes prédominants. (ITA)
3 Exemple d'une série d'annonces polychromes pour les produits laitiers frais de la centrale de marketing de l'agriculture allemande; thèmes tirés de contes de fées. (GER)
4 Annonce de magazine pour une boisson à base d'orge. Série de devinettes. (GBR)
5 Annonce pleine page pour les biscuits *Bahlsen*, avec coupon pour un tirage au sort d'échantillons. Biscuit brun doré, marque bleu-blanc-rouge. (GER)
6 Annonce sur double page pour le chocolat *Milka*. La vache violette renvoie à la couleur standardisée de l'emballage, un thème publicitaire utilisé depuis des années. (GER)

3

Advertisements

Anzeigen

Annonces

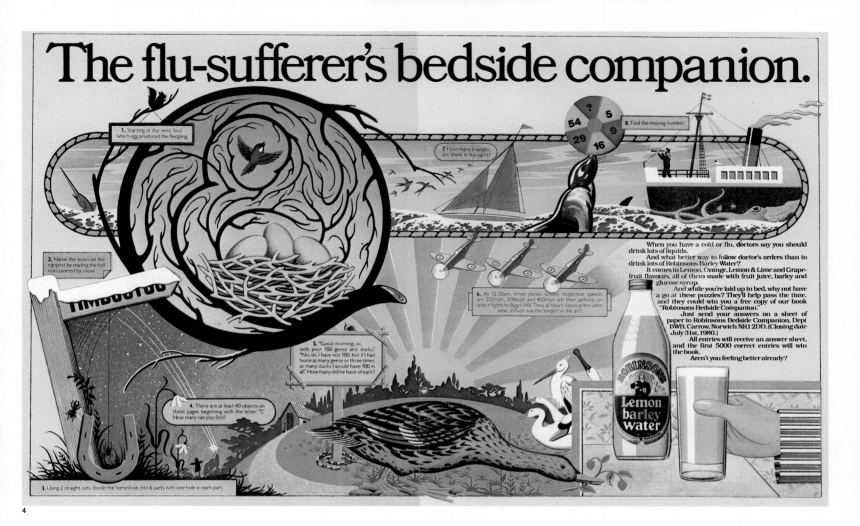

The flu-sufferer's bedside companion.

1. Starting at the nest, find which egg produced the fledgling.

2. Name the town on the signpost by reading the half not covered by snow.

3. Using 2 straight cuts, divide the horseshoe into 6 parts with one hole in each part.

4. There are at least 40 objects on these pages beginning with the letter "S". How many can you find?

5. "Good morning, sir, with your 100 geese and ducks." "No, sir, I have not 100, but if I had twice as many geese or three times as many ducks I would have 100 in all." How many did he have of each?

6. At 12.30am, three planes whose respective speeds are 250mph, 300mph and 400mph left their airfields on direct flights to Biggin Hill. They all touch down at the same time. Which was the longest in the air?

7. How many triangles are there in the yacht?

8. Find the missing number.

When you have a cold or flu, doctors say you should drink lots of liquids.

And what better way to follow doctor's orders than to drink lots of Robinsons Barley Water?

It comes in Lemon, Orange, Lemon & Lime and Grapefruit flavours, all of them made with fruit juice, barley and glucose syrup.

And while you're laid up in bed, why not have a go at these puzzles? They'll help pass the time, and they could win you a free copy of our book "Robinsons Bedside Companion".

Just send your answers on a sheet of paper to Robinsons Bedside Companion, Dept BWB, Carrow, Norwich NR1 2DD. (Closing date July 31st, 1980.)

All entries will receive an answer sheet, and the first 5000 correct entries will win the book.

Aren't you feeling better already?

4

Der Reise-Keks.

5

ARTIST / KÜNSTLER / ARTISTE:

1 Oskar Weiss
2 A. Tamagnone/G. Ferrari
3 Tomi Ungerer
4 Tony Meeuwissen
6 Dieter Ziegenfeuter

DESIGNER / GESTALTER / MAQUETTISTE:

1 Fredy Steiner
2 Italo Cammarata
4 John Horton
5 Günter Herrmann

ART DIRECTOR / DIRECTEUR ARTISTIQUE:

1 Fredy Steiner
2 Giampiero Ferrari
3 Robert Pütz
4 John Horton
5 Günter Herrmann/Emilio Sanchez
6 Maria-Christina Sennefelder

AGENCY / AGENTUR / AGENCE – STUDIO:

1 Gisler & Gisler
2 Armando Testa S.p.A.
3 Robert Pütz GmbH & Co.
4 Collett Dickenson Pearce & Partners
5 GWA Werbeagentur
6 Young & Rubicam GmbH

Die Zartheit dieser Schokolade nehmen sich viele zum Vorbild.

6

7

BIOTRONIK
Le pacemaker du rythme retrouvé

8

Advertisements
Anzeigen
Annonces

9

10

ARTIST / KÜNSTLER / ARTISTE:

7, 8 Tudor Mironesco
9–12 Tadashi Ohashi

DESIGNER / GESTALTER / MAQUETTISTE:

9–12 Tadashi Ohashi

ART DIRECTOR / DIRECTEUR ARTISTIQUE:

9–12 Tadashi Ohashi

11

12

7, 8 Illustration and complete full-page advertisement for *Biotronik* heart pacemakers. (FRA)
9, 10 From a series of full-page advertisements using the slogan "The proverb of Japan" for the *Kikkoman* company, manufacturers of sauces and seasoning. Fig. 9 in shades of yellow, brown and green; Fig. 10 mostly in blue shades. (JPN)
11, 12 Two further full-page advertisements for *Kikkoman* sauces, with the same slogan: "The tastes of Japan." Fig. 11 with whitish radish turning into red, with greenish-brown leaves; Fig. 12 in shades of green. (JPN)

7, 8 Illustration und vollständige, ganzseitige Anzeige für *Biotronik*-Herzschrittmacher. (FRA)
9, 10 Aus einer Serie von ganzseitigen Anzeigen unter dem Slogan «Die Sprichwörter Japans», für Produkte der Firma *Kikkoman*, Hersteller von Saucen und Gewürzen. Abb. 9 in Gelb-, Braun- und Grüntönen, Abb. 10 vorwiegend in Blautönen. (JPN)
11, 12 Zwei weitere Anzeigen für *Kikkoman*-Saucen. Der gemeinsame Slogan lautet: «Die Geschmäcke Japans.» Abb. 11 mit weisslichem, in Rot übergehenden Rettich mit grünbraunen Blättern, Abb. 12 in Grüntönen. (JPN)

7, 8 Illustration et annonce pleine page complète pour un pacemaker *Biotronik*. (FRA)
9, 10 Exemples d'une série d'annonces pleine page sous la devise «Les proverbes du Japon», réalisée pour les produits du fabricant de sauces et condiments *Kikkoman*. La fig. 9 est exécutée en tons jaunes, bruns et verts, la fig. 10 surtout en tons bleus. (JPN)
11, 12 Deux autres annonces pleine page pour les sauces *Kikkoman*, cette fois-ci sous la devise «Les goûts du Japon». Fig. 11: raifort blanchâtre à rougeâtre, feuilles vert-brun; fig. 12 exécutée en divers tons verts. (JPN)

13

14

13–17 Illustrations and complete advertisement from an advertising campaign for wines produced by the Clos Du Val Wine Co., Ltd., California, and Taltarni Moonambel, Australia. Fig. 13: "The Annual Non-arrival of the English Grape Ceremony"; Fig. 14: "Blessing the Grapes, California style"; Fig. 15: "The Nobel Grape"; Figs. 16, 17: "Connoisseurs". All advertisements are in full colour and appeared also as posters. (USA)

13–17 Illustrationen und eine vollständige Anzeige aus einer Werbekampagne für Weine der Firma Clos Du Val Wine Co., Ltd., Kalifornien, und Taltarni Moonambel, Australien. Abb. 13: «Das jährliche Nicht-Stattfinden der englischen Trauben-Zeremonie»; Abb. 14: «Lobgesang auf die kalifornischen Trauben»; Abb. 15: «Die vornehme Traube»; Abb. 16, 17: «Kenner». Alle Illustrationen in Farbe. Sie sind auch als Plakate erschienen. (USA)

13–17 Illustrations et annonce complète pour une campagne en faveur des vins de la Clos du Val Wine Co., Ltd. (Californie) et de Taltarni Moonambel (Australie). Fig. 13: «La non-cérémonie annuelle du raisin anglais»; fig. 14: «Hymne au raisin de Californie»; fig. 15: «Le noble raisin»; fig. 16, 17: «Les Connaisseurs». Toutes ces annonces polychromes ont également été utilisées sous forme d'affiches. (USA)

15

ARTIST / KÜNSTLER / ARTISTE:
13–17 Ronald Searle

ART DIRECTOR / DIRECTEUR ARTISTIQUE:
13–17 John Locke

AGENCY / AGENTUR / AGENCE – STUDIO:
13–17 John Locke Studios, Inc.

16

18 Large-format newspaper advertisement for a department store's spring sales: "Hippopotamus in Spring." (JPN)
19, 20 From a comprehensive *Ciba-Geigy* campaign for a medicament to combat worms. Light brown with dark brown. (SWI)
21 Newspaper advertisement for the time recording and checking systems of the Union Kassenfabrik AG company. (SWI)
22 Full-page newspaper advertisement for a film entitled "The Black Hole", *Walt Disney Productions*. (GBR)
23 Double-spread advertisement for storage tanks manufactured by the GATX Terminals Corp. (USA)
24 Double-spread, full-colour advertisement for a computer system called MCS Computers, manufactured by *Compugraphics*. (USA)

18 Grossformatiges Zeitungsinserat eines Kaufhauses für den Frühjahrsausverkauf: «Flusspferde im Frühling.» (JPN)
19, 20 Aus einer umfassenden Kampagne von *Ciba-Geigy* für das Wurmmittel *Lopatol*. Hellbraun mit Dunkelbraun. (SWI)
21 Zeitungsinserat für Zeiterfassungs- und Kontrollsysteme der Firma Union Kassenfabrik AG. (SWI)
22 Ganzseitiges Zeitungsinserat für einen Film der *Walt Disney Productions* mit dem Titel «Das schwarze Loch». (GBR)
23 «Wir haben was Sie brauchen, wo Sie es brauchen.» Doppelseitige Anzeige für Tanks der Firma GATX. (USA)
24 «Passt wie ein Handschuh.» Doppelseitige, farbige Anzeige für ein Computer-System von *Compugraphics*. (USA)

18 Annonce de journal au grand format pour la saison de printemps d'un grand magasin: «Hippopotames au printemps.» (JPN)
19, 20 Annonces illustrant une vaste campagne de *Ciba-Geigy* pour le vermifuge *Lopatol*. Brun clair, avec du brun foncé. (SWI)
21 Annonce de journal pour les systèmes de saisie de données et de contrôle de l'Union Kassenfabrik AG. (SWI)
22 Annonce de journal pleine page pour un film des *Walt Disney Productions*, «Le Trou noir». (GBR)
23 «Nous avons ce qu'il vous faut. Là où il vous le faut.» Annonce double page pour les réservoirs de la GATX Corp. (USA)
24 «Ça vous va comme un gant.» Annonce couleur sur double page pour un système informatique de *Compugraphics*. (USA)

ARTIST / KÜNSTLER / ARTISTE:

18 Takanori Asaeda
19, 20 Christian Lang
21 Jenny Leibundgut
23 Harlan Scheaffler
24 Terry Allen

DESIGNER / GESTALTER / MAQUETTISTE:

18 Yasuo Okubo
19, 20 Christian Lang
21 Fritz Gottschalk/Jenny Leibundgut
22 Peter Maisey
23 Robert Qually
24 Terry Allen

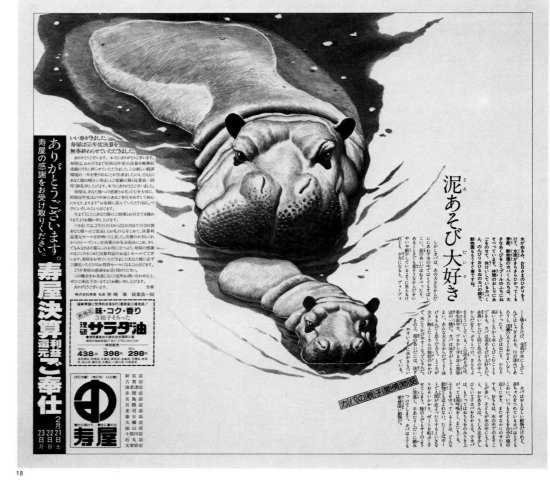

18

19

20

21

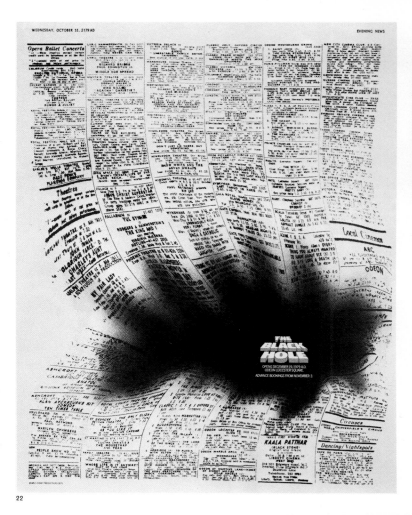

23

ART DIRECTOR / DIRECTEUR ARTISTIQUE:

18 Yoshitaka Ueda
19, 20 Christian Lang
21 Gottschalk & Ash Int'l
22 Peter Maisey
23 Robert Qually
24 Jim Richards

AGENCY / AGENTUR / AGENCE – STUDIO:

18 Dentsu Advertising
19, 20 Ciba-Geigy/Zentrale Werbung
21 Adolf Wirz & Partner AG/
    Gottschalk & Ash Int'l
22 First City Advertising
23 Lee King & Partners
24 Media Concepts

22

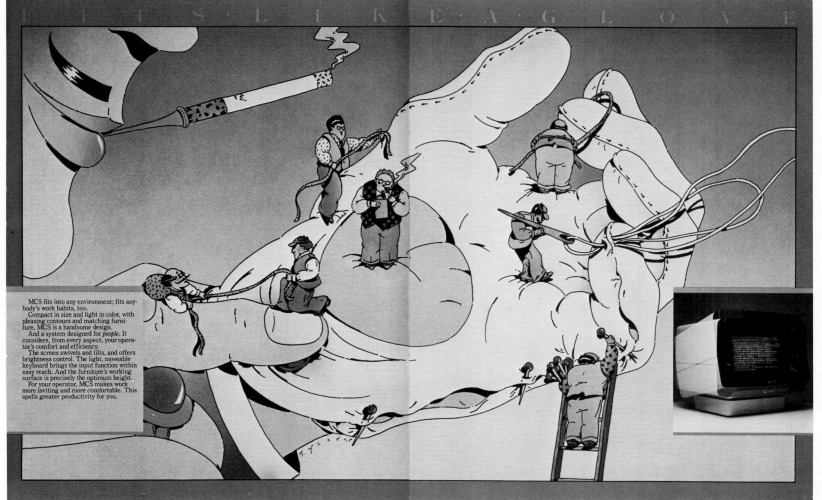

24

Baa baa black sheep
Have you any wool?
Yes sir, yes sir
Three bags full:
One for the master,
One for the dame,
But none for the
little boy....

25

Save pounds, not pennies

27

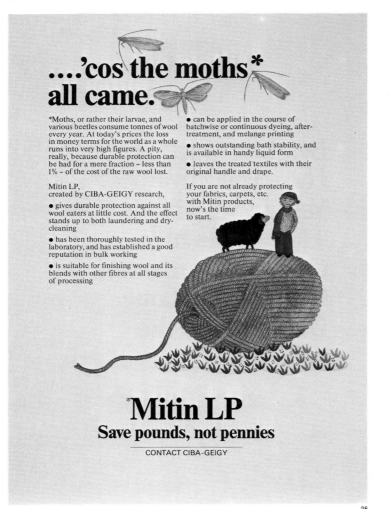

....'cos the moths*
all came.

*Moths, or rather their larvae, and various beetles consume tonnes of wool every year. At today's prices the loss in money terms for the world as a whole runs into very high figures. A pity, really, because durable protection can be had for a mere fraction – less than 1% – of the cost of the raw wool lost.

Mitin LP, created by CIBA-GEIGY research,

● gives durable protection against all wool eaters at little cost. And the effect stands up to both laundering and dry-cleaning

● has been thoroughly tested in the laboratory, and has established a good reputation in bulk working

● is suitable for finishing wool and its blends with other fibres at all stages of processing

● can be applied in the course of batchwise or continuous dyeing, after-treatment, and melange printing

● shows outstanding bath stability, and is available in handy liquid form

● leaves the treated textiles with their original handle and drape.

If you are not already protecting your fabrics, carpets, etc. with Mitin products, now's the time to start.

Mitin LP
Save pounds, not pennies

CONTACT CIBA-GEIGY

26

ARTIST / KÜNSTLER / ARTISTE:

25–27 Christine Tillard
28 Mamoru Shimokochi
29 Ken Laidlaw

DESIGNER / GESTALTER / MAQUETTISTE:

25–27 Christian Lang
28 Paul Pruneau

ART DIRECTOR / DIRECTEUR ARTISTIQUE:

25–27 Christian Lang
28 Douglas Boyd
29 Dennis Wheelan

AGENCY / AGENTUR / AGENCE – STUDIO:

25–27 Ciba-Geigy/Zentrale Werbung
28 Douglas Boyd Design & Marketing

WEST WEEK 1982

March 19, 20, 21

Pacific Design Center

Gateway to the Pacific

The Market Event of the West

28

29

Ken Laidlaw

25, 26 Recto and verso of a *Ciba-Geigy* advertisement for *Mitin LP*, a moth-protector outfit for wool and other fibres. A rhyme on the recto points out that the sheep has enough wool for the lady and the gentleman but none for the child. The reason for the latter is on the verso: because the moths came. (SWI)
27 A *Ciba-Geigy* promotional gift in the form of a money-box referring to the *Mitin* moth-protector outfit (see Figs. 25, 26). (SWI)
28 Trade magazine advertisement for an exhibition of design on America's West Coast. Mainly in shades of blue. (USA)
29 Trade magazine advertisement for sleeping pills, from a series showing animals that hibernate. (GBR)

25, 26 Vorder- und Rückseite eines Inserats von *Ciba-Geigy* für *Mitin LP*, eine Mottenschutzausrüstung für Wolle und andere Fasern. Auf der Vorderseite ein Reim, der besagt, dass das Schaf zwar Wolle für den Herrn und die Dame, aber keine für den Jungen habe; auf der Rückseite der Grund: weil die Motten kamen. (SWI)
27 Kundengeschenk von *Ciba-Geigy* in Form einer Sparbüchse als Werbung für *Mitin*-Mottenschutzausrüstung (s. Abb. 25, 26). (SWI)
28 Fachzeitschriften-Inserat für eine Design-Ausstellung an der Westküste der USA. Vorwiegend in Blautönen. (USA)
29 Fachzeitschriften-Inserat für Schlaftabletten, aus einer Serie mit Tieren, die einen Winterschlaf machen. (GBR)

25, 26 Recto et verso d'une annonce de *Ciba-Geigy* pour le *Mitin LP*, un apprêt antimite pour la laine et d'autres fibres textiles. Au recto, une poésie disant que le mouton a bien de la laine pour madame et monsieur, mais pas pour leur garçon; explication au verso: parce que les mites ont passé par-là. (SWI)
27 Cadeau pour la clientèle de *Ciba-Geigy*: une tirelire évoquant l'apprêt antimite *Mitin* (cf. les fig. 25, 26). (SWI)
28 Annonce de revue professionnelle pour une exposition de design sur la côte ouest des Etats-Unis. Tons bleus surtout. (USA)
29 Annonce de revue spécialisée pour un somnifère, parue dans une série où l'on voit hiberner des animaux. (GBR)

30

32

30–34 Full-page illustrations and a complete double spread from an advertising campaign in magazines for the *Siegwerk Farbenfabrik*. The distinctive symbol, the rainbow, has been interpreted already by various artists in advertisements for these printing inks; here some examples from a series by the French artist André François. (GER)

30–34 Ganzseitige Illustrationen und eine vollständige Doppelseite aus einer Anzeigenkampagne in Zeitschriften für die *Siegwerk Farbenfabrik*. Das Wahrzeichen, der Regenbogen, wurde bereits von verschiedenen Künstlern in Anzeigen für diese Druckfarben interpretiert; hier einige Beispiele aus einer Serie des Franzosen André François. (GER)

30–34 Illustrations pleine page et une double page complète tirées d'une campagne d'annonces de magazines réalisée pour la fabrique d'encres d'imprimerie *Siegwerk*. L'emblème de l'arc-en-ciel a déjà été interprété par divers artistes dans la publicité de cette entreprise. Voici plusieurs exemples d'une série conçue par le Français André François. (GER)

ARTIST / KÜNSTLER / ARTISTE:
30–34 André François

ART DIRECTOR / DIRECTEUR ARTISTIQUE:
30–34 Robert Pütz

AGENCY / AGENTUR / AGENCE – STUDIO:
30–34 Robert Pütz GmbH & Co.

31

33

テトン

株式会社 竹月

Advertisements
Anzeigen
Annonces

ARTIST / KÜNSTLER:

35 Kazumasa Nagai
36 John Rombola
37 Seymour Chwast
38 Daniele Morini
39 Walter Lienert

DESIGNER / GESTALTER:

35 Kazumasa Nagai
36 Leora M. Sies
37 Richard Mantel
39 Walter Lienert

ART DIRECTOR:

35 Kazumasa Nagai
36 Leora M. Sies
37 Seymour Chwast
38 Roberta Stabilini
39 Walter Lienert

AGENCY / AGENTUR / AGENCE:

35 Nippon Design Center
36 Larry Aaron Adv.
37 Push Pin Studios
38 Young & Rubicam Italia SpA
39 Ciba-Geigy/Zentrale Werbung

36

37

38

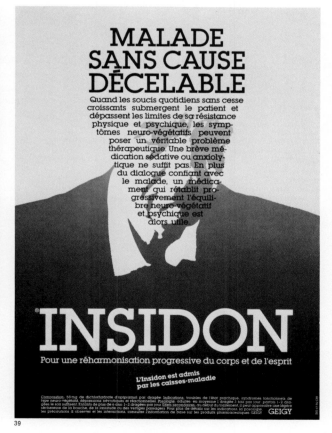

39

35 Newspaper advertisement for the *Takeo Paper Company*. (JPN)
36 Full-page, full-colour advertisement for the *Royce Chemical Co.* (USA)
37 Full-page advertisement for Litho Prepsters Inc. The suit is in the standard colours of a litho. (USA)
38 A *Bayer* advertisement for soluble aspirin tablets with Vitamin C for children. The orange and green on the packing are repeated on the clothing. (ITA)
39 Black-and-white advertisement for *Insidon*, a *Geigy* medicament. (SWI)

35 Zeitschriftenanzeige für eine Papierfabrik. (JPN)
36 Ganzseitiges, farbiges Inserat für ein Chemie-Unternehmen: «Wir sind alles andere als ein Papiertiger.» (USA)
37 «Massgeschneiderter Service für Vier-Farben-Filme.» Ganzseitiges Inserat für

einen Lithographen. Anzug in den Standardfarben eines Lithos. (USA)
38 Inserat von *Bayer* für Aspirin-Brausetabletten mit Vitamin C für Kinder. Das Orange und Grün der Packung wiederholt sich in der Kleidung. (ITA)
39 Anzeige in Schwarzweiss für das Medikament *Insidon* von *Geigy*. (SWI)

35 Annonce de journal pour un papetier. (JPN)
36 «Nous sommes tout, sauf des tigres en papier.» Annonce couleur pleine page pour une fabrique de produits chimiques. (USA)
37 «Service sur mesure pour typons tramés.» Annonce pleine page pour un atelier de lithographie. Complet en quadrichromie type litho. (USA)
38 Annonce *Bayer* pour une aspirine effervescente à la vitamine C. (ITA)
39 Annonce noir et blanc pour le médicament *Insidon* de *Geigy*. (SWI)

FOR THE CROPS THAT
COVER AMERICA'S TABLES

KOCIDE
The Walnut Fungicide

No other copper
fungicide covers like
KOCIDE 101, the finest
money can buy.

P.O. Box 45539,
Houston, TX 77045
Tel. 713/433-6404
TWX 910-881-2737

KOCIDE Chemical Corporation

40

FOR THE CROPS THAT
COVER AMERICA'S TABLES

KOCIDE
The Almond Fungicide

No other copper
fungicide covers like
KOCIDE 101, the finest
money can buy.

P.O. Box 45539,
Houston, TX 77045
Tel. 713/433-6404
TWX 910-881-2737

KOCIDE Chemical Corporation

41

44

40, 41 From a series of small-format advertisements for *Kocide 101*, a plant-protecting agent. Here two examples from the range of application. In full colour. (USA)
42, 43 These advertisements for *Voetbal International*, a football magazine for men, present the rare male representatives of the population who pay no attention to this periodical. They serve the ends of space promotion and refer to the magazine's high circulation. (NLD)
44, 45 Complete trade magazine advertisement and illustration for *Ludiomil*, a *Ciba* medicament for the treatment of depression. The rose was to be established as a logo for the product. (USA)

40, 41 Aus einer Serie kleinformatiger Anzeigen für *Kocide 101*, ein Pflanzenschutzmittel. Hier zwei Beispiele aus dem Anwendungsbereich. In Farbe. (USA)
42, 43 In diesen Anzeigen für *Voetbal International*, eine Fussballzeitschrift für Männer, werden jene seltenen Vertreter der männlichen Bevölkerung vorgestellt, die nichts von der Zeitschrift halten. Mit Hinweis auf die hohe Auflage wird um Inserenten geworben. (NLD)
44, 45 Vollständiges Fachzeitschrifteninserat und Illustration für das Medikament *Ludiomil* von *Ciba* gegen Depressionen. Die Rose wird hier als Symbol für das Medikament eingeführt. (USA)

40, 41 Exemples d'annonces au petit format, série réalisée en faveur du produit phytosanitaire *Kocide 101*. On montre ici deux domaines d'application de ce produit. En couleur. (USA)
42, 43 Dans ces annonces pour *Voetbal International*, un magazine de football pour hommes, on présente les rares spécimens de la population masculine qui ne s'intéressent pas à ce type de journal. Campagne mettant en évidence l'intérêt du fort tirage pour les annonceurs. (NLD)
44, 45 Illustration et annonce complète de revue spécialisée où elle figure. Antidépresseur *Ludiomil* de *Ciba*. La rose est introduite comme emblème caractéristique du médicament. (USA)

Advertisements / Anzeigen / Annonces

42

43

ARTIST / KÜNSTLER / ARTISTE:

46 Clark Robinson
47 Bjarne Norking
50–52 J. Robert Faulkner
53 Scott Eggers
54 Nancy Hoefig

DESIGNER / GESTALTER / MAQUETTISTE:

46 Clark Robinson
48 Gary Goldsmith
49 Horst Hellmund
50–52 J. Robert Faulkner
53 Stephen Miller
54 D. C. Stipp/Nancy Hoefig

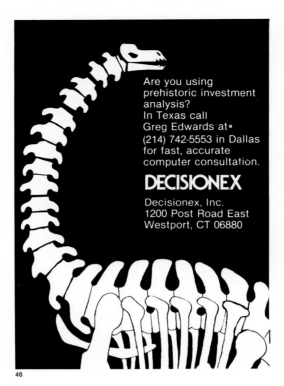

46

47

46 Newspaper advertisement for *Decisionex* computers which are recommended for modern investment analyses. (USA)
47 Magazine advertisement for *Volkswagen* in Brazil. (BRA)
48 A *Volkswagen* model, known in the United States as the "rabbit", is here claimed to be the best mileage car. (USA)
49 Advertisement from a campaign for *Volkswagen*, here in conjunction with a Swiss dealer. The copy says that the twenty millionth "beetle" has just left the Mexican plant. (GER)
50–52 Full-page newspaper advertisement for *Picadilly Square*, a shopping centre in Santa Barbara, California. (USA)
53, 54 Full-page, three-colour ads for *Governor's Square*, a department store in Dallas. Fig. 53 deals with a sale; Fig. 54: goods that can be purchased for thirty dollars. (USA)

46 «Arbeiten Sie mit prähistorischen Investitions-Analysen?» Zeitungsinserat für *Decisionex*-Computer. (USA)
47 Zeitschrifteninserat des *Volkswagenwerks* in Brasilien. (BRA)
48 «Rabbit» (Kaninchen) ist in den USA die Bezeichnung des VW-«Polo». Es geht hier um den niedrigen Verbrauch. (USA)
49 Inserat aus einer Kampagne des *Volkswagenwerkes*, hier zusammen mit einem Schweizer Händler. Thema ist die Fertigstellung des zwanzigmillionsten «Käfers» in Mexiko. (GER)
50–52 Ganzseitige Zeitungsinserate für ein Einkaufszentrum, mit Hinweis auf besondere Gelegenheiten und Veranstaltungen. (USA)
53, 54 Ganzseitige, dreifarbige Inserate für ein Kaufhaus. In Abb. 53 geht es um einen Ausverkauf, in Abb. 54 um verschiedene Dinge, die für dreissig Dollars zu haben sind. (USA)

46 «Travaillez-vous avec des analyses d'investissements préhistoriques?» Annonce de journal. Ordinateurs *Decisionex*. (USA)
47 Annonce de magazine de *Volkswagen* au Brésil. (BRA)
48 «La voiture la plus économique d'Amérique», «pour aller de a à b»: la «Rabbit», nom américain de la «Polo» de VW. (USA)
49 Annonce pour une campagne *Volkswagen*, en coopération avec un importateur suisse. Le thème: la 20 000 000e «Coccinelle» sortie de l'usine de Mexico. (GER)
50–52 Annonces de journal pleine page pour un centre commercial annonçant des occasions et manifestations particulières. (USA)
53, 54 Annonces trois couleurs, pleine page, pour un grand magasin. La fig. 53 se rapporte aux soldes, la fig. 54 à tout ce qui ne coûte que trente dollars. (USA)

50

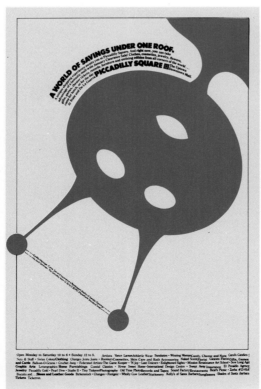

51

52

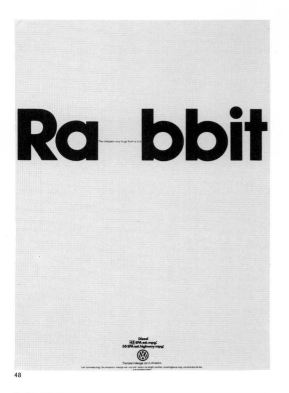

Ra bbit

The cheaper way to go from a to b

Diesel
45 EPA est. mpg'
58 EPA est. highway mpg'

🔵 The best mileage car in America

Use estimated mpg 'EA comparison mileage cost vary with speed, trip length, weather, actual highway mpg will probably be less

48

Unica.
20 milioni
di volte.

L'automobile più riuscita di tutti i tempi è una Volkswagen: il 15 maggio 1981 il 20.000.000° Maggiolino ha lasciato le catene di montaggio della Volkswagen de Mexico. Una cifra record, mai raggiunta da un'auto, prima del Maggiolino.

Con il primato dei 20.000.000 la Volkswagen fornisce la «prova vivente» dell'unicità e della giustezza del suo concetto costruttivo: migliorare continuamente ogni modello Volkswagen, per corrispondere alle mutevoli condizioni del traffico e dell'ambiente e alle esigenze dei suoi Clienti. Questo concetto vale – più che mai – anche per l'attuale generazione di modelli Volkswagen. Pur essa simbolo di qua-

lità, indistruttibilità, raziocinio, resistenza, economia e costanza di valore.
Così la Volkswagen non è solo in testa nella tecnica delle costruzioni automobilistiche, ma ha dato anche la possibilità di guadagnare bene agli uomini di molti Paesi: nelle costruzioni automobilistiche, nel Service Volkswagen e nelle industrie fornitrici – per citare solo alcuni settori.

Volkswagen ha dato a molti più mobilità e la vettura sognata. 20 milioni di volte: finora ce l'ha fatta solo il Maggiolino.

Volkswagenwerk AG

49

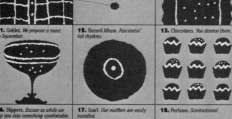

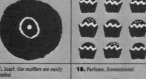

ART DIRECTOR / DIRECTEUR ARTISTIQUE:

46 Clark Robinson
47 Bjarne Norking
48 Gary Goldsmith
49 Horst Hellmund
50–52 J. Robert Faulkner
53 Stephen Miller
54 D. C. Stipp

AGENCY / AGENTUR / AGENCE – STUDIO:

46 Clark L. Robinson Inc.
47 Alcantara Machado, Periscinoto Comunicações Ltda.
48 Doyle Dane Bernbach
50–52 Garth DeCew Group
53, 54 Richards, Sullivan, Brock & Associates

55

56

55, 56 Newspaper advertisements for spring articles and for a spring sale. They were also used as posters in various shopping centres. Green, yellow and beige. (USA)
57, 58 Examples from a series of newspaper advertisements for the Union Bank of Switzerland. (SWI)
59 Newspaper advertisement of the *Seibu* department store, drawing attention to an exhibition by Tadanori Yooko. (JPN)
60 From a series of newspaper advertisements for *Asian-Paints* that have become No. 1 on the market. (IND)
61, 62 Advertisements of the *I. Magnin* department store. (USA)
63, 64 Examples from a series of seven advertisements by *Nippon Electronics*, explaining here the astounding communication systems of dolphins and birds. (JPN)

55, 56 Zeitungsinserate für Frühjahrsartikel und einen Frühjahrsausverkauf. Sie wurden auch als Plakate in verschiedenen Einkaufszentren verwendet. Grün, gelb, beige. (USA)
57, 58 Beispiele aus einer Serie von Zeitungsinseraten der Schweizerischen Bankgesellschaft. (SWI)
59 Zeitungsinserat des *Seibu*-Kaufhauses, mit Hinweis auf eine Ausstellung des Künstlers Tadanori Yooko. (JPN)
60 Aus einer Serie von Zeitungsinseraten für *Asian-Paints*-Farben, die zur Nr. 1 auf dem Markt geworden sind. (IND)
61, 62 Anzeigen des Kaufhauses *I. Magnin* für das Weihnachtsgeschäft mit Parfüms. (USA)
63, 64 Beispiele aus einer Serie von sieben Inseraten von *Nippon Electronics*. Hier geht es um die erstaunlichen Kommunikationssysteme der Delphine und Vögel. (JPN)

55, 56 Annonces de journaux pour des articles de printemps et des soldes de printemps, utilisées aussi comme affiches dans des centres commerciaux. Vert, jaune, beige. (USA)
57, 58 Exemples d'une série d'annonces de journaux de l'Union de Banques Suisses. (SWI)
59 Annonce de journal du grand magasin *Seibu*; référence est faite à une exposition de l'artiste Tadanori Yooko. (JPN)
60 Exemple d'une série d'annonces de journaux pour les couleurs *Asian-Paints* devenues le leader du marché. (IND)
61, 62 Annonces du grand magasin *I. Magnin* pour la campagne de vente de parfums à Noël. (USA)
63, 64 Exemples tirés d'une série de sept annonces de *Nippon Electronics*. Il y est question des systèmes de communication extraordinaires propres aux dauphins et aux oiseaux. (JPN)

57

Man kann nicht das zweite wollen, ohne das erste zu tun.

58

Zeit zerrinnen lassen kostet Geld. Besonders bei Wertschriften.

59

ART DIRECTOR / DIRECTEUR ARTISTIQUE:

55, 56 Nancy Hoefig
57, 58 Ernst Herzog
59 Tadanori Yokoo
60 Bahadur Merwan
61, 62 Kay Architect
63, 64 Takanori Asaeda

AGENCY / AGENTUR / AGENCE – STUDIO:

55, 56 Richards, Sullivan, Brock & Associates
57, 58 Advico
60 Ogilvy Benson & Mather
61, 62 I. Magnin/Adv. Dept.
63, 64 Dentsu Advertising

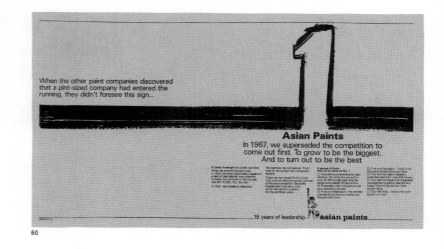

60

Advertisements / Anzeigen / Annonces

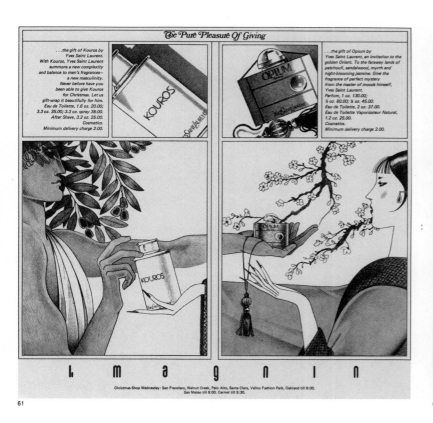

61

62

63

64

45

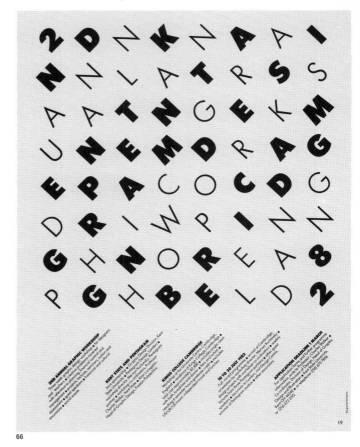

65 Newspaper advertisement for *Barney's*, a clothing store, with an appeal to vote in national elections by using the argument that one vote is of course futile until others of the same persuasion are counted with it. (USA)

66 Magazine advertisement for a graphic-design course organized by Kent State University and *Pentagram Design*. (USA)

67 Advertisement by the First Tennessee Banks for a tax-saving program called the first Tennessee Money Shelter for tax relief on Individual Retirement Accounts. Black and white with brownish orange. (USA)

68 Advertisement for *Governor's Square* summer offers. (USA)

69 Trade magazine advertisement for DKG zippers. (USA)

70, 71 Examples from a series of full-colour advertisements for *The Mall in Columbia*, a shopping centre to be expanded by seventy stores. (USA)

72 Full-page newspaper advertisement for the opening of the *White Marsh* shopping centre. In full colour. (USA)

ARTIST / KÜNSTLER / ARTISTE:

65 Milton Glaser
67 Phil Wende
70, 71 Brian Boyd
72 Ron Sullivan

DESIGNER / GESTALTER / MAQUETTISTE:

65 Tom Woolsley
66 Mervin Kurlansky / Robert Maude
67 Jerry Sullivan
68 Dick Mitchell
69 Tony DiSpigna
70, 71 Stephen Miller / Brian Boyd
72 Ron Sullivan

ART DIRECTOR / DIRECTEUR ARTISTIQUE:

65 Tom Woolsley
66 Mervyn Kurlansky
67 Jerry Sullivan
68 Dick Mitchell
70, 71 Stephen Miller
72 Ron Sullivan

AGENCY / AGENTUR / AGENCE – STUDIO:

65 Ally & Gargano
66 Pentagram
67 Burton Campbell
68, 70–72 Richards, Sullivan, Brock & Assoc.
69 Lubalin Peckolick Assoc. Inc.

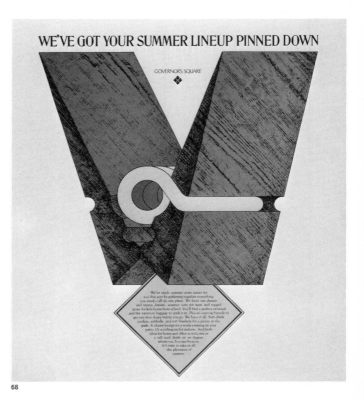

IF THE ZIPPERS IN YOUR DRESSES DON'T SLIDE, YOUR SALES MIGHT.

65 «Natürlich zählt eine Stimme nicht. Bis Sie alle die Leute zählen, die so denken.» Zeitungsinserat eines Bekleidungsgeschäftes, mit Aufruf zur Stimmabgabe bei nationalen Wahlen. (USA)
66 Zeitschriften-Inserat für einen Graphik-Design-Kurs, organisiert von der Kent State University und *Pentagram Design*. (USA)
67 «Man muss kein grosses Tier sein, um Steuervorteile zu geniessen.» Anzeige einer Bank, die hier steuergünstige Spareinlagen anbietet. Schwarzweiss mit bräunlichem Orange. (USA)
68 Inserat für das Sommersortiment eines Kaufhauses. (USA)
69 Fachzeitschriften-Anzeige für DKG-Reissverschlüsse. (USA)
70, 71 Beispiele aus einer Serie von farbigen Anzeigen für ein Einkaufszentrum, das um siebzig neue Läden erweitert wird. (USA)
72 Ganzseitiges Zeitungsinserat für die Eröffnung des Einkaufszentrums *White Marsh*. Mehrfarbig. (USA)

65 «Bien sûr, une voix isolée ne compte pas. Jusqu'à ce que vous comptiez tous ceux qui pensent de même.» Annonce de journal d'un magasin de confection sur les devoirs civiques. (USA)
66 Annonce de magazine pour un cours d'art graphique organisé par l'Université d'Etat Kent et *Pentagram Design*. (USA)
67 «On n'a pas besoin d'être un gros bonnet («une grosse bête») pour obtenir des avantages fiscaux.» Annonce d'une banque offrant des livrets d'épargne. Noir et blanc, orange brun. (USA)
68 Annonce pour l'assortiment d'été d'un grand magasin. (USA)
69 Annonce professionnelle: fermetures à glissière DKG. (USA)
70, 71 Exemples d'annonces: série couleur pour un centre commercial où s'ouvrent soixante-dix nouveaux magasins. (USA)
72 Annonce de journal pleine page pour l'inauguration du centre commercial *White Marsh*. En polychromie. (USA)

Advertisements
Anzeigen
Annonces

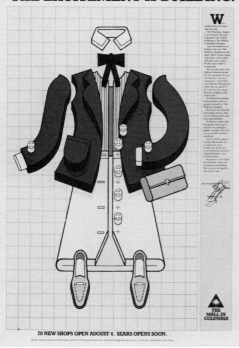

73

Advertisements
Anzeigen
Annonces

74

73, 74 Illustration and complete newspaper advertisement by the department store *I. Magnin* for an Italian perfume. (USA)
75–78 Full-page newspaper advertisements from various campaigns for the *Eaton* department store. Figs. 75 and 76 deal with extended opening hours before Christmas so that customers can do last-minute shopping; Fig. 77: the opening of a special *Steinway* piano salon in the store; Fig. 78 appeared on the occasion of the national holiday of the Canadian province of Québec which, as an acknowledgement of the ties with Québec and its traditions, was also declared a holiday by *Eaton*. (CAN)

73, 74 Illustration und vollständiges Zeitungsinserat des Kaufhauses *I. Magnin* für ein italienisches Parfum. (USA)
75–78 Ganzseitige Zeitungsinserate aus verschiedenen Kampagnen des Kaufhauses *Eaton*. In Abb. 75 und 76 geht es um die verlängerten Öffnungszeiten vor Weihnachten für die Einkäufe in letzter Minute; in Abb. 77 wird die Eröffnung eines speziellen *Steinway*-Salons des Kaufhauses bekanntgegeben; Abb. 78 erschien anlässlich des Nationalfeiertages des kanadischen Bundesstaates Québec, der auch von *Eaton*, als Zeichen der Verbundenheit mit Québec und seinen Traditionen, zum Feiertag erklärt wird. (CAN)

73, 74 Illustration et annonce de journal complète du grand magasin *I. Magnin* pour un parfum italien. (USA)
75–78 Annonces de journaux pleine page extraites de diverses campagnes du grand magasin *Eaton*. Les fig. 75 et 76 traitent de l'ouverture nocturne à la veille des fêtes de Noël pour permettre les achats de dernière minute; la fig. 77 annonce l'ouverture d'un salon *Steinway*; la fig. 78 représente l'annonce publiée pour la fête nationale de la province du Québec déclarée jour férié par *Eaton* en vertu de l'importance reconnue aux traditions et à la politique de la province. (CAN)

75

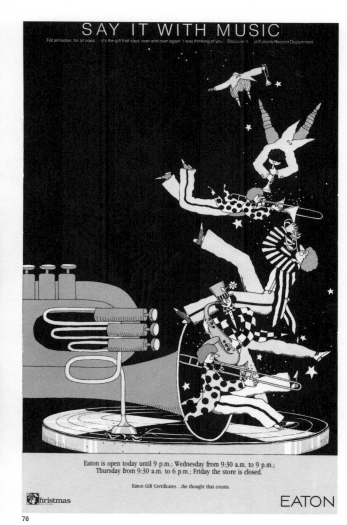

76

77

78

49

ZOEK DE BESTE CASSETTE.

Als u 'n cassette koopt, kunt u het beste de Sony Metallic nemen.

En denkt u nu niet meteen: „Dat is weer zo'n reklamepraatje."

Want wij zeggen niet dat onze Metallic cassette verreweg de beste is. Het bekende muziekblad Disk zegt 't. Die heeft alle cassettes uit en te na getest. De konklusie liet niets aan duidelijkheid te wensen over:

„Sony Metallic is royaal de beste cassette uit de test."

Nou heeft u gelijk dat één test van één tijdschrift niet alles zegt.

Andere bladen als Hifi Choice en Stereo komen echter tot dezelfde konklusie.

Sony Metallic is gewoon de beste cassette die er op dit moment te koop is.

Maar belangrijker dan wat zij er van vinden, is wat u van deze Sony cassette vindt. Daar gaat 't per slot om.

En er is maar één manier om daar achter te komen. 'n Keer proberen, die Sony Metallic. Mits uw cassettedeck 'n metaltapestand heeft.

Is dat niet het geval, dan is er nog geen man overboord. Sony heeft alle soorten cassettes. Maar wat had u anders verwacht van de grootste tapefabrikant ter wereld? SONY

– Sony Metallic verdient in deze test duidelijk de gouden medaille. Hij steekt op de wezenlijke punten met kop en schouders boven de rest uit.
– Opvallend genoeg en eigen
(DISK MAART 1981).

SONY CASSETTES, JE HOORT 'T METEEN.

79

ARTIST / KÜNSTLER / ARTISTE:

79 Pauline Ellison/Chris Lewis
81, 82 Dick Mitchell
83, 84 Dick Sakahara

DESIGNER / GESTALTER / MAQUETTISTE:

79 Hans Goedicke
80 Joe Feigenbaum
81, 82 Dick Mitchell
83 Jim Adair
84 Wayne Butler

79 "Search for the best cassette." Black-and-white *Sony* advertisement. (NLD)
80 Double-spread ad for a new typeface designed by Tom Carnase for the World Typeface Center. *Favrile* was chosen from names suggested by the public. ((USA)
81, 82 Illustration and complete trade magazine advertisement for the Schroder Real Estate Corp., referring here to its growth. (USA)
83, 84 *Life* magazine advertisements aimed at the pharmaceutical and entertainment industries and serving the ends of space promotion. (USA)

79 «Suche die beste Kassette.» Inserat in Schwarzweiss für *Sony*-Kassetten. (NLD)
80 Doppelseitiges Inserat für einen neuen Schrifttyp, entworfen von Tom Carnase und aufgrund eines Vorschlags aus der Öffentlichkeit *Favrile* genannt. Es werden hier alle vorgeschlagenen Namen aufgeführt. (USA)
81, 82 Illustration und vollständiges Fachzeitschriften-Inserat für ein Immobilienunternehmen, das hier auf sein Wachstum hinweist. (USA)
83, 84 Inserate der Zeitschrift *Life*, die hier um Anzeigen aus der Pharma-Branche und der Unterhaltungsindustrie wirbt. (USA)

79 «Choisis la meilleure cassette.» Annonce noir-blanc. Cassettes *Sony*. (NLD)
80 Annonce double page en faveur d'un nouveau caractère créé par Tom Carnase et baptisé *Favrile* sur une proposition venue du public. Sont ici énumérés tous les autres noms proposés pour cette nouvelle famille de caractères. (USA)
81, 82 Illustration et annonce complète de revue professionnelle pour un promoteur immobilier fier de sa croissance rapide. (USA)
83, 84 Annonces du magazine *Life* destinées aux annonceurs potentiels dans le secteur des produits pharmaceutiques et de l'industrie des loisirs. (USA)

80

81

82

ART DIRECTOR / DIRECTEUR ARTISTIQUE:

79 Hans Goedicke
80 Tom Carnase
81, 82 Dick Mitchell
83, 84 Jim Adair

AGENCY / AGENTUR / AGENCE – STUDIO:

79 KVH/GGK International B. V.
80 Carnase, Inc.
81, 82 Richards, Sullivan, Brock & Associates
83, 84 Geer, DuBois Inc.

Your drug advertising feels better in the one magazine where you get fast, fast results. **LIFE**

83

Your entertainment advertising makes a big entrance in the one magazine with more show per page. **LIFE**

84

Advertisements
Anzeigen
Annonces

ARTIST / KÜNSTLER / ARTISTE:

85 Carlo Pollastrini
86 Jean Munier
87 Patrick Gaudard
88 Centrokappa Visual Production
89, 90 Mark Hess

DESIGNER / GESTALTER / MAQUETTISTE:

85 Carlo Pollastrini
88 Centrokappa Srl

ART DIRECTOR / DIRECTEUR ARTISTIQUE:

85 Carlo Pollastrini
86 Philippe Arnal
87 Daniel Pilloud
88 Centrokappa

AGENCY / AGENTUR / AGENCE – STUDIO:

85 Ferrante Pollastrini
86 Non Stop
87 Patrick Gaudard
88 Centrokappa Srl

85

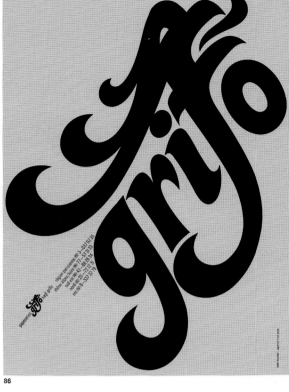

86

87

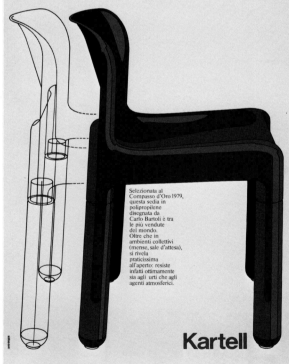

88

85 Advertisement for a roofing system which requires only one layer. (ITA)
86 Trade magazine advertisement in black and white for *Grifo* paper. (FRA)
87 Full-page, full-colour advertisement of the American-Swiss concern, Autologic S.A., manufacturers of photo-typesetting equipment. It was published on the occasion of a trade fair in Lausanne. (SWI)
88 Example from a series of advertisements for a *Kartell* chair, designed by Carlo Baroli. Chair in green chades. (ITA)
89, 90 Illustration and complete advertisement for the Alcan Aluminum Corp., pointing out that growth is the sign of something that lives. (USA)

85 Inserat für ein Dachdecksystem, bei dem eine Schicht genügt. (ITA)
86 Fachzeitschrifteninserat in Schwarzweiss für *Grifo*-Papier. (FRA)
87 Ganzseitige, mehrfarbige Anzeige eines amerikanisch-schweizerischen Unternehmens, der Autologic S.A., anlässlich einer Messe in Lausanne. Es stellt vor allem Photosatz-Anlagen her. (SWI)
88 Beispiel aus einer Serie von Anzeigen für einen *Kartell*-Stuhl, der von Carlo Baroli entworfen wurde. Stuhl in Grüntönen. (ITA)
89, 90 Illustration und vollständiges Inserat für die *Alcan*-Aluminiumwerke. Thema des Inserates ist das Wachsen durch Erfahrung. (USA)

85 Annonce pour un système de couverture de toit monocouche. (ITA)
86 Annonce professionnelle noir et blanc pour les papiers *Grifo*. (FRA)
87 Annonce polychrome pleine page d'une entreprise américano-helvé-
tique, l'Autologic S.A., publiée à l'occasion d'une exposition à Lausanne. Ses
fabrications: surtout des équipements de photocomposition. (SWI)
88 Exemple d'une série d'annonces pour une chaise *Kartell* conçue par Carlo
Baroli. Chaise aux tons verts. (ITA)
89, 90 Illustration et annonce complète pour les usines d'aluminium *Alcan*:
«La croissance est le signe caractéristique d'un organisme vivant.» (USA)

90

89

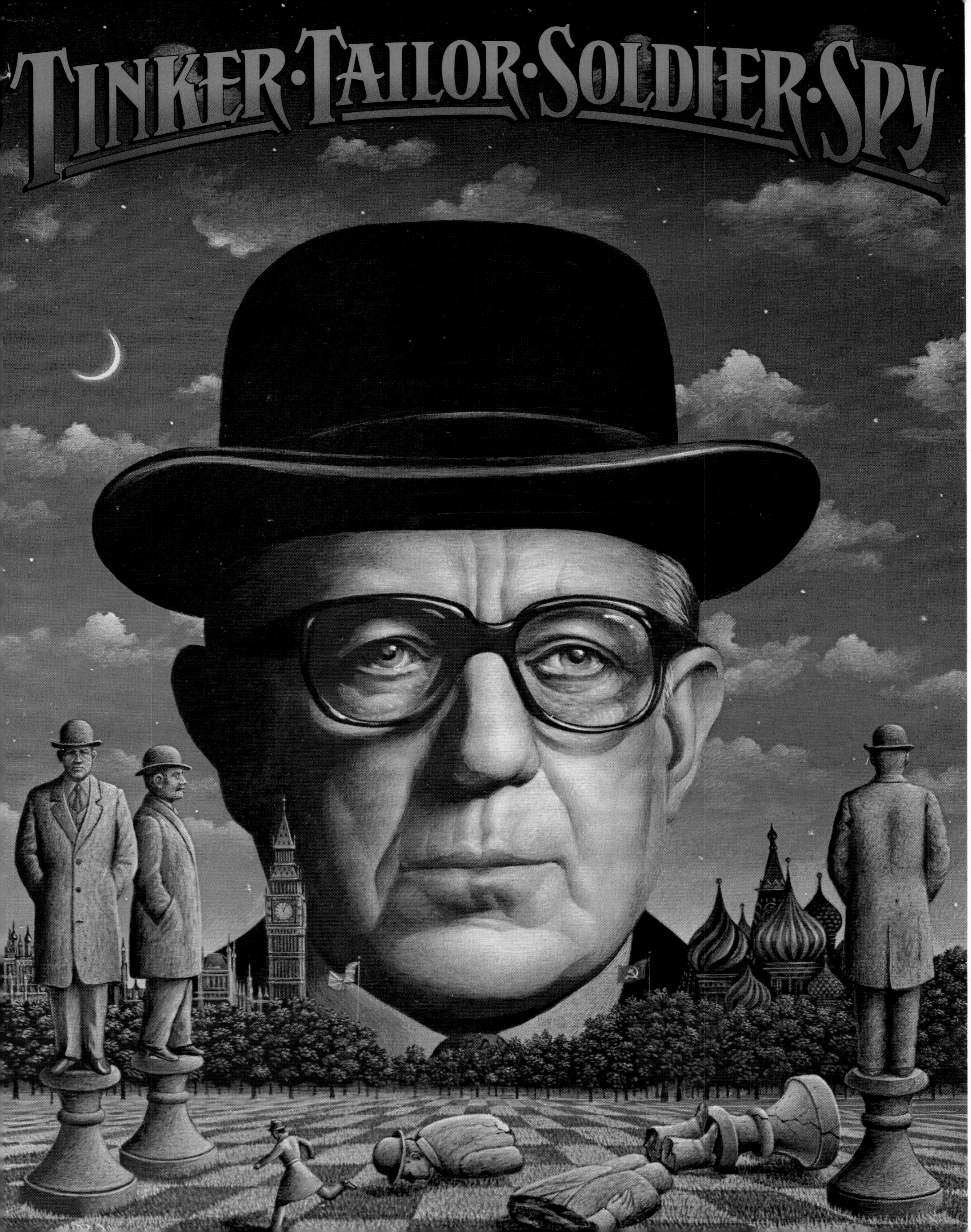
TINKER·TAILOR·SOLDIER·SPY

91, 92 Illustration and complete advertisement for a television series based on the well-known spy novel by John le Carré, with Sir Alec Guinness playing the role of George Smiley. The production was financed by the *Exxon* company. (USA)
93, 94 Complete advertisement and illustration for *Dioressence* perfume by *Christian Dior*. (FRA)

91, 92 Illustration und vollständiges Inserat für eine Fernsehsendung des Films nach einem Spionageroman von John le Carré, mit Sir Alec Guinness in der Rolle des berühmten George Smiley. Finanziert wurde die Aufführung von *Exxon*. (USA)
93, 94 Vollständiges Inserat und Illustration für das Parfum *Dioressence* von *Christian Dior*. (FRA)

91, 92 Illustration et annonce complète pour la programmation à la télévision du film tiré du roman d'espionnage de John Le Carré, avec sir Alec Guinness dans le rôle de George Smiley. L'émission a été financée par Exxon Corporation. (USA)
93, 94 Illustration et annonce complète pour le parfum *Dioressence* de *Christian Dior*. (FRA)

ARTIST / KÜNSTLER / ARTISTE:

91, 92 Richard Hess
93, 94 Gruau

DESIGNER / GESTALTER / MAQUETTISTE:

91, 92 Susan Lyster

ART DIRECTOR / DIRECTEUR ARTISTIQUE:

91, 92 Jack Sidebotham/Ted Shaw

AGENCY / AGENTUR / AGENCE – STUDIO:

91, 92 McCaffrey & McCall, Inc.
93, 94 Alice

94

92

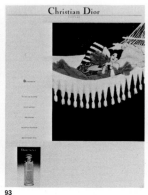

93

Advertisements
Anzeigen
Annonces

95 a

95–100 Double spreads and full-page illustrations from a *Champion International* image campaign, using the general slogan "Planting seeds for the future" to convey the corporation's wide-ranging plans and thoughts for the future. The different subjects are: "The seeds of thought" (Fig. 95, 95a); "Our growing thirst for water" (Fig. 96); "Facing tomorrow today" (Fig. 97); "Human Engineering" (Fig. 98) and (Fig. 99, 100) "In the future, nations will be dividing up mankind's common inheritance: the vast wealth of the oceans. But will we do it recklessly or with vision?" These subjects are dealt with in more detail in a brochure that is available from *Champion International*. (USA)

95–100 Doppelseiten und ganzseitige Illustrationen aus einer Image-Kampagne von *Champion International*. Der gemeinsame Slogan, «Champion pflanzt für die Zukunft», soll das weitsichtige Planen und Zukunftsdenken der Forstgruppe des Papierherstellers verdeutlichen. Die einzelnen Themen sind: «Samen des Denkens» (Abb. 95, 95a); «Unser wachsender Durst nach Wasser» (Abb. 96); «Heute der Zukunft ins Auge sehen» (Abb. 97); «Menschliches Wachstum» (Abb. 98) und (Abb. 99, 100) «In der Zukunft werden die Nationen das gemeinsame Erbe der Menschheit aufteilen: den immensen Reichtum der Meere. Aber werden wir es rücksichtslos oder mit Umsicht tun?» Abhandlungen zu diesem Themenkreis sind auch in einer Broschüre zusammengefasst und bei *Champion International* erhältlich. (USA)

95–100 Doubles pages et illustrations pleine page tirées d'une campagne d'image globale de marque de *Champion International* placée sous la devise «Champion plante pour l'avenir» et tendant à démontrer la vision prospective et le sens profond des responsabilités incombant au groupe forestier de ce grand papetier. Les sujets sont les suivants: «Semences de la pensée» (Fig. 95, 95a); «Notre soif d'eau croissante» (96); «Regarder aujourd'hui l'avenir dans les yeux» (97); «Croissance humaine» (98). Fig. 99, 100: «L'avenir verra les nations se partager l'héritage collectif de l'humanité: l'immense richesse des mers. Mais ce partage se fera-t-il sans ménagement ou judicieusement?» Ces sujets sont aussi traités dans une brochure *Champion*. (USA)

95

96

97

98

99

100

ARTIST / KÜNSTLER / ARTISTE:

95, 95a Robert Giusti
96, 98–100 Wilson McLean
97 Richard Hess

ART DIRECTOR:

95–100 Len Sirowitz

AGENCY / AGENTUR / AGENCE:

95–100 Rosenfeld, Sirowitz
      & Lawson, Inc.

101

102

A slip of the code can sink a ship

Industry in the eighties cannot afford the computer programming statistics of the seventies.

If, for example, the technology of shipbuilding were at the same level of sophistication as computer programming in the 1970's, a significant percentage of the world's ocean-going vessels would sink upon launch.

But this is the eighties, and ITT is programming for the eighties with new commitments to reliability in all product lines, from microprocessor-based telephone switching systems to computerized delivery routes for our bakeries.

To keep us on an even keel, we're building a programming research center in Stratford, Connecticut, staffed with a crew of scientists, engineers and other specialists from around the world. Programming competency centers have been established in countries ranging from Norway to the Mediterranean Sea; and from England to California and beyond. We're determined to maintain ITT's world-class competitiveness and technological leadership.

The future demands it!

ITT Programming

103

A big byte of profits

Any high-technology corporation, with a population of 100,000 or more, is likely to have generated at least 10 million source lines of computer code, at a cost of between $500 million and $1 billion.

The amount of data these programs manipulate is considerable. Corporations typically have multiple data base and data dictionary systems with access to billions of bytes of information.

At the ITT programming research center in Stratford, Connecticut, our emphasis is on introducing new productivity techniques and developing innovative programming environments for transfer to all ITT units. The resultant, worldwide technology exchanges have become one of our primary means of managing this expensive new realm of evolving human enterprise.

We've recognized that it's time to bring programming into control; contributing to profits, not costs.

The future demands it!

ITT Programming

104

A leg up.

TRW distributors not only have fast delivery . . . usually same day . . . but they have the most complete resistor choice.

Carbon Comps, Metal Film, Thick and Thin Film Networks, General Purpose Wirewound, and Hi-Rel resistors. He has them all . . . on the shelf, ready to go. At the most competitive prices around.

Fast delivery. Complete resistor choice. Competitive prices. One-stop shopping. You can see why we have a leg up on the competition.

See your local distributor or contact:
TRW Fixed Resistor Distributor Operation.
P.O. Box 12867, Phila., PA 19108.
Or call (215) 923-8230. TWX-710-670-3370.

TRW IRC RESISTORS
ANOTHER PRODUCT OF A COMPANY CALLED TRW

Advt. 2800-81-1 — 1 page, 10" x 13-1/2"
Electronic Buyers' News — June 1, 1981

105

You spoke. We listened.

You asked for a line of general purpose and semi-precision resistors with the quality and characteristics of metal film, not carbon.

You wanted cost savings, but also better performance.

Meet our GP-1/4W. It's metal film . . . not carbon. It's dual rated for both 1/4 W and 1/2 W applications, yet it is a drop-in replacement for other 1/4 W resistors.

At TRW you don't always get what you ask for . . . sometimes you get more.

CARBON COMPOSITION • WIREWOUNDS • METAL FILM • ULTRA-PRECISION • HI-VOLTAGE •
THICK & THIN FILM NETWORKS • SPECIAL APPLICATION RESISTOR PRODUCTS

For detailed information and literature contact:
TRW/IRC Resistors, 401 N. Broad St., Phila., PA 19108.
Or call (215) 922-8900. TWX-170-670-2286.
Or see your local TRW distributor.

TRW/IRC Resistors, 401 N. Broad St., Phila., PA 19108

Talk to us. We'll not only listen, we'll respond.
☐ Send data on the next generation metal film resistors for general purpose and semi-precision applications.
☐ Call me and let's talk.

Name _____
Company _____ Title _____
Address _____
City _____ State ____ Zip ____
Phone Number _____

TRW IRC RESISTORS
ANOTHER PRODUCT OF A COMPANY CALLED TRW

Adst. 2800-81-3 — 1 page — 10" x 15½"
Electronic Buyers' News — To be determined

106

59

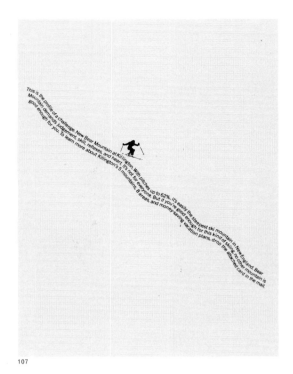

107

As cinco regiões do Brasil.

Este anúncio é uma homenagem da Fokker aos cinco anos da aviação regional no Brasil e às suas cinco companhias aéreas regionais.

Em 1976 nascia, no Brasil, o Transporte Aéreo Regional. Seus principais objetivos - ligar as pequenas e médias comunidades aos pólos geoeconômico do País; promover a integração social do homem do interior; e massificar produtivamente o uso do transporte aéreo, em benefício da racionalização de combustível - estão

sendo brilhantemente realizados. Hoje, as cinco companhias aéreas regionais - TAM, TABA, VOTEC, RIO-SUL e NORDESTE - atendem a mais de 170 cidades em praticamente todos os estados brasileiros, encurtando as distâncias e aumentando, cada vez mais, o ritmo do progresso e do desenvolvimento do Brasil.

A FOKKER é a fabricante do Fokker F27, o avião especialmente projetado para vôos regionais. Com capacidade para 44 a 60 passageiros, o F27 tem espaço para bagagem, inclusive de mão, toda a estrutura necessária para o serviço de bordo, e conta ainda com uma grande porta lateral, para facilitar a carga e descarga de mercadorias. Rentável, econômico, confortável e versátil, o Fokker F27 pode operar de qualquer tipo de pista,

mesmo as mais curtas, e rudimentares. A TAM já tem três e está esperando o quarto chegar.

Fokker B.V.
P.O. Box 7600 - 1117 ZJ Schiphol
Holanda
Uma família holandesa com certeza.

109

Imagine your worst fear a reality.

THE HOWLING

A DANIEL H. BLATT PRODUCTION "THE HOWLING" Starring DEE WALLACE · PATRICK MACNEE
DENNIS DUGAN · CHRISTOPHER STONE · BELINDA BALASKI · KEVIN McCARTHY · JOHN CARRADINE
SLIM PICKENS And introducing ELISABETH BROOKS Executive Producers DANIEL H. BLATT and STEVEN A. LANE
Screenplay by JOHN SAYLES and TERENCE H. WINKLESS Based on the novel by GARY BRANDNER
Music by PINO DONAGGIO Produced by MICHAEL FINNELL and JACK CONRAD Directed by JOE DANTE
Presented by AVCO EMBASSY, INTERNATIONAL FILM INVESTORS and WESCOM PRODUCTIONS
ORIGINAL MOTION PICTURE SOUNDTRACK ALBUM AVAILABLE ON VARÉSE SARABANDE RECORDS
R RESTRICTED
AVCO EMBASSY PICTURES Release

SOON AT THEATRES EVERYWHERE.

108

107 Magazine advertisement for a ski-resort region. (USA)
108 Full-page magazine advertisement for "The Howling", a horror film supposed to make people's worst fears a reality. (USA)
109 Double-spread advertisement for *Fokker* aeroplanes, offered for the national airline routes in Brazil's five regions and the airline companies situated there. Light and dark blue with red and white. (BRA)
110, 111 "Dawn Chorus." Illustration and full-page advertisement for TDK tape cassettes. In full colour. (GBR)
112 Full-page advertisement for Continental Corporation, an insurance company. Black and white with a red telephone. (USA)
113 Self-promotional advertisement of a graphic production studio called *Midnight Oil.* In black and white. (USA)
114, 115 Magazine advertisements for *Decisionex* computers. (USA)

110

112

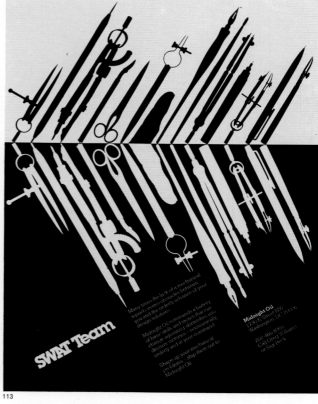

113

111

114

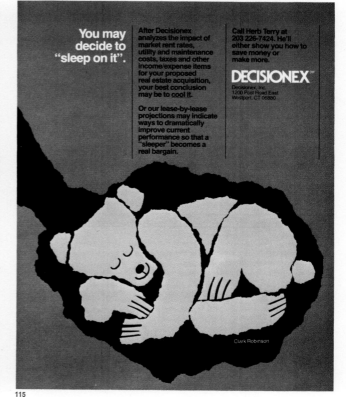

115

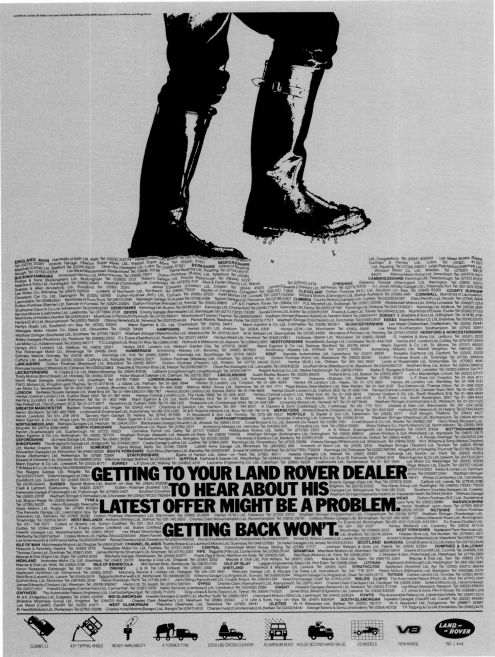

ARTIST / KÜNSTLER / ARTISTE:

117, 118 Colin Mier
119, 120 Robert Giusti

DESIGNER / GESTALTER / MAQUETTISTE:

116 Brian Morrow
117, 118 Hans Goedicke

ART DIRECTOR / DIRECTEUR ARTISTIQUE:

116 Brian Morrow
117, 118 Hans Goedicke
119, 120 Ted Curl

AGENCY / AGENTUR / AGENCE – STUDIO:

116 TBWA Ltd.
117, 118 KVH/GGK International B.V.
119, 120 Magnus Nankervis & Curl

116 Full-pages, black-and-white newspaper advertisement about the *Land Rover*, listing addresses of dealers. (GBR)
117, 118 From a series of full-page advertisements for the Dutch National Railways. The full-colour illustrations show the Dutch tracks and railway trains to the Hook of Holland, English ones from Harwich to London, and in between the sea route. (NLD)
119, 120 Illustration and complete double-spread advertisement for *Thai Airlines* referring to a new route to Canton. (THAI)

116 Ganzseitiges Zeitungsinserat für den *Land Rover*, mit Angabe der Adressen von Verkaufsstellen in Grossbritannien. (GBR)
117, 118 Aus einer Serie von vier ganzseitigen Inseraten der holländischen Eisenbahnen unter dem Motto «Englisch-Lektionen». Die farbigen Illustrationen zeigen jeweils die holländischen Transportmittel und -wege nach Hoek van Holland, die englischen von Harwich nach London und dazwischen den Seeweg. (NLD)
119, 120 Illustration und vollständiges, doppelseitiges Inserat für *Thai Airlines,* hier für eine neue Route nach Kanton. (THAI)

116 Annonce de journal pleine page pour la *Land Rover*, avec la liste des concessionnaires en Grande-Bretagne. (GBR)
117, 118 Exemples d'une série de quatre annonces pleine page des Chemins de fer néerlandais intitulée «Leçons d'anglais». Les illustrations couleur montrent les moyens et voies de transport hollandais jusqu'à Hoek van Holland, les anglais de Harwich à Londres et le transport maritime. (NLD)
119, 120 Illustration et annonce double page complète pour *Thai Airlines,* annonçant une nouvelle liaison avec Canton. (THAI)

119

121

122

123

ARTIST / KÜNSTLER / ARTISTE:

122 Craig Carl
123 Centrokappa Visual Production
124 Eraldo Carugati
125, 128 Alex Ebel
126, 127 Pascal Lamorinière

DESIGNER / GESTALTER / MAQUETTISTE:

121 Dietrich Ebert
122 Craig Carl
123 Centrokappa Srl
124, 125, 128 Gail Daniels
126, 127 Jean Verecchia

ART DIRECTOR / DIRECTEUR ARTISTIQUE:

121 Dietrich Ebert
122 Martin Wolff
123 Centrokappa Srl
124 Angus McQueen/Gail Daniels
125, 128 Angus McQueen/Mark Keller
126, 127 Louis Alloing

AGENCY / AGENTUR / AGENCE – STUDIO:

121 Alain Fion
122 Wolff, Whitehill Advertising Inc.
123 Centrokappa Srl
124, 125, 128 Ackerman & McQueen Advertising Inc.
126, 127 Safronoff & Associés

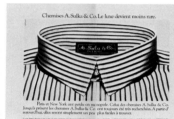

126

127

124

125

128

121 Full-page magazine advertisement for *Lacoste* clothing, alluding to the popularity of its trademark, the crocodile. (GER)
122 Full-page trade magazine advertisement for the introduction of a new name in girls' fashions. In full colour. (USA)
123 Full-colour trade magazine advertisement with a red border for a manufacturer of lamps and other furnishings. (ITA)
124 Double-spread magazine advertisement for *Resistol* cowboy hats. Mainly in shades of brown and yellow, blue river. (USA)
125, 128 Examples from a series of full-page advertisements for *Nacona* cowboy boots. In full colour. (USA)
126, 127 Double-spread trade magazine advertisement for *Sulka* shirts, on the occasion of a trade fair. In black and white. (FRA)

121 Ganzseitiges Zeitschriften-Inserat für *Lacoste*-Kleidung; mit dem Markenzeichen, das wie ein Maskottchen behandelt wird. (GER)
122 Mehrfarbiges, ganzseitiges Fachzeitschriften-Inserat für die Einführung einer neuen Marke in der Mädchen-Oberbekleidung. (USA)
123 Rot umrandetes, mehrfarbiges Fachzeitschriften-Inserat eines Herstellers von Lampen und anderen Einrichtungsdingen. (ITA)
124 Doppelseitiges Zeitschriften-Inserat für *Resistol*-Cowboy-Hüte. Vorwiegend Braun- und Gelbtöne, blauer Fluss. (USA)
125, 128 Beispiele aus einer Serie von ganzseitigen, farbigen Anzeigen für *Nacona*-Cowboy-Stiefel. (USA)
126, 127 Doppelseitiges Fachzeitschriften-Inserat in Schwarzweiss anlässlich einer Messe, für Hemden von *Sulka*. (FRA)

121 Annonce de magazine pleine page pour les vêtements *Lacoste*, avec l'animal-mascotte de la marque. (GER)
122 Annonce de revue professionnelle, polychrome, pleine page, pour le lancement d'une nouvelle marque de vêtements pour filles. (USA)
123 Annonce polychrome de revue professionnelle, encadrée de rouge, pour un fabricant de lampes et autres articles d'équipement. (ITA)
124 Annonce de magazine double page pour les chapeaux de cow-boys *Resistol*. Tons bruns et jaunes prédominants, fleuve bleu. (USA)
125, 128 Exemples d'annonces figurant dans une série polychrome sur pleine page en faveur des bottes de cow-boys *Nacona*. (USA)
126, 127 Annonce de revue professionnelle, double page, pour les chemises *Sulka*, publiée à l'occasion d'une foire. Noir, blanc. (FRA)

Advertisements
Anzeigen
Annonces

Startling. Piped kidskin or snakeskin pumps by Casadei. Downtown Seattle only in Salon Shoes.

nordstrom
Washington/California/Oregon/Utah/Alaska

129

PENDLETON, USA

PURE WOOL   FOR FURTHER INFORMATION WRITE   PENDLETON WOOLEN MILLS, PORTLAND, OREGON 97201

130

131

The Eagle and the Penguin

The Penguin and the Owl were both courting the Bird of Paradise. The Penguin came to the Eagle for advice. "I'm not getting anywhere," he said. "I'd like to take her dancing every night, but she seems to prefer helping the Owl study for his courses at night school."

"Be patient," said the Eagle, with his renowned sense of style. "The owl is a dull fellow and your natural elegance will surely win out in the end."

It didn't work out that way. The Bird of Paradise married the Owl as soon as he finished school and they settled down in Venice, Florida, and raised 38 kids, all of whom worked their way through college and got post-graduate degrees.

The penguin never married. He moved to Hollywood where he went dancing every night and, during the day, made a decent living playing the butler in some pretty good B movies.

MORAL: You can't win them all, but you can sure look good trying.

Good days, bad days—ups and downs, there's an important satisfaction in knowing you look good, no matter what.

We've been helping people look good since 1867. Our shirts are known for classic cut and fit. Fabrics that are custom-woven and custom-dyed. The extra care in cutting and stitching, right here in Pennsylvania, that make an Eagle feel comfortable and improve over the years.

That's why, no matter how things are going, an Eagle shirt can help you look good—without even trying.

One more thing. Some fine stores like our shirts so much they have us sew in their labels. If you're dead set on buying an Eagle shirt, with or without a real Eagle label, just drop us a card and we'll let you know where you can. Miss Afflerbach, P.O. Box 180, Quakertown, PA 18951

132

The Eagle and the Jaybird

Once on a business trip to the Coast, the Eagle and the Jaybird were invited to a cocktail party at a movie producer's home. "We must dress for the occasion," said the Jay, and went out and spent $369 on a new outfit.

"How do you like my threads?" he asked the Eagle. "One of them is loose," replied the Eagle, who has a keen eye for craftsmanship. "Get your money back." "Nonsense," said the Jay. "Details, details, details. All I care about is the broad strokes. One little thread won't stop me."

Sure enough, the loose thread got caught in an assistant casting director's gold chain at the party and began to unravel. The Eagle was too busy getting the phone number of Second Runner-up Miss Anaheim to notice that the unravelling continued until the Jaybird was as naked as an oven roaster.

The L.A. police arrested the Jaybird and locked him up for 90 days on an indecent exposure charge.

MORAL: Sometimes, hanging by a thread is as bad as hanging by a noose.

Every Eagle shirt goes through 72 separate phases of manufacture and inspection before it ever leaves our Pennsylvania factory.

We check to make sure every button fits every buttonhole. We stitch the buttonholes so it's impossible for them to fray. Threads? We have lots of nice ladies who spend their entire day checking for loose threads… not only at the seams, but even *inside* the collar before it is sewn to the band.

Our point is this: some birds may be generous to a fault, but an Eagle overlooks nothing.

Now, where to find our shirts. It may be a problem since a lot of fine stores like them so much they have us sew in their labels. Same shirt, different name. If you're dead set on buying an Eagle shirt, with (or without) a real Eagle label, just drop us a card and we'll let you know where you can. Miss Afflerbach, P.O. Box 180, Quakertown, PA 18951

133

The Eagle and the Goose

Before taking off on his annual winter flight to South America, the Goose stopped by to show the Eagle his vacation wardrobe: white patent leather loafers, purple slacks and silk shirts of all colors.

"These outfits aren't you," said the Eagle, who's a stickler for taste. "It's silly for a goose to try to look like a cockatoo. Stay with what suits you." "Out of the question," said the Goose. "I'm tired of being just one of the flock. This year, I'm going to stand out."

And stand out he did. Somewhere over West Virginia, a hunter selected him out of two thousand other geese and let him have it. In the wing. The Goose crash landed in Wheeling, where he spent the winter in a convalescent home while all the other geese were in Rio, taking Portuguese lessons and drinking Pina Coladas.

MORAL: If you're dressed to kill, somebody may very well take a shot at you.

Mercifully the days of blatant overstatement in men's fashions are gone. Today most men (and women) want what Eagle has been known for through the years: shirts that can become old friends. The colors of our custom-woven fabrics are unusual but never gaudy. Sometimes classic, sometimes bold, but never overwhelming. And because the parts of every Eagle shirt are cut out by hand (at the same time and from the same bolt) the color of each section of an Eagle shirt exactly matches that of every other. That's why, no matter how styles may change, nobody ever shoots down an Eagle.

Now, where to find our shirts. It may be a problem since a lot of fine stores like them so much they have us sew in their labels. Same shirt, different name. If you're dead set on buying an Eagle shirt, with or without a real Eagle label, just drop us a card and we'll let you know where you can. Miss Afflerbach, P.O. Box 180, Quakertown, PA 18951

134

---

129 Full-page advertisement for women's shoe stores. (USA)
130 From a series of full-page advertisements for *Pendleton* woolen clothing. In brown shades with a blue label. (USA)
131 From a campaign for a chain of bookshops, using the slogan "Give your imagination a chance". (SWE)
132–135 Examples from a series of full-page advertisements in black and white for *Eagle* shirts, showing Fig. 132 in detail. Each advertisement is comprised of a witty story in the form of a fable, using the eagle as a central character. (USA)

129 Ganzseitige Anzeige für Damenschuh-Geschäfte. (USA)
130 Aus einer Serie von ganzseitigen Inseraten für *Pendleton*-Wollwaren. In Brauntönen, Etikett blau. (USA)
131 Aus einer Kampagne für eine Kette von Buchläden unter dem Motto «Gib Deiner Phantasie eine Chance». (SWE)
132–135 Beispiele aus einer Serie von ganzseitigen Anzeigen in Schwarzweiss für Hemden der Marke *Eagle* (Adler) und Detail von Abb. 132. Alle enthalten eine lustige, kleine Geschichte, wobei der Adler jeweils Ratgeber und Experte in Sachen Mode ist. (USA)

129 Annonce pleine page. Magasins de chaussures dames. (USA)
130 Exemple d'une série d'annonces pleine page pour les lainages *Pendleton*. Tons bruns, étiquette bleue. (USA)
131 Elément d'une campagne pour une chaîne de librairies, intitulée «Donne une chance à ton imagination». (SWE)
132–135 Exemples d'une série d'annonces pleine page, en noir et blanc, pour les chemises de la marque *Eagle* (aigle), ainsi que le détail de la fig. 132. Toutes ces annonces contiennent des historiettes où l'aigle joue au conseiller de mode. (USA)

ARTIST / KÜNSTLER / ARTISTE:

129 Joseph Sellars
130 David Grove
131 Leif Eriksson
132–135 R. O. Blechman

DESIGNER / GESTALTER:

130 Cal Anderson
132–135 William McCaffery

ART DIRECTOR:

129 Claudia Milne/Joseph Sellars
130 Cal Anderson
131 Ted Bates
132–135 William McCaffery

AGENCY / AGENTUR / AGENCE:

130 Cunningham & Walsh
131 Ted Bates AB
132–135 William McCaffery, Inc.

Advertisements
Anzeigen
Annonces

135

2

Booklets

Folders

Catalogues

Programmes

Broschüren

Faltprospekte

Kataloge

Programme

Brochures

Dépliants

Catalogues

Programmes

136

137

Booklets
Prospekte
Brochures

ARTIST / KÜNSTLER / ARTISTE:

136 Helmut Kraft
137 Ephraim Eyal
138 Dominic Scibilia
139, 140 Barbara Geissler
142 Alan Patton/Whole Hog Studio

DESIGNER / GESTALTER / MAQUETTISTE:

136 Helmut Kraft
137 Jack Jaget/David Margolin
138 Ray Chuhay
139, 140 Barbara Geissler
141 Bruno K. Wiese
142 Chris Polito

ART DIRECTOR / DIRECTEUR ARTISTIQUE:

136 Helmut Kraft
137 Jack Jaget/David Margolin
138 Ray Chuhay
139, 140 Horst Rickmann
142 Chris Polito

AGENCY / AGENTUR / AGENCE – STUDIO:

136 Kraftdesign
137 Duographix Ltd.
138 Lang, Fisher & Stashower Advt. Inc.
139, 140 Geissler Design
142 Hanley Partnership

138

136 Full-colour cover of a folder for holiday hotels. (GER)
137 Recto and an unfolding menu of the Carlton Penta Hotel, Tel Aviv. Bright colours. (ISR)
138 Illustration in brown and beige for the breakfast menu of Dutch Pantry Restaurants. (USA)
139, 140 Vignette for a menu from a series for the holiday-cruise ship "MS Europa", and full-colour cover of the wine list. (GER)
141 Card with the symbol of this year's "Kiel Weeks", celebrating its 100th anniversary. (GER)
142 Direct mail from the *Natural Light Beer* company addressed to wholesalers. (USA)

136 Mehrfarbiger Umschlag eines Faltprospektes mit Ferienhotels. (GER)
137 Vorderseite einer aufklappbaren Menukarte eines Hotels in Tel Aviv. Leuchtende Farben. (ISR)
138 Illustration in Braun und Beige für die Frühstückskarte einer Restaurantkette. (USA)
139, 140 Vignette für eine Menukarte aus einer Serie für das Kreuzfahrtenschiff «MS Europa» und mehrfarbige Umschlagseite der Weinkarte. (GER)
141 Karte mit dem Symbol der diesjährigen «Kieler Woche», die zum 100. Mal stattfindet. (GER)
142 An Grossverteiler gerichtete Werbesendung eines Bierherstellers. (USA)

141

136 Couverture polychrome d'un dépliant touristique comportant une liste d'hôtels. (GER)
137 Recto d'un menu dépliable aux couleurs brillantes réalisé pour un hôtel de Tel Aviv. (ISR)
138 Illustration pour la carte des petits déjeuners d'une chaîne de restaurants. (USA)
139, 140 Vignette pour un menu figurant dans une série réalisée pour le paquebot de croisière «MS Europa», et couverture polychrome de la carte des vins. (GER)
141 Carte ornée de l'emblème de la Semaine de Kiel, semaine internationale de régates organisée cette année pour la centième fois. (GER)
142 Publicité directe d'une brasserie adressée aux grands distributeurs. (USA)

139

MS Europa Weinkarte

140

142

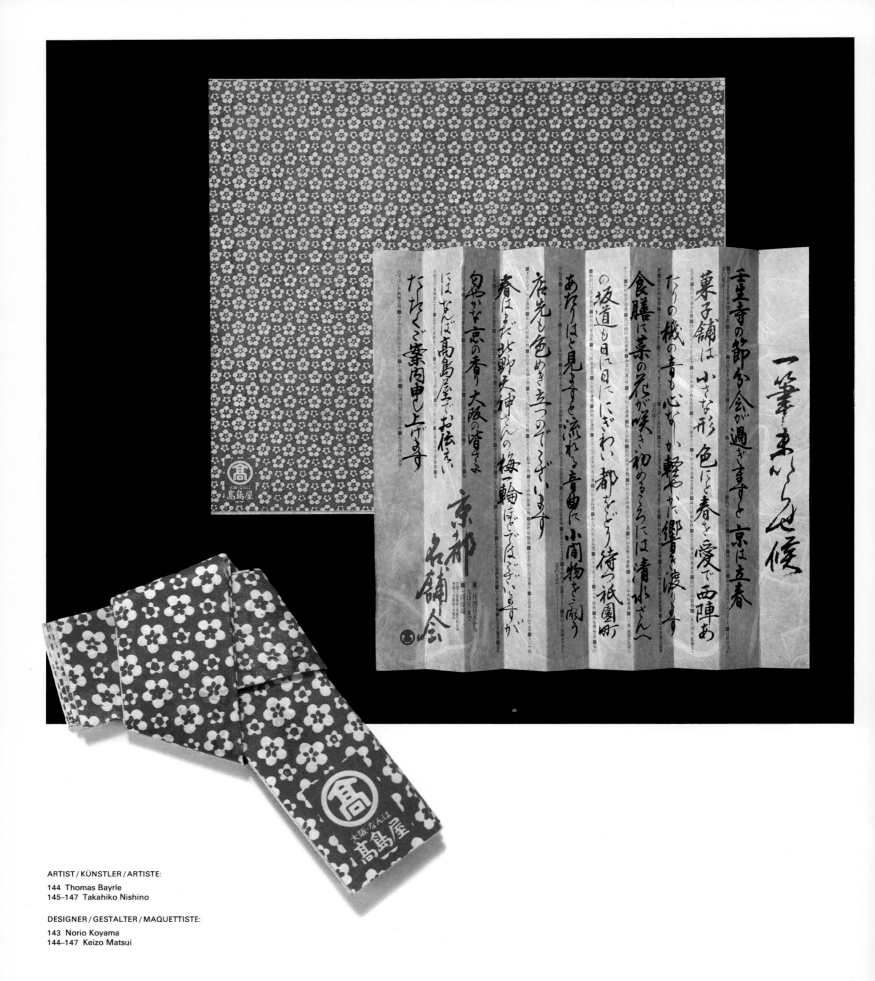

ARTIST / KÜNSTLER / ARTISTE:

144 Thomas Bayrle
145–147 Takahiko Nishino

DESIGNER / GESTALTER / MAQUETTISTE:

143 Norio Koyama
144–147 Keizo Matsui

143 Folded and unfolded direct advertising of *Takashimaya*, a Japanese department store. The photograph shows the recto with lettering and the flowered verso. (JPN)
144, 145 Illustration for the announcement of an art exhibition, and complete double spread from a fashion prospectus of the *Takashimaya* department store. (JPN)
146, 147 Double spreads from another fashion prospectus of the *Takashimaya* department store (see Figs. 143–145). All illustrations are in full colour. (JPN)

143 Auseinander- und zusammengefaltete Direktwerbung des japanischen Kaufhauses *Takashimaya*. Die Aufnahme zeigt neben der beschrifteten Vorderseite auch die geblümte Rückseite. (JPN)
144, 145 Illustration für die Ankündigung einer Kunstausstellung und vollständige Doppelseite aus einem Modeprospekt des Kaufhauses *Takashimaya*. (JPN)
146, 147 Doppelseiten aus einem weiteren Modeprospekt des Kaufhauses *Takashimaya* (s. Abb. 143–145). Alle Illustrationen sind mehrfarbig. (JPN)

143 Publicité directe, dépliée et repliée, pour le grand magasin japonais *Takashimaya*. On voit sur la photo le recto avec le texte et le verso fleuri. (JPN)
144, 145 Illustration pour l'annonce d'une exposition d'art et page double complète où elle figure. Prospectus de mode du grand magasin *Takashimaya*. (JPN)
146, 147 Pages doubles d'un autre prospectus de mode du grand magasin *Takashimaya* (cf. les fig. 143–154). Toutes les illustrations sont exécutées en polychromie. (JPN)

ART DIRECTOR / DIRECTEUR ARTISTIQUE:

143 Koichi Yokoi
144–147 Keizo Matsui

AGENCY / AGENTUR / AGENCE – STUDIO:

143 Takashimaya Design Studio

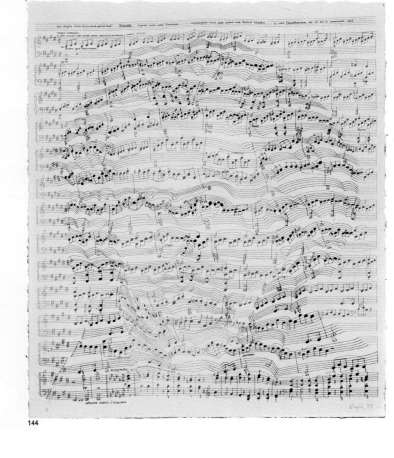

144

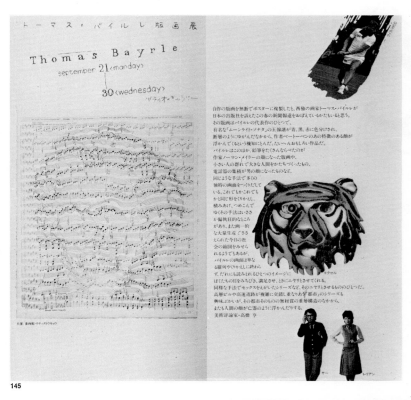

145

Booklets / Prospekte / Brochures

146

147

als Loipentiger

auf 195 PS

von Loch zu Loch

auf 1 PS

von Gipfel zu Gipfel

und auch im Büro

148

148 Illustrations in actual size from a publication for business friends of the company Yellowsport GmbH, dealing with the *Lacoste* collection and the trademark. Here, various sports for which *Lacoste* clothing is suitable. (GER)
149–151 From a point-of-purchase campaign for records of modern music by Ligeti. Black and white. (USA)
152 Closed and open press folder as advertising for *Swakara* furs. It contains a writing-pad. (GER)
153 Cover of a *U. S. Invest* sales brochure which deals with investments in the American real-estate market. (USA)
154, 155 Sell-in brochure to announce new collections of sports clothes by *Adidas*, sent to retailers. Here, the top sheet contained in the folder and the folder cover. (AUS)

148 Illustrationen in Originalgrösse aus einer Publikation für Geschäftsfreunde der Firma Yellowsport GmbH, in der es um die *Lacoste*-Kollektion und das Markenzeichen geht. Hier verschiedene Sportarten, bei denen man *Lacoste* trägt. (GER)
149–151 Verkaufshelfer aus einer Kampagne für Schallplatten mit moderner Musik von Ligeti. In Schwarzweiss. (USA)
152 Zusammen- und aufgeklappte Pressemappe als Werbung für *Swakara*-Pelze. Die Mappe enthält einen Schreibblock. (GER)
153 Umschlag einer Verkaufsbroschüre von *U. S. Invest*, bei der es um Investitionen auf dem US-Immobilienmarkt geht. (USA)
154, 155 An den Einzelhandel gerichtete Werbesendung für eine neue *Adidas*-Sportkleidungskollektion. Hier das oberste in der Faltmappe enthaltene Blatt und Vorderseite der Mappe. (AUS)

148 Illustrations (au format original) pour une publication de la Yellowsport S. à. r. l. où ce distributeur présente à ses correspondants la collection *Lacoste*. Sous le célèbre emblème, on visualise les disciplines sportives qu'habille *Lacoste*. (GER)
149–151 Eléments d'une campagne P. L. V. pour les disques de musique moderne de György Ligeti. En noir et blanc. (USA)
152 Dossier de presse ouvert et fermé. Publicité pour les fourrures *Swakara*. Le dossier comprend un bloc-notes. (GER)
153 Couverture d'une brochure de vente d'*U. S. Invest* qui recommande les investissements dans l'immobilier américain. (USA)
154, 155 Publicité adressée aux détaillants pour une nouvelle collection de tenues sport *Adidas*. Nous montrons ici la première feuille et le recto du portefeuille. (AUS)

ARTIST / KÜNSTLER / ARTISTE:

148 Dietrich Ebert
149–151 Barbara Field
152 Lutz Reinhardt
153 Sandra Higashi

DESIGNER / GESTALTER / MAQUETTISTE:

148 Dietrich Ebert
149–151 Barbara Field
152 Lutz Reinhardt
153 Marty Neumeier
154, 155 Heinz Grunwald

154

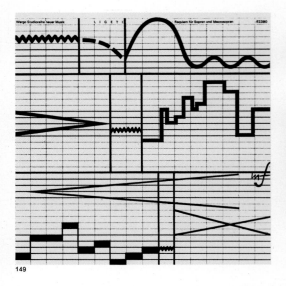

149

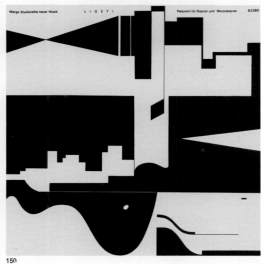

150

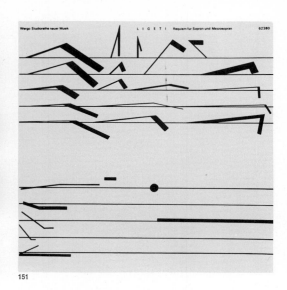

151

Booklets
Prospekte
Brochures

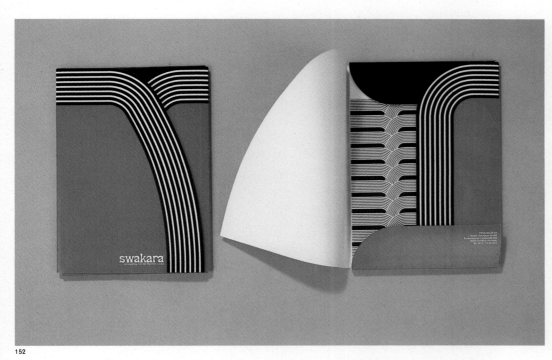

152

153

155

ART DIRECTOR / DIRECTEUR ARTISTIQUE:

148 Dietrich Ebert
149–151 Barbara Field
152 Lutz Reinhardt
153 Marty Neumeier
154, 155 Heinz Grunwald

AGENCY / AGENTUR / AGENCE – STUDIO:

148 Alain Fion
149–151 Field Design
152 Swakara-Team, J. Walter Thompson GmbH
153 Neumeier Design Team
154, 155 NTG Advertising

156

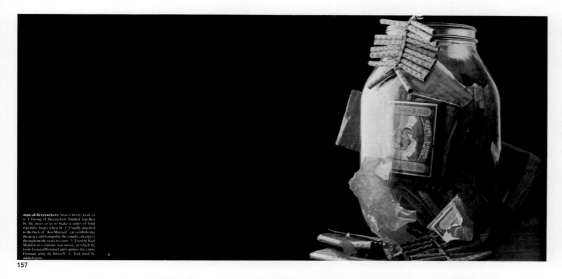

157

158

ARTIST / KÜNSTLER / ARTISTE:

156 Richard Hess
157 Phil Marco
158 Seymour Chwast
160, 161 Stephane Papounaud

DESIGNER / GESTALTER / MAQUETTISTE:

156–159 Thomas Geismar/Hoi Ling Chu
160, 161 Jean François Vautrin

ART DIRECTOR / DIRECTEUR ARTISTIQUE:

156–159 Thomas Geismar
160, 161 Jean François Vautrin

AGENCY / AGENTUR / AGENCE – STUDIO:

156–159 Chermayeff & Geismar Associates
160, 161 Extension

156–159 Illustration, two double spreads and cover of a brochure for *Matte* paper manufactured by *Westvaco.* On the cover spread (Fig. 159) the various definitions of the word matte, matt, or mat as found in the dictionary are presented while all illustrations have something to do with this word, one way or the other. In Fig. 156, it is the Christian name of Matt Dillon, hero of a TV series. (USA)
160, 161 Opened and closed brochure in which various small *Renault* vans and lorries are shown. (FRA)

156–159 Illustration, Doppelseiten und Umschlag einer Broschüre für die Papierqualität *Matte* von *Westvaco.* Auf dem Umschlag (Abb. 159) werden Lexikon-Definitionen des Wortes Matte, matt oder mat im englischen Sprachgebrauch aufgeführt, während alle Illustrationen ebenfalls etwas mit diesem Wort zu tun haben. Bei Abb. 156 ist es der Vorname von Matt Dillon, Held einer TV-Serie. (USA)
160, 161 Geschlossene und geöffnete Broschüre, in der verschiedene Kleintransporter von *Renault* angeboten werden. (FRA)

156–159 Illustration, deux doubles pages et couverture d'une brochure pour la qualité de papier *Matte* de *Westvaco.* La couverture (fig. 159) porte différentes définitions lexicologiques des mots Matte, matt, mat en anglais, auxquels se réfèrent également les illustrations. Ainsi, la fig. 156 représente Matt Dillon, le héros populaire d'une série télévisée de «Western». (USA)
160, 161 Brochure ouverte et fermée pour les petits transporteurs *Renault.* (FRA)

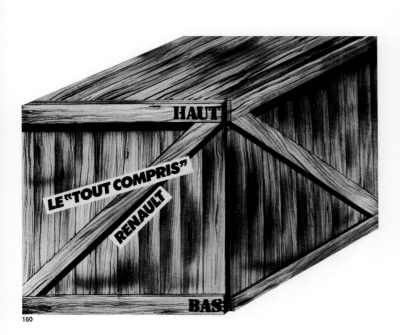

160

161

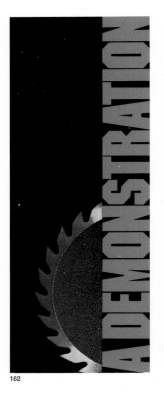

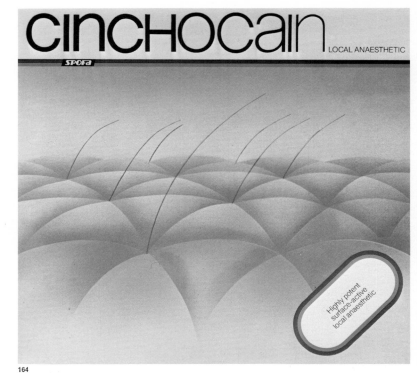

162

163

164

166

167

162 Recto of a folder for *Sanblade*—a combination of disc sander and saw blade. (USA)
163 Cover of a small *Wolf* customer-brochure, a manufacturer of envelopes. (USA)
164, 165 Covers of prospectuses for a local anaesthetic and a vein tonic. (CSR)
166, 167 Double spread and illustration from a small *Ciba-Geigy* dog breviary, with advice and information on the co-existence of man and dog. (SWI)
168 Design used on the front of a folder for publications dealing with the problems of heart disorders, issued by the *Squibb* pharmaceutical company. (USA)
169–172 Examples from a campaign for the *Ciba-Geigy* medicament *Ludiomil*. Various manifestations of depression are shown here. Black on tinted paper. (SWI)

162 Vorderseite eines Faltprospekts für ein spezielles Sägeblatt mit Reibefläche. (USA)
163 Umschlag einer kleinen Kundenbroschüre von *Wolf*, Hersteller von Briefumschlägen. (USA)
164, 165 Vorderseiten von Prospekten für eine Hautsalbe und ein Venentonikum. (CSR)
166, 167 Doppelseite und Illustration aus einem kleinen Hundebrevier von *Ciba-Geigy*, mit Ratschlägen und Informationen über das Zusammenleben von Mensch und Hund. (SWI)
168 Illustration auf der Vorderseite einer Mappe für Publikationen über Probleme im Zusammenhang mit Herzbeschwerden, herausgegeben von dem pharmazeutischen Unternehmen *Squibb*. (USA)
169–172 Beispiele aus einer Kampagne für das Medikament *Ludiomil* von *Ciba-Geigy*. Hier werden verschiedene Erscheinungsformen der Depression dargestellt. Schwarz auf farbigem Papier. (SWI)

162 Recto d'un dépliant pour une combinaison de scie sauteuse et de ponceuse. (USA)
163 Couverture d'une petite brochure pour la clientèle du fabricant d'enveloppes *Wolf*. (USA)
164, 165 Recto de deux prospectus pour une pommade pour la peau et un tonique veineux. (CSR)
166, 167 Double page et illustration tirées d'un petit bréviaire du chien de *Ciba-Geigy*, où l'on trouve des conseils et informations sur la cohabitation du chien et de l'homme. (SWI)
168 Composition de couverture d'un classeur de publications sur les problèmes cardiovasculaires diffusé par la société pharmaceutique *Squibb*. (USA)
169–172 Exemples d'une campagne en faveur du médicament *Ludiomil* de *Ciba-Geigy*, actif dans diverses formes de dépression. Noir sur papier couleur. (SWI)

168

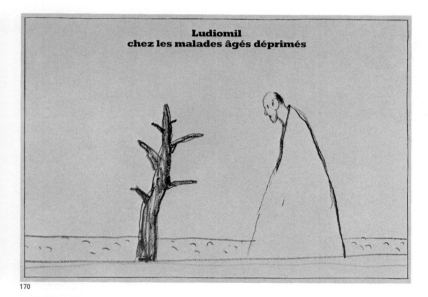

Booklets / Prospekte / Brochures

ARTIST / KÜNSTLER / ARTISTE:

163 Elaine & Dorothy Wozniak
164, 165 Milan Kolář
166, 167, 169–172 Christian Lang

DESIGNER / GESTALTER / MAQUETTISTE:

162 Dennis Peter Barnett
163 Ray Chuhay
164, 165 Milan Kolář
166, 167 Christian Lang
168 Roger Cook/Don Shanosky
169–172 Hanspeter Eisenhut

ART DIRECTOR / DIRECTEUR ARTISTIQUE:

162 Dennis Peter Barnett
163 Ray Chuhay
164, 165 Jaroslav Neubauer
166, 167, 169–172 Christian Lang
168 Roger Cook/Don Shanosky

AGENCY / AGENTUR / AGENCE – STUDIO:

162 Barnett Design Group
163 Lang, Fisher & Stashower Advt. Inc.
166, 167, 169–172 Ciba-Geigy/
    Zentrale Werbung
168 Cook & Shanosky Associates

165

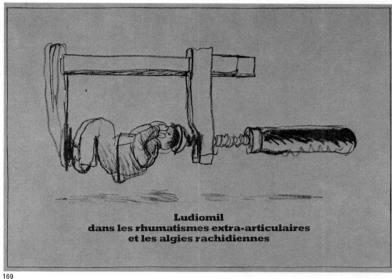

Ludiomil
dans les rhumatismes extra-articulaires
et les algies rachidiennes

169

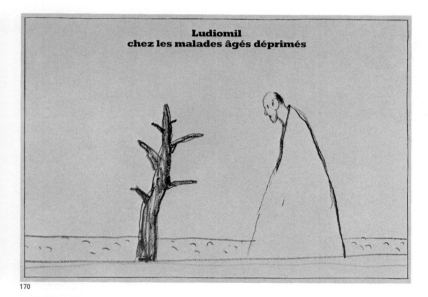

Ludiomil
chez les malades âgés déprimés

170

Ludiomil
chez les alcooliques et les drogués déprimés

171

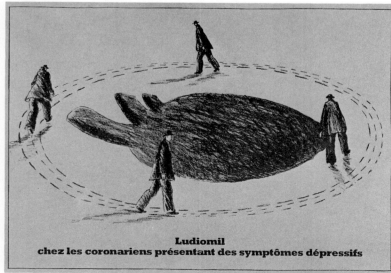

Ludiomil
chez les coronariens présentant des symptômes dépressifs

172

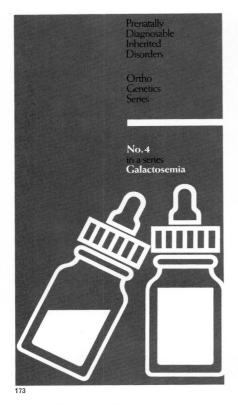

Prenatally
Diagnosable
Inherited
Disorders

Ortho
Genetics
Series

No. 4
in a series
Galactosemia

173

K⁺News

NO.11 IN A SERIES

CURRENT INFORMATION ON THE DIAGNOSIS AND MANAGEMENT OF POTASSIUM DEFICIENCY

"Subtotal" parenteral nutrition
leads to K⁺ starvation
Page 2

Unexplained hypokalemia:
a systematic diagnostic approach
Page 7

Medicine for "women's problems"
causes potassium problems
Page 8

174

gti installatietechniek

gti amsterdam
een grote installateur
en toch flexibel

175

ARTIST / KÜNSTLER / ARTISTE:

173 Jim Joseph
174 Bob Alcorn
175 Jan Lepair
176 Mickey Patel

DESIGNER / GESTALTER / MAQUETTISTE:

173 Donna Hersh
174 Wally Young
175 Jan Lepair
177 S. Odermatt
178 Harry Metzler
179 Michelle Evola
180 Stan Brod
181 Cyril John Schlosser

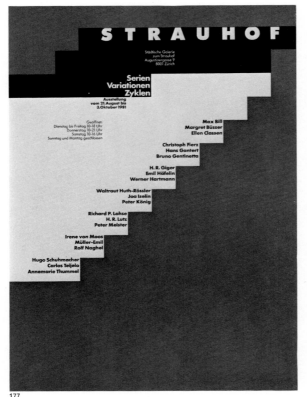

STRAUHOF

Städtische Galerie
zum Strauhof
Augustinergasse 9
8001 Zürich

Serien
Variationen
Zyklen

Ausstellung
vom 21. August bis
3. Oktober 1981

Geöffnet:
Dienstag bis Freitag 10–18 Uhr
Donnerstag 10–21 Uhr
Samstag 10–16 Uhr
Sonntag und Montag geschlossen

Max Bill
Margret Büsser
Ellen Classen

Christoph Fierz
Hans Gantert
Bruno Gentinetta

H. R. Giger
Emil Häfelin
Werner Hartmann

Waltraut Huth-Rössler
Joa Iselin
Peter König

Richard P. Lohse
H. R. Lutz
Peter Meister

Irene von Moos
Müller-Emil
Rolf Naghel

Hugo Schuhmacher
Carlos Teljelo
Annemarie Thummel

177

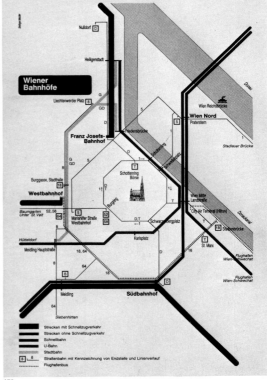

178

180

ART DIRECTOR / DIRECTEUR ARTISTIQUE:

173 Donna Hersh
174 Wally Young
175 Hans Welling/Jan Lepair
176 Mickey Patel
178 Peter Simlinger
179 Andrew Kner
180 Christine Mathews
181 Cyril John Schlosser

176

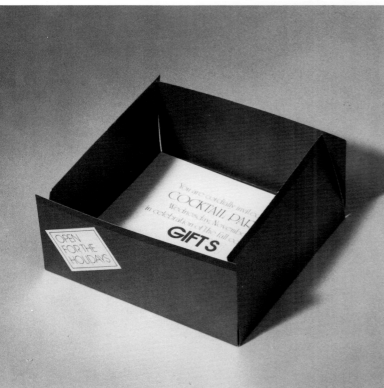

179

173 Cover of a brochure from a series by the pharmaceutical company *Ortho* dealing with genetics. The subject here is galactosemia. White on olive-green. (USA)
174 Recto of a *Ciba* brochure on the diagnosis and management of potassium deficiency. (USA)
175 Cover of a brochure of a firm for electrical and heating installations. (NLD)
176 Cover of an *Air India* brochure with some amusing comments and comparisons regarding the subject of uniforms. Full-colour illustrations. (IND)
177 Invitation to an exhibition at the Strauhof municipal gallery in Zurich. (SWI)
178 Card with a location plan of Vienna's railway stations. Red, blue and grey on white. (AUT)
179 Opened cover of an invitation card to a cocktail party organized by the *New York Times*. Copper-colour on the outside, red inside. White card with red lettering. (USA)
180 Recto of a greeting card for the Jewish New Year. (USA)
181 Opened brochure of the "Minnesota Future Problem Solving Program". (USA)

173 Umschlag einer Broschüre aus einer Serie des pharmazeutischen Unternehmens *Ortho* über Genetik, hier zum Thema Galactosämie. Weiss auf Olivgrün. (USA)
174 Vorderseite einer *Ciba*-Broschüre über Kaliummangel und dessen Behandlung. (USA)
175 Umschlag der Broschüre einer Firma für elektro- und wärmetechnische Installationen. (NLD)
176 Umschlag einer Broschüre der *Air India* mit einigen lustigen Kommentaren und Vergleichen zum Thema Uniform. Mehrfarbige Illustrationen. (IND)
177 Einladung zu einer Ausstellung der Städtischen Galerie zum Strauhof, Zürich. (SWI)
178 Karte mit einem Lageplan der Wiener Bahnhöfe. Rot, blau und grau auf Weiss. (AUT)
179 Geöffneter Umschlag für eine Einladungskarte der *New York Times* zu einer Cocktail-Party. Aussen kupferfarben, innen rot. Karte weiss mit roter Schrift. (USA)
180 Vorderseite einer Glückwunschkarte zum jüdischen Neujahrsfest. (USA)
181 Geöffnete Broschüre über ein Lehrprogramm, dessen Gegenstand Problemlösungen sind. (USA)

173 Couverture d'une brochure de la société pharmaceutique *Ortho* publiée dans une série consacrée aux affections héréditaires, ici la galactosémie. Blanc sur vert olive. (USA)
174 Recto d'une brochure de *Ciba* sur le traitement de la kaliopénie. (USA)
175 Couverture de la brochure d'une entreprise d'électricité et de chauffage. (NLD)
176 Couverture d'une brochure où *Air India* se livre à des commentaires et comparaisons amusants dans le domaine des uniformes. Illustrations en polychromie. (IND)
177 Invitation au vernissage d'une exposition à la Galerie municipale du Strauhof, Zurich. (SWI)
178 Carte avec un plan de situation des gares de Vienne. Rouge, bleu et gris sur blanc. (AUT)
179 Enveloppe ouverte pour une carte d'invitation du *New York Times* à un cocktail. Extérieur cuivre, intérieur rouge. Carte blanche, texte en rouge. (USA)
180 Recto d'une carte de vœux pour le Jour de l'An israélite. (USA)
181 Brochure ouverte. Programme d'enseignement des techniques de solution de problèmes. (USA)

AGENCY / AGENTUR / AGENCE – STUDIO:

173 Kallir, Philips, Ross, Inc.
174 William Douglas McAdams Inc.
175 Anema & Hageman
177 Odermatt & Tissi
180 Lipson Assoc. Inc.

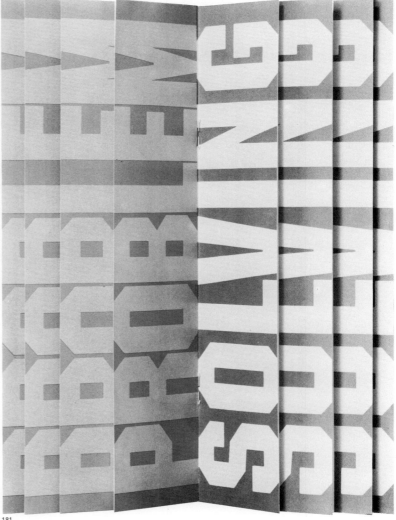

181

Form A — 5 IPNS '80

Active Member Registration
Please complete this form in block letters.

○ Dr. ○ Prof. ○ Mr. ○ Ms.
Name
Last   First and initial
Address

Country   Telephone
Institutional affiliation

Accompanying persons

Last   First and initial

First and initial
Number of children

Accommodations
○ I plan to stay at the Hilton Hotel.
○ I shall make my own arrangements.
○ I shall require camping facilities.

Arrival date

Travel
○ I shall arrive in Philadelphia by air.
○ I shall arrive in Philadelphia by train.
○ I shall arrive in Philadelphia by automobile

Approximate time

Payment

	Active member	Accompanying person	Number of persons	Total
○ Before March 7, 1980	$225.00	$145.00		$
○ After March 7, 1980	$280.00	$180.00		$

○ I enclose a remittance of $_____ (check or money order) payable to the Fifth International Pediatric Nephrology Symposium (IPNS 80).
○ I have arranged a direct bank transfer to Provident National Bank, Children's Hospital Office, in the amount of $_____

Signature   Date

Mail to:
Michael E. Norman, M.D.
Secretary-General, IPNS '80
Room 6237
Children's Hospital of Philadelphia
34th & Civic Center Blvd.
Philadelphia, PA 19104
USA

Form B — 5 IPNS '80

Hotel Registration
Hilton Hotel of Philadelphia

I want to reserve _____ rooms for _____ persons.

Arrival day and date   Arrival time

Departure day and date   Departure time

Range of rates (check preferred rate)*

1 person	○ $40.00	○ $44.00	○ $48.00	○ $50.00	○ $52.00
2 persons	○ $50.00	○ $54.00	○ $58.00	○ $60.00	○ $62.00

*The higher the room location, the higher the room rate.

Additional adults in room (up to four persons) – $10.00 per person.

Children (under 18 years) in same room with parents are free.

Children in their own room (up to four children) pay the 1 person rate.

Rooms will be held until 6:00 pm on date of arrival unless a later time is confirmed or reservation guaranteed.

Check-out time is 12:00 noon.

Forms must be received by September 1, 1980 to guarantee reservations.

All rates subject to applicable taxes.

If the rate requested is not available, the closest available rate will be assigned.

Name

Address

Country

Home telephone   Business telephone

Return this form to: Reservations
                                        Hilton Hotel of Philadelphia
                                        34th & Civic Center Blvd.
                                        Philadelphia, PA 19104
                                        USA

182, 183 Registration forms for a Pediatric Nephrology Symposium and for hotel reservations. (USA)
184 Inside spread of a prospectus for the *Mountain-Bell*'s teleconferencing apparatus. (USA)
185 From a humorous publication on the subject of sport arising from a design conference organized by the Centro Sportivo "Riviera del Conero", Ancona. (ITA)
186 For a show of the Push Pin Studios in Paris. (FRA)
187, 188 Prospectuses of the Chicago Board of Trade on markets and education. (USA)

182, 183 Formulare für die Anmeldung zu einem Ärzte-Symposium und Hotelreservation. (USA)
184 Innenseite eines Prospekts für Konferenzschaltungen der *Mountain-Bell*-Telephongesellschaft. (USA)
185 Illustration aus einer humoristischen Publikation zum Thema Sport, aufgrund einer vom Centro Sportivo «Riviera del Conero», Ancona, organisierten internationalen Messe der Sport-Karikatur. (ITA)
186 Für eine Graphik- und Plakatausstellung. (FRA)
187, 188 Prospekte der Handelskammer von Chicago. Themen: Handelsinformationen und Ausbildung. (USA)

182, 183 Formules d'inscription à un symposium médical, avec réservation de l'hôtel. (USA)
184 Intérieur d'un prospectus de la société des téléphones *Mountain-Bell* sur les téléconférences. (USA)
185 Extrait d'une publication humoristique consacrée au sport, inspirée par une exposition de caricatures sportives organisée à Ancône par le Centro Sportivo «Riviera del Conero». (ITA)
186 Pour une exposition graphique et affichiste. (FRA)
187, 188 Prospectus de la Chambre de commerce de Chicago: l'état des marchés; cours de formation. (USA)

ARTIST / KÜNSTLER / ARTISTE:

184 Etienne Delessert/Patrick Gaudard
185 Yutenji Saburo
186 Seymour Chwast

DESIGNER / GESTALTER / MAQUETTISTE:

182, 183 Joel Katz
184 Rita Marshall
187, 188 Richard Prey

ART DIRECTOR / DIRECTEUR ARTISTIQUE:

182, 183 Joel Katz
184 Rita Marshall
186 Robert Delpire
187, 188 Richard Prey

AGENCY / AGENTUR / AGENCE – STUDIO:

182, 183 Katz Wheeler Design
184 Tracy-Locke
186 Ideodis
187, 188 CBT Publication Services

185

With Teleconferencing, your company has a communications bridge that connects you with a whole new way of doing business. A way where the telephone, and the Bell System's information management network, is a meeting ground. A way you can do business more efficiently and economically than ever before.

On the following pages, you'll see six examples of Teleconferencing at work. And how companies used their equipment and services to increase productivity and reduce operating costs. Listed after these examples are five kinds of business situations Teleconferencing can help most. If your company faces any one of these situations, we'd like to hear from you. So we can tell you how the Bell System can help you build a bridge to better business communications with Teleconferencing.

The knowledge business

Teleconferencing. Your bridge to better business communications.

Booklets
Prospekte
Brochures

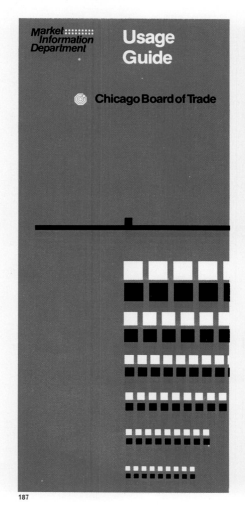

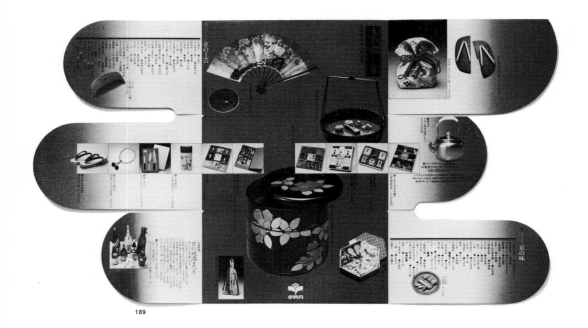

189

ICA
Institute of Contemporary
Art
University of Pennsylvania

**Urban
Encounters**

A Map of
Public Art in Philadelphia
1959-1979

190

ARTIST / KÜNSTLER / ARTISTE:

189 Naoki Nishi
190 Joel Katz
192 Michael Mathias Prechtl
193 Jan Sawka

DESIGNER / GESTALTER / MAQUETTISTE:

189 Kenzo Nakagawa/Hiro Nobuyama
190 Joel Katz
191 Tony Woodward
194 W. H. Stegelmann

193

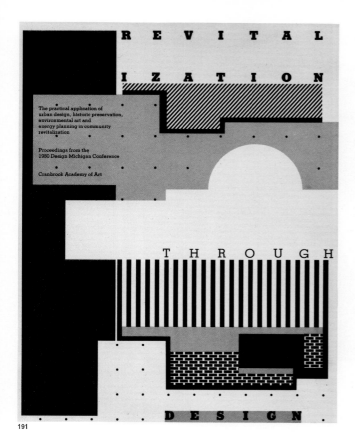

191

192

189 Opened folder of the *Isetan* department store in Tokyo, on the occasion of a trade fair in Kyoto. Middle part in red, sides in violet and white. (JPN)
190 Cover of a prospectus containing maps that locate sixty art works that have been installed since 1959 in public spaces in Philadelphia. (USA)
191 Cover of a brochure dealing with a summary of presentations made at the 1980 Design Michigan Conference. Black and white with beige and brown. (USA)
192 Invitation to a Prechtl exhibition in the Nuremberg Art Gallery. (GER)
193 Invitation to a Jan Sawka exhibition in the André Zarre Gallery. (USA)
194 Leporello prospectus of a union for tax officers and employees. (GER)

189 Aufgeklappter Faltprospekt des *Isetan*-Kaufhauses, Tokio, anlässlich einer Messe in Kyoto. Mittlerer Teil rot, Seitenteile violett und weiss. (JPN)
190 Umschlag eines Prospektes mit Lageplänen der in verschiedenen Stadtteilen von Philadelphia vorhandenen, öffentlich zugänglichen Kunstwerke. (USA)
191 «Wiederbelebung durch Design.» Umschlag einer Broschüre, die eine Zusammenfassung von Präsentationen zu diesem Thema enthält. (USA)
192 Einladung zu einer Prechtl-Ausstellung in der Kunsthalle Nürnberg. (GER)
193 Einladung zu einer Ausstellung von Jan Sawka in New York. (USA)
194 Prospekt einer Gewerkschaft für Angestellte der Steuerbehörde. (GER)

189 Dépliant (déplié) du grand magasin *Isetan* de Tokyo publié à l'occasion d'une foire à Kyoto. Partie centrale rouge, volets violet et blanc. (JPN)
190 Couverture d'un prospectus comportant des plans de situation des sculptures du domaine public réparties dans les divers quartiers de Philadelphie. (USA)
191 «L'action revitalisante du design.» Couverture d'une brochure de résumés de communications à la Design Michigan Conference. Noir-blanc, beige et brun. (USA)
192 Invitation à une exposition de Prechtl à la Kunsthalle de Nuremberg. (GER)
193 Invitation à une exposition de Jan Sawka dans une galerie newyorkaise. (USA)
194 Prospectus en accordéon pour un syndicat d'employés fiscaux. (GER)

194

ART DIRECTOR:

189 Kenzo Nakagawa
190 Joel Katz
191 Katherine McCoy
194 W. H. Stegelmann

AGENCY / AGENTUR / AGENCE:

189 Nippon Design Center
190 Katz Wheeler Design
191 Cranbrook Academy of Art/ Design Dept.
194 W. H. Stegelmann

195

196

195, 196 Open and closed folding box in traditional Japanese style meant for the presentation and storage of ancient folk toys. (JPN)
197 Invitation to a banquet given by Burns, Cooper, Hynes Ltd., an advertising agency. (CAN)
198 For an invitation to a Celestino Piatti exhibition in the Munich municipal museum. The Swiss graphic designer is known above all for his cover designs for the *dtv* paperback series. (GER)
199 Cover for the catalogue of an exhibition of Duo's—single works representing the combined efforts of two craftsmen. (AUS)
200, 201 Double spreads from a brochure issued by the Council of Ministers of Education as a metric style guide for the conversion from feet and inches as well as temperature grading. (CAN)

199

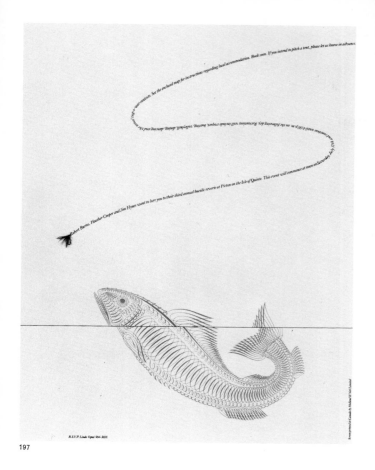

197

198

195, 196 Geöffnete und geschlossene Schachtel im traditionellen japanischen Stil, die zum Aufbewahren und Präsentieren von altem, volkstümlichem Spielzeug verwendet wird. (JPN)
197 Grossformatige Einladung zu einem Festessen einer Werbeagentur. (CAN)
198 Illustration für die Einladung zu einer Ausstellung von Celestino Piatti im Münchner Stadtmuseum. Der Schweizer Graphiker wurde vor allem durch seine *dtv*-Umschläge bekannt. (GER)
199 Umschlag für den Katalog einer Ausstellung von kunstgewerblichen Gegenständen, die jeweils in Zusammenarbeit von zwei Personen entstanden sind. (AUS)
200, 201 Doppelseiten aus einer Broschüre des kanadischen Ministeriums für Erziehung über die Einführung des metrischen Systems, das auch die Umstellung auf Celsius bedeutet. (CAN)

195, 196 Boîte pliante japonaise de style traditionnel, ouverte et fermée, servant à la présentation et à la conservation de jouets folkloriques anciens. (JPN)
197 Invitation (au grand format) à un banquet organisé par une agence publicitaire. (CAN)
198 Illustration pour l'invitation à une exposition de Celestino Piatti au Musée municipal de Munich. Ce graphiste suisse s'est surtout signalé par ses couvertures de livres *dtv*. (GER)
199 Couverture du catalogue d'une exposition de créations artisanales en équipes de deux personnes, chaque groupe de deux artistes formant un «duo». (AUS)
200, 201 Doubles pages d'une brochure du ministère canadien de l'Education nationale concernant l'adoption du système métrique, y inclus aussi les mesures de température. (CAN)

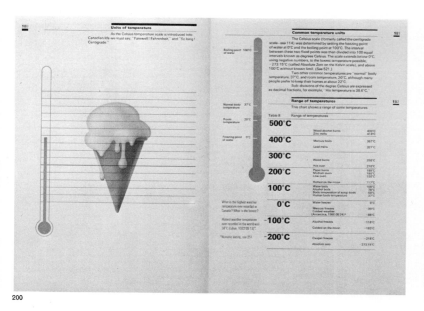

200

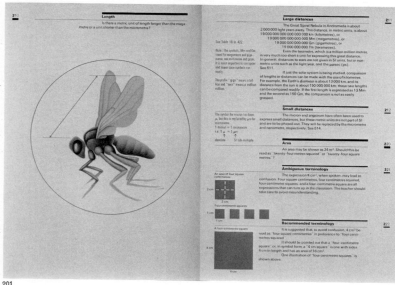

201

202

203

205

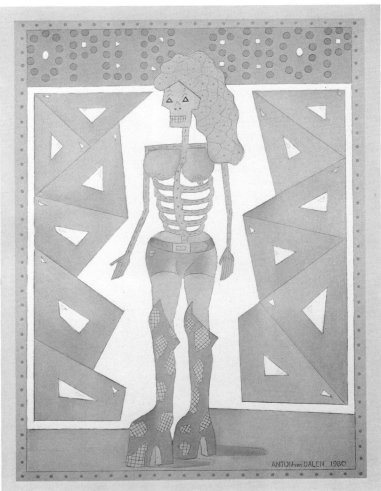

206

We still have those who believe in the archaic traditions of the 1880s and 1890s; those who believe that America is built from the top down, that if you keep the great corporations fat and wealthy, enough will trickle down to keep those at the lower level of our economic structure happy and contented.
—George Meany

Painting by Honoré Sharrer

204

202 Cover of a Bulgarian publication entitled "A Propos". In full colour. (BUL)
203, 204, 206 From a catalogue entitled "Images of Labor", issued by District 1199, National Union of Hospital and Health Care Employees. Each picture refers to a text dealing with this subject and has been commissioned within the framework of the union's cultural "Bread and Roses" programme. (USA)
205 Cover of a *New York Times* spectators' guide for the New York Marathon. (USA)
207 Invitation to an exhibition in New York of work by Tim, political cartoonist of *L'Express*. (USA)
208 Prospectus with information for students about governmental job opportunities. (CAN)

202 Umschlag einer bulgarischen Publikation mit dem Titel «A Propos». In Farbe. (BUL)
203, 204, 206 Aus einem Katalog mit dem Titel «Bilder der Arbeit». Jedes Bild bezieht sich auf einen Text zu diesem Thema und wurde innerhalb des Kulturprogramms einer Gewerkschaft in Auftrag gegeben. (USA)
205 Umschlag einer der *New York Times* beigelegten Broschüre über den Stadt-Marathonlauf. (USA)
207 Einladung zu einer Ausstellung des politischen Karikaturisten Tim in New York. (USA)
208 Informationsprospekt für Studenten über offene Stellen in der Verwaltung. (CAN)

202 Couverture d'une publication bulgare. En polychromie. (BUL)
203, 204, 206 Images accompagnant des textes syndicaux dans un catalogue, «Images du travail». (USA)
205 Couverture d'une brochure du *New York Times* commentant le marathon newyorkais. (USA)
207 Invitation à une exposition du caricaturiste de *L'Express*, Tim, organisée à New York. (USA)
208 Prospectus renseignant les étudiants et lycéens sur les possibilités de stages pratiques. (CAN)

207

Expérience pratique pour le premier emploi

l'Opération
expérience
p r a t i q u e
Ontario

Secrétariat Jeunesse   Ministère des Collèges et Universités
Ontario

208

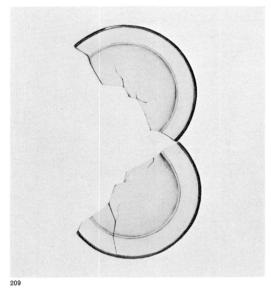

209

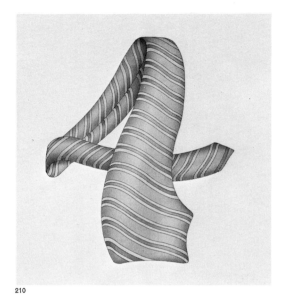

210

211

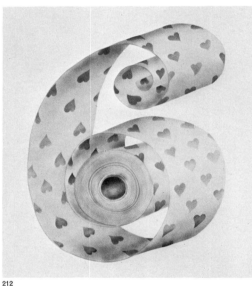

212

213

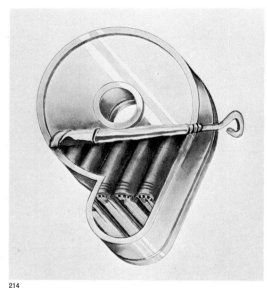

214

209–214 Examples of illustrations dealing with the subject of numerals, from an image folder of the course of study in graphic design at a college of art in Pforzheim. (GER)
215 Illustration on the fourth cover spread of a book catalogue issued by the MIT Press, taken from a book entitled *The Spirit of Colors—The Art of Karl Gerstner*. (USA)
216 Cover of the catalogue for a Savignac exhibition in the poster museum, Paris. (FRA)
217 Verso of an empty envelope in black and white serving as an invitation to a Christo exhibition at the Ziegler Gallery, Zurich. Letterpress printing, heightened by the inserted flap, emphasizes the typical contours of the envelope. (SWI)

209–214 Beispiele von Illustrationen zum Thema Ziffern, aus einer Image-Mappe des Studiengangs Grafik-Design der Fachhochschule für Gestaltung, Pforzheim. (GER)
215 Illustration der vierten Umschlagseite eines Buchkatalogs der technischen Hochschule MIT. Sie wurde dem Buch *Der Geist der Farbe, Karl Gerstner und seine Kunst* entnommen. (USA)
216 Umschlag des Katalogs anlässlich einer Savignac-Ausstellung im Pariser Plakatmuseum. (FRA)
217 Rückseite eines leeren Briefumschlags in Schwarzweiss als Einladung zu einer Christo-Ausstellung in der Galerie Ziegler, Zürich. Dank Buchdruck, verstärkt duch die hereingesteckte Lasche, werden die typischen Konturen des Umschlages hervorgehoben. (SWI)

209–214 Exemples d'illustrations de chiffres tirés d'un portefeuille iconographique du cours d'art graphique de l'Université de design de Pforzheim (Fachhochschule für Gestaltung). (GER)
215 Illustration de la 4e page de couverture d'un catalogue d'édition de l'Université technologique MIT, empruntée à l'ouvrage *L'Esprit des couleurs – L'Art de Karl Gerstner*. (USA)
216 Couverture du catalogue de l'exposition Savignac au Musée de l'Affiche de Paris. (FRA)
217 Verso d'une enveloppe vide en noir et blanc servant d'invitation à une exposition Christo à la galerie zurichoise Ziegler. Les contours typiques de l'enveloppe sont soulignés par la languette escamotée et l'emploi de l'impression typographique. (SWI)

216

Booklets / Prospekte / Brochures

215

217

Booklets
Prospekte
Brochures

219–221 Illustrations from a booklet to commemorate the Illustrators and Designers Workshop held in Paris. (USA)
222 Announcement of a creative competition for students, sponsored by the Dallas Society of Visual Communications. (USA)
223 Cover of a catalogue of regional books. (GER)
224 Cover of a brochure in which an artist and an engineer present their proposal for a new middle spire of the Sankt Servaas cathedral in Maestricht. (NLD)

219–221 Illustrationen von vier Künstlern (Abb. 219 ist eine Gemeinschaftsarbeit) zum Thema Paris, aus einer Mappe in Erinnerung an einen dort veranstalteten Design-Workshop. (USA)
222 Ankündigung eines kreativen Wettbewerbs für Studenten, von der Dallas Society of Visual Communications. (USA)
223 Umschlag eines Katalogs für regionale Bücher. (GER)
224 Umschlag einer Broschüre, in der ein Künstler und ein Ingenieur ihren Vorschlag für einen neuen Mittelturm des Sankt-Servaas-Doms in Maastricht präsentieren. (NLD)

219–221 Illustrations par quatre artistes (la fig. 219 est une œuvre collective) sur le thème de Paris tirées d'une portefeuille commémoratif d'un atelier de design à Paris. (USA)
222 Annonce d'un concours de créativité organisé pour les étudiants par la Dallas Society of Visual Communications. (USA)
223 Couverture d'un catalogue d'ouvrages régionaux. (GER)
224 Couverture d'une brochure présentant le projet d'un artiste et d'un ingénieur pour l'érection d'une nouvelle tour centrale de la cathédrale Saint-Servais de Maëstricht. (NLD)

ARTIST / KÜNSTLER / ARTISTE:

219 Soizick Leporcher / Katharina Buechler
220 Reymond Knowlton
221 Fred Otnes
222 Dick Mitchell
223 Albert Kohlmeier
224 Dré Devens / Han de Vrede

DESIGNER / GESTALTER / MAQUETTISTE:

219–221 John DeCesare
222 Dick Mitchell
223 Albert Kohlmeier
224 Bear Cornet

ART DIRECTOR / DIRECTEUR ARTISTIQUE:

219–221 John DeCesare
222 Dick Mitchell
223 Albert Kohlmeier

AGENCY / AGENTUR / AGENCE – STUDIO:

219–221 DeCesare Design Assoc.
222 Richards, Sullivan, Brock & Associates
223 Fantasy Factory

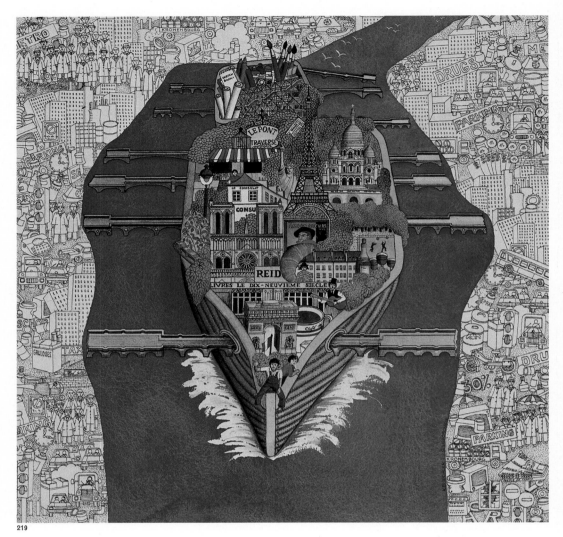

219

220

221

222

223

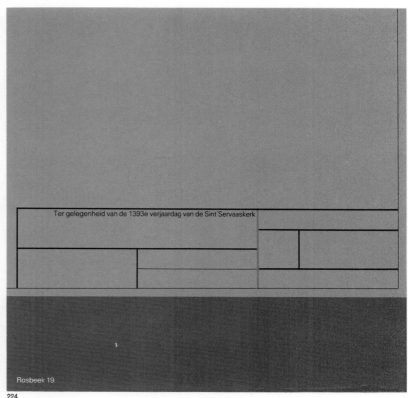

224

225

ARTIST / KÜNSTLER / ARTISTE:

225 Milou Hermus
226, 227 Bob Fortier
229 Oswaldo Miranda (Miran)

DESIGNER / GESTALTER / MAQUETTISTE:

226, 227 Bruce Mau
228, 230 Melissa Moger
229 Oswaldo Miranda
231 Emil Micha

ART DIRECTOR / DIRECTEUR ARTISTIQUE:

226, 227 Bruce Mau
229 Oswaldo Miranda
231 Andrew Kner

225 "Trying to get out." Illustration of an Amnesty International card. (NLD)
226, 227 Illustrations from a brochure dealing with the subject of physical fitness, issued by the Occidental Life Insurance Company of Canada. Two problems out of the ten most common problems that stand beween people and fitness are detailed here. (CAN)
228, 230 Detail of the cover and spread listing members of the staff, from an edition of Portfolio, the students' yearbook of the Rhode Island School of Design. (USA)
229 Recto of a large envelope with an invitation to a typography competition. (BRA)
231 A New York Times supplement with details about this newspaper introducing standard modular advertising units. Blue and grey. (USA)

225 «Versuch herauszukommen» ist der Titel dieser Illustration einer Karte für die Gefangenen-hilfsorganisation Amnesty International. (NLD)
226, 227 Illustrationen aus der Broschüre einer Versicherungsgesellschaft, zum Thema der körperlichen Fitness. Hier zwei der Probleme, die bei der Erlangung dieses Ziels häufig im Wege stehen: Trägheit und Hemmungen. (CAN)
228, 230 Detail des Umschlags einer Ausgabe von Portfolio, Jahrbuch einer Design-Schule, und Doppelseite daraus, mit Porträts und Namen der Mitglieder der Schulleitung. (USA)
229 Vorderseite eines grossformatigen Umschlags mit Einladung zu einem Typographie-Wettbewerb. (BRA)
231 Beilage der New York Times mit Angaben über neue Standardgrössen für Anzeigen. Blau und Grau. (USA)

225 «Essai de libération» – voici la légende de cette illustration pour une carte de l'organisation d'aide aux prisonniers Amnesty International. (NLD)
226, 227 Illustrations réalisées pour la brochure d'une compagnie d'assurances consacrée à la forme physique de ses assurés. On y évoque deux problèmes majeurs: l'inertie et les inhibitions. (CAN)
228, 230 Détail de la couverture d'une édition de Portfolio, l'annuel d'une école de design, et double page de ce même annuel avec les noms et les portraits des membres de la direction. (USA)
229 Recto d'une enveloppe au grand format: invitation à un concours de typographie. (BRA)
231 Supplément du New York Times: indications sur les nouveaux formats d'annonces. Bleu et gris. (USA)

226

227

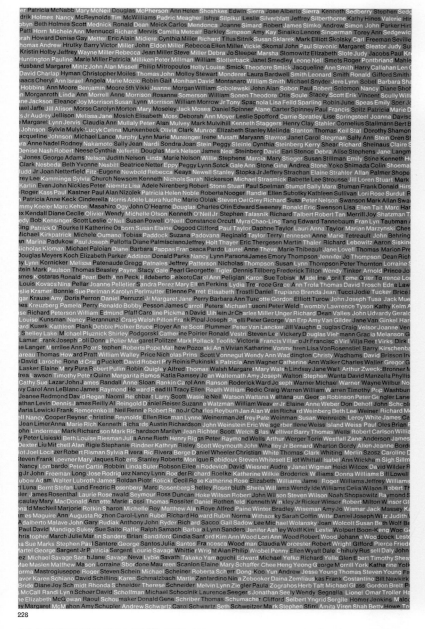

AGENCY / AGENTUR / AGENCE – STUDIO:

226, 227 Fifty Fingers Inc.
229 Umuarama Publicidade

228

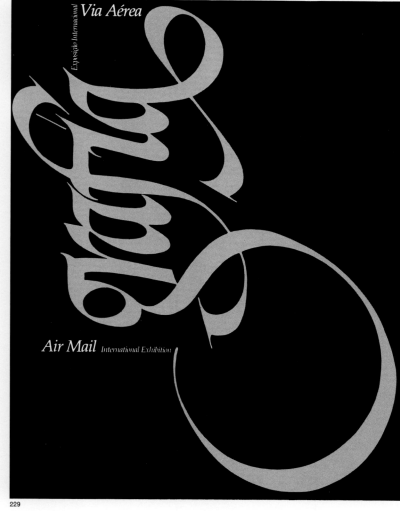

Via Aérea
Exposição Internacional

Air Mail *International Exhibition*

229

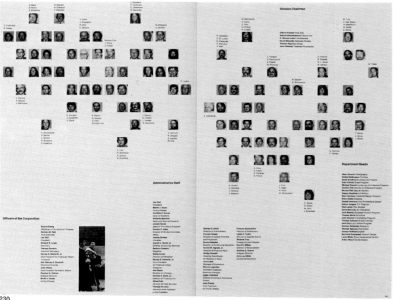

230

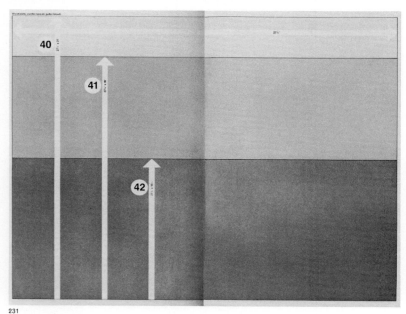

231

Booklets
Prospekte
Brochures

232

233

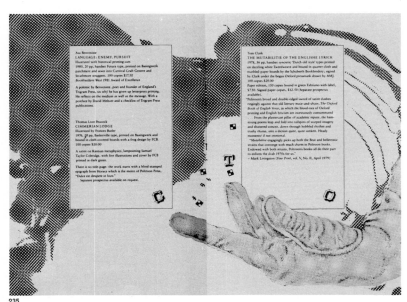

235

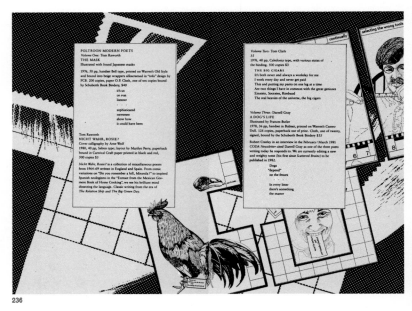

236

237

232–234 From *Donkey-Post*, a small self-promotion booklet of the graphic artist E. Prüssen, printed on a hand press. Figs. 232 and 234: Signature-writing machines and the wish of agricultural experts to furnish old sheep with false teeth; Fig. 233: Vignettes for the Frankfurt Book Fair. (GER)
235, 236, 238 Double spreads and introductory spread of a Poltroon Press catalogue listing new books. This small publishing company deals mostly with bibliophile books. (USA)
237 "Let us paint a world of peace." Christmas card from a wholesaler. (BRA)
239 Self-promotion of *Funny Business*, an agency for illustrators. (GBR)

232–234 Aus *Donkey-Post*, die auf einer Handpresse abgezogene Hauszeitschrift des Graphikers Eduard Prüssen. Themen zu Abb. 232 und 234: Unterschriftsmaschinen und der Wunsch von Landwirtschaftsexperten, alten Schafen Gebisse einzusetzen; Abb. 233: Aus «Bibliokomik», ein Sonderdruck mit sechs Vignetten zur Frankfurter Buchmesse. (GER)
235, 236, 238 Doppelseiten und einleitende Seite aus einem Katalog mit Neuerscheinungen eines kleinen Verlages, der grösstenteils bibliophile Bücher herstellt. (USA)
237 «Lasst uns eine Welt des Friedens malen.» Weihnachtskarte eines Grosshändlers. (BRA)
239 Die Zukunft war das Thema dieser Eigenwerbung von einer Agentur für Illustratoren. (GBR)

232–234 Extraits de *Donkey-Post*, le house organ du graphiste Eduard Prüssen fabriqué sur une presse à bras. Fig. 232, 234: les machines à signer; les dentiers dont les experts agricoles vont doter les vieux moutons. Fig. 233: vignettes pour la Foire du livre de Francfort. (GER)
235, 236, 238 Doubles pages et page d'introduction d'un catalogue des nouveautés publié par un petit éditeur spécialisé dans les productions bibliophiles. (USA)
237 «Peignons un monde de paix.» Carte de vœux de Noël d'un grossiste. (BRA)
239 Ce qu'apportera l'avenir: auto-promotion d'une agence regroupant des illustrateurs. (GBR)

234

ART DIRECTOR / DIRECTEUR ARTISTIQUE:

235, 236, 238 Poltroon Press
239 Ian Chambers

AGENCY / AGENTUR / AGENCE – STUDIO:

235, 236, 238 Poltroon Press

Booklets
Prospekte
Brochures

238

239

CONTINUED ON PAGE 10...

BELGIUM: Rue Du Grand Duc, 63 Bruxelles 1040 02 640 9222. HOLLAND: Weesperzijde 85 Amsterdam. 020 681551 SCANDINAVIA: HC Andersens Boulevard 17 1553 Copenhagen V. 148852.

240

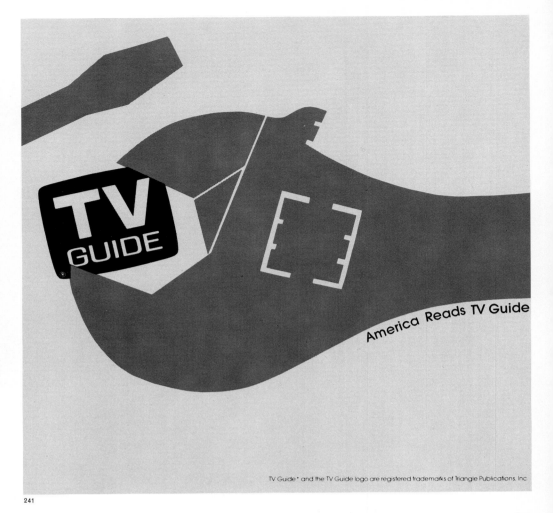

241

ARTIST / KÜNSTLER / ARTISTE:

242 Anita Siegel
243 James Endicott
244, 246 Heather Cooper
245 Dagmar Frinta

DESIGNER / GESTALTER / MAQUETTISTE:

240 Fred Rosato
241 Bobbi Adair
244, 246 Heather Cooper
245 Cheryl Lewin

240, 241 Ad for *TV Guide* serving the ends of space promotion. Reference is made to the magazine's high circulation and the possibilities of target-oriented advertising as opposed to haphazard methods and the hammering together of a media plan. (USA)
242 Self-promotion of Anita Siegel, an illustrator. Collage and drawing on black construction paper. (USA)
243 Christmas card issued by Portal Publications Ltd. (USA)
244, 246 Full-colour Valentin's Day cards. (USA)
245 Illustration used on Christmas packages and displays by *Conran's*, the American branch of the British *Habitat*, home furnishers. (USA)

240, 241 Inserenten-Werbung der Fernsehprogramm-Zeitschrift *TV Guide*. Hier geht es um die breite Streuung und die Möglichkeiten gezielter Werbung – im Gegensatz zur Flaschenpost – sowie um das richtige «Zusammenbauen» eines Mediaplans. (USA)
242 Eigenwerbung einer Illustratorin. Zeichnung und Collage auf schwarzem Karton. (USA)
243 Weihnachtskarte von einer Verlagsgesellschaft. (USA)
244, 246 Mehrfarbige Grusskarten zum Valentinstag. (USA)
245 Für verschiedene Weihnachtsaussendungen und Dekorationen eines Einrichtungsgeschäftes verwendete Illustration. (USA)

240, 241 Publicité annonceurs du magazine de programmes télévisés *TV Guide*. Il y est question d'une large diffusion, de la possibilité d'atteindre des cibles précises – contrairement à la «bouteille à la mer» – et de l'assemblage d'un plan médias. (USA)
242 Elément autopromotionnel d'une illustratrice. Collage et dessin sur carton noir. (USA)
243 Carte de vœux de Noël d'un éditeur. (USA)
244, 246 Cartes de vœux polychromes pour la Saint-Valentin. (USA)
245 Illustration utilisée pour divers envois publicitaires à Noël ainsi que pour la décoration d'un magasin d'ameublement. (USA)

242

243

244

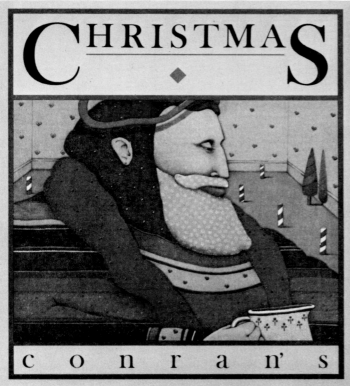

245

246

ART DIRECTOR / DIRECTEUR ARTISTIQUE:

240, 241 John William Brown
244, 246 Heather Cooper
245 Cheryl Lewin

AGENCY / AGENTUR / AGENCE – STUDIO:

244, 246 Burns, Cooper, Hynes Ltd.
245 Conran's

247

Markt für den Blauen Dunst:
Das bewährte, erfolgreiche Duo.
Für Besseres gibt's nichts Besseres.

DIE ZEIT
ZEITmagazin

248

Booklets
Prospekte
Brochures

249

247, 249 Spreads from a graphic designer's self-promotional folder, showing here examples of constructions for the 1980 Annual Report of the Philadelphia National Corporation, a banking institution. Fig. 247 refers to the variety and depth of personnel; Fig. 249 is the folder's cover art emphasizing a new decade. In full colour. (USA)
248, 250 Examples from a series of advertising spreads for the weekly newspaper *Die Zeit* and its magazine, for the purpose of space promotion. Fig. 248 with a cut-out "burnt hole" is aimed at the tobacco industry; Fig. 250 is meant for home furnishers. (GER)
251, 252 Double spread and illustration on the cover of a brochure about annual report presentation, belonging to the design series issued by the Potlatch Corporation. (USA)

247, 249 Blätter aus der Eigenwerbungsmappe eines Graphikers. Er zeigt hier Beispiele aus dem Jahresbericht für eine Bank. Abb. 247 bezieht sich auf ein Kapitel über das Personal, Abb. 249 diente als Umschlag – ein Hinweis auf das neue Jahrzehnt. In Farbe. (USA)
248, 250 Beispiele aus einer Serie von Werbeblättern für die Inserentenwerbung der Wochenzeitung *Die Zeit* und des *Zeitmagazins*. Abb. 248, mit ausgestanztem «Brand-Loch», richtet sich an die Tabakindustrie, Abb. 250 an Wohnungsausstatter. (GER)
251, 252 Doppelseite und Illustration des Umschlags einer Broschüre des Papierherstellers Potlatch Corporation, über die Präsentation von Jahresberichten. In Abb. 251 geht es um die Zusammenarbeit zwischen den Gestaltern und der Firmenleitung. (USA)

247, 249 Deux feuilles d'un portefolio autopromotionnel d'un graphiste avec des exemples d'illustrations pour le rapport annuel d'une banque. La fig. 247 accompagne un chapitre consacré au personnel, la fig. 249 sert de couverture en annonçant la décennie à venir. En couleurs. (USA)
248, 250 Exemples d'une série de feuillets publicitaires destinés aux annonceurs potentiels de l'hebdo *Die Zeit* et du *Zeitmagazin*. La fig. 248, avec un trou central de «brûlure», s'adresse à l'industrie du tabac, la fig. 250 aux ensembliers. (GER)
251, 252 Double page et illustration de la couverture d'une brochure du fabricant de papier Potlatch Corporation consacrée à la présentation des rapports annuels. La fig. 251 vise la collaboration entre les artistes (un peu marginaux) et la direction. (USA)

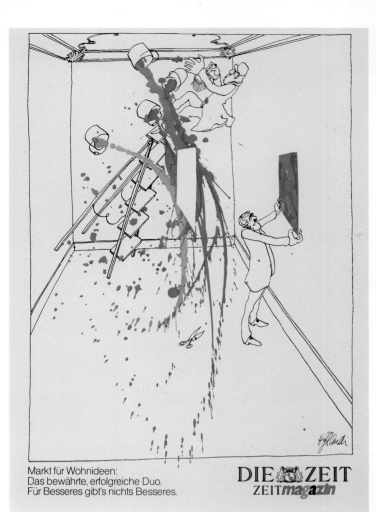

Markt für Wohnideen:
Das bewährte, erfolgreiche Duo.
Für Besseres gibt's nichts Besseres.

DIE ZEIT
ZEIT*magazin*

250

251

252

253

254

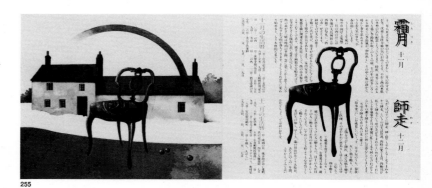

255

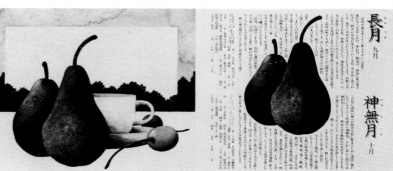

256

ARTIST / KÜNSTLER / ARTISTE:

253–256 Shigeo Okamoto

DESIGNER / GESTALTER / MAQUETTISTE:

253–256 Shigeo Okamoto
257–259 Christof Gassner
260 Lanny Sommese

ART DIRECTOR / DIRECTEUR ARTISTIQUE:

253–256 Shigeo Okamoto
260 Lanny Sommese

AGENCY / AGENTUR / AGENCE – STUDIO:

253–256 Shigeo Okamoto Design Center
260 Lanny Sommese Design

257

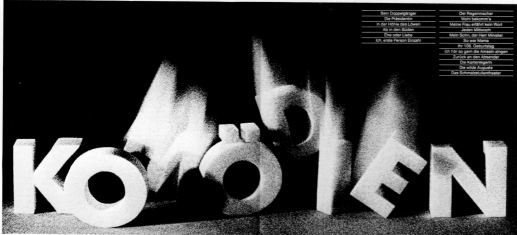

258

253–256 Full-page illustration and complete double spreads from a bank's brochure. As shown in these examples, throughout the brochure an element of the illustration is repeated and integrated in the text on the opposite page. All illustrations are in full colour. (JPN)
257–259 Introductory double spreads to the chapters "Neuroses of bourgeois society" and "Comedies", and cover of the brochure of German television's second channel, containing a summary and brief descriptions of the plays on its programme for 1982. (GER)
260 Cover of a summer festival's programme. (US)

253–256 Ganzseitige Illustration und vollständige Doppelseiten aus der Broschüre einer Bank. Wie bei diesen Beispielen wird auf jeder Doppelseite ein Element der Illustration auf der gegenüberliegenden Textseite wiederholt und integriert. Alle Illustrationen sind mehrfarbig. (JPN)
257–259 Doppelseiten als Einleitung zu den Kapiteln über die Schauspiele der entsprechenden Kategorie und Umschlag der Broschüre des Zweiten Deutschen Fernsehens. Sie enthält eine Übersicht und kurze Abhandlungen über die Aufführungen auf dem Sendeplan für 1982. (GER)
260 Umschlag eines Prospektes mit einem speziellen Kultur-Programm für den Sommer. (USA)

253–256 Illustration pleine page et doubles pages complètes d'une brochure de banque. Comme on le voit par ces exemples, un élément de l'illustration est repris sur la page opposée et intégré dans le texte. (JPN)
257–259 Doubles pages introduisant les chapitres des différents genres théâtraux figurant dans les émissions de la 2e chaîne de TV allemande, et couverture de la même brochure-programme pour 1982. (GER)
260 Couverture d'un dépliant avec le programme d'un festival d'été des arts visuels et de spectacle. (USA)

259

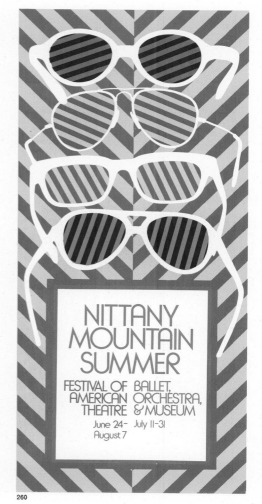

260

261

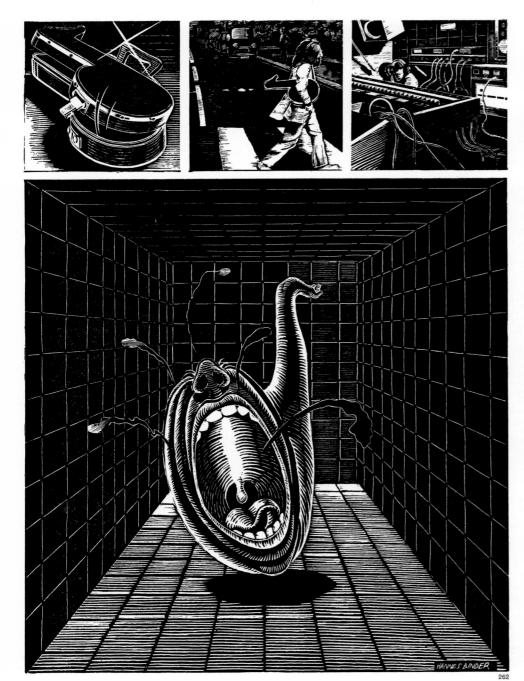

262

Listen

263

ARTIST / KÜNSTLER / ARTISTE:

261 Randall Enos
262 Hannes Binder
263 John O'Leary
264 Studio 6

DESIGNER / GESTALTER / MAQUETTISTE:

263 John O'Leary
264 Miodrag Mijatović-Mijat

AGENCY / AGENTUR / AGENCE – STUDIO:

264 Studio 6

Booklets / Prospekte / Brochures

264

ART DIRECTOR / DIRECTEUR ARTISTIQUE:

261 Michael Brent
263 John O'Leary
264 Jean-Claude Widmer

261 Illustration of the *Tennis and Golf Digests'* New Year greetings, with a calendar of events. (USA)
262 Illustration in black and white from a publication in newspaper style issued by the city of Zurich, with information about the International Jazz Festival, Zurich. (SWI)
263 Self-promotion by John O'Leary, an illustrator. (USA)
264 Embossed cover, with affixed card, of a brochure for Radio "Suisse Romande" for a two-day classical music concert. (SWI)

261 Illustration des Neujahrsgrusses einer Golf- und einer Tennis-Zeitschrift mit Veranstaltungskalender. (USA)
262 Illustration in Schwarzweiss aus einer zeitungsähnlich aufgemachten Publikation der Stadt Zürich mit Informationen zum Internationalen Jazz-Festival in Zürich. (SWI)
263 «Hör zu.» Eigenwerbung eines Illustrators. (USA)
264 Geprägter Umschlag, mit aufgeklebter Karte, von einer Broschüre des Westschweizer Radios zur «Schubertiade». (SWI)

261 Illustration de la carte de Nouvel An d'un magazine de golf et d'un autre de tennis, avec calendrier sportif. (USA)
262 Illustration noir et blanc d'une publication de la ville de Zurich présentant sous une forme apparentée à un journal des renseignements sur le festival international de jazz. (SWI)
263 «Ecoute.» Autopromotion d'un illustrateur. (USA)
264 Couverture gaufrée (avec carte encollée) d'une brochure de Radio Suisse Romande pour la «Schubertiade» de Moudon. (SWI)

3

Newspaper Illustrations
Magazine Illustrations
Magazine Covers
Trade Magazines
House Organs
Corporate Publications
Annual Reports
Book Covers

Zeitungs-Illustrationen
Zeitschriften-Illustrationen
Zeitschriften-Umschläge
Fachzeitschriften
Hauszeitschriften
Firmenpublikationen
Jahresberichte
Buchumschläge

Illustrations de journaux
Illustrations de périodiques
Couvertures de périodiques
Revues professionnelles
Journaux d'entreprise
Publications d'entreprise
Rapports annuels
Couvertures de livres

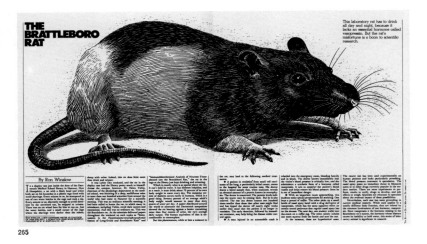

265

ARTIST / KÜNSTLER / ARTISTE:

265 Doug Smith
266, 269 Henrik Drescher
267 Jamie Hogan
268 Andrzej Dudzinski
270 John Gentile
271 Terry Allen

DESIGNER / GESTALTER:

265, 268–271 Ronn Campisi
266 Lynn Staley
267 Elizabeth Williams

ART DIRECTOR:

265, 267–271 Ronn Campisi
266 Lynn Staley

AGENCY / AGENTUR / AGENCE:

267 Elizabeth Williams

PUBLISHER / VERLEGER:

265–271 The Boston Globe

266

267

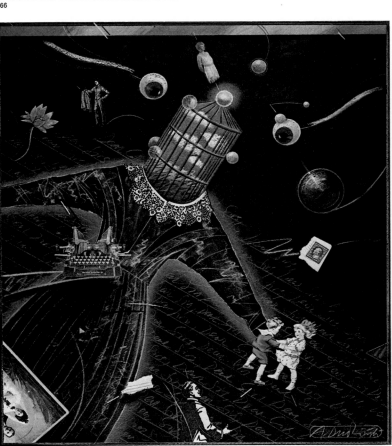

268

269

270

Newspaper Illustrations
Zeitungs-Illustrationen
Illustrations de journaux

265, 267 Double spreads from the *Boston Globe Magazine*, supplement of *The Boston Globe*. The subjects are the rat used for medical experiments, and gardening in autumn. (USA)
266 Spread from *The Boston Globe* on the subject of collecting doll's house furnishings. (USA)
268, 269 Illustrations from the *Boston Globe Magazine*. Fig. 268 is the introductory illustration for a story about the unearthing of the mysterious history of a great-grandmother; Fig. 269 is an illustration introducing a short story. (USA)
270, 271 Black-and-white illustration from an article in the *Boston Globe Magazine* about a Swede who rescued numerous Jews from the Nazi terror, and a full-colour cover illustration from an issue containing an article about the powers of judges. (USA)

265, 267 Doppelseiten aus dem *Boston Globe Magazine*, Beilage der Zeitung *Boston Globe*. Themen: Die Ratte als medizinisches Versuchstier (Abb. 265), und Gartenarbeit im Herbst (Abb. 267). (USA)
266 Für einen Beitrag in *Boston Globe* über das Sammeln von Puppenstubenmöbeln. (USA)
268, 269 Illustrationen aus dem *Boston Globe Magazine*. In Abb. 268 handelt es sich um die einleitende Illustration zu einer Geschichte über das geheimnisvolle Schicksal einer Urgrossmutter; Abb. 269 leitet eine Kurzgeschichte ein. (USA)
270, 271 Schwarzweiss-Illustration zu einem Artikel im *Boston Globe Magazine* über einen Schweden, der zahlreiche Juden vor den Nazis gerettet hat, und mehrfarbige Umschlagillustration einer Ausgabe mit einem Artikel über die Macht der Richter. (USA)

265, 267 Doubles pages du *Boston Globe Magazine*, supplément du journal *The Boston Globe*. Sujets: le rat en tant qu'animal de laboratoire; le jardinage en automne. (USA)
266 Pour un article du *Boston Globe* sur la collection de meubles de maisons de poupées. (USA)
268, 269 Illustrations du *Boston Globe Magazine*. La fig. 268 accompagne le début d'un récit consacré au destin mystérieux d'une arrière-grand-maman. La fig. 269 introduit une nouvelle. (USA)
270, 271 Illustration noir et blanc pour un article du *Boston Globe Magazine* qui met à l'honneur un Suédois qui réussit à tirer nombre de juifs des griffes des nazis, et illustration polychrome de couverture pour un numéro où l'on discute du pouvoir des juges. (USA)

271

109

Newspaper Illustrations
Zeitungs-Illustrationen
Illustrations de journaux

ARTIST / KÜNSTLER / ARTISTE:

272, 274 Steve Guarnaccia
273 Vivienne Flesher
275 Jamie Hogan
276, 277 Karen Watson

DESIGNER / GESTALTER / MAQUETTISTE:

272–277 Ronn Campisi

272, 273 Black-and-white illustrations from short stories in the *Boston Globe Magazine*. (USA)
274, 275 Covers of the *Boston Globe Magazine*. These issues contain articles about the marketing of leisure-time clothes, and about Vietnam war crimes. (USA)
276, 277 Full-page illustration and complete introductory double spread for a short story about music lessons. Taken from the *Boston Globe Magazine*. (USA)

272, 273 Schwarzweiss-Illustrationen zu Kurzgeschichten im *Boston Globe Magazine*. Die Themen: Utopische «Marschbefehle» (Abb. 272) und ein Mann, der sein Augenlicht verliert (Abb. 273). (USA)
274, 275 Umschläge des *Boston Globe Magazine*. Die Ausgaben enthalten Artikel über das Marketing von Freizeitkleidung und über Straftaten in Vietnam. (USA)
276, 277 Ganzseitige Illustration und vollständige, einleitende Doppelseite zu einer Kurzgeschichte über Musikunterricht. Aus dem *Boston Globe Magazine*. (USA)

272, 273 Illustrations noir et blanc pour des nouvelles publiées dans le *Boston Globe Magazine*. Sujets: «ordres de marche» utopiques (fig. 272); un homme perd la vue (fig. 273). (USA)
274, 275 Couvertures du *Boston Globe Magazine*. Les numéros en question contiennent des articles sur la commercialisation de vêtements de loisirs et les crimes commis au Viêt-nam. (USA)
276, 277 Illustration pleine page et double page initiale complète d'une nouvelle où il est question de leçons de musique. Extrait du *Boston Globe Magazine*. (USA)

272

273

274

275

276

277

ART DIRECTOR / DIRECTEUR ARTISTIQUE:
272–277 Ronn Campisi

PUBLISHER / VERLEGER / EDITEUR:
272–277 The Boston Globe

278

279

ARTIST / KÜNSTLER / ARTISTE:

278, 279 Braldt Bralds
280 Jan Sawka
281 Terry Allen
282 Cathy Hull

DESIGNER / GESTALTER / MAQUETTISTE:

280, 281 Ronn Campisi

ART DIRECTOR / DIRECTEUR ARTISTIQUE:

278, 279 Ed Schneider
280, 281 Ronn Campisi
282 John McCleod

PUBLISHER / VERLEGER / EDITEUR:

278, 279 The Washington Post
280, 281 The Boston Globe
282 The New York Times

280

282

281

Newspaper Illustrations
Zeitungs-Illustrationen
Illustrations de journaux

278, 279 Illustration and complete cover of the *Washington Post Magazine*. Subject is a book by admiral Hyman G. Rickover. (USA)
280 Illustration for an article in the *Boston Globe Magazine* about South African writers who oppose the Apartheid politics of their country. In black and white. (USA)
281 Full-colour illustration for an article in the *Boston Globe Magazine* about growing vegetables indoors in winter. (USA)
282 Illustration from the Home Section, Hers Column, in *The New York Times*. The Subject: "Marriage, a psychological trap." (USA)

278, 279 Illustration und vollständiger Umschlag des *Washington Post Magazine*. Thema ist das Buch eines Admirals. (USA)
280 Illustration zu einem Artikel im *Boston Globe Magazine* über südafrikanische Schriftsteller, die gegen die Apartheidspolitik sind. In Schwarzweiss. (USA)
281 Mehrfarbige Illustration für einen Artikel im *Boston Globe Magazine* über den winterlichen Gemüseanbau im Hause. (USA)
282 Illustration aus der *New York Times*, Rubrik für die Frau. Das Thema: Heirat, eine psychologische Falle. (USA)

278, 279 Illustration et couverture complète du *Washington Post Magazine*. Sujet: un livre de l'amiral Rickover. (USA)
280 Illustration pour un article du *Boston Globe Magazine* sur des écrivains sud-africains hostiles à la politique de l'apartheid. Noir et blanc. (USA)
281 Illustration polychrome pour un article du *Boston Globe Magazine* sur la culture des légumes à l'abri, en hiver. (USA)
282 Illustration du *New York Times*, section Pour la Femme: «le mariage, un piège psychologique.» (USA)

113

283–285 Illustrations from *The Boston Globe* daily newspaper. Fig. 283: Review of a book about Franklin D. Roosevelt; Fig. 284: Review of a new book written by Philip Roth; Fig. 285: from an article about how parents suffer when their children divorce. (USA)
286 Illustration from a calendar of children's events in *The New York Times*. (USA)
287 From a *New York Times* article about censorship in the Caribbean press. (USA)
288, 289 Illustrations from *The New York Times*. Fig. 288 belongs to the Dining Out Guide for restaurants specialising in fish and seafood; Fig. 289: recipes for cooking sea urchins. (USA)

283–285 Illustrationen aus der Zeitung *Boston Globe*. Abb. 283 bezieht sich auf die Besprechung eines Buches von Joseph Alsop über Franklin D. Roosevelt; Abb. 284 auf ein Buch von Philip Roth. Abb. 285 gehört zu einem Artikel, der sich mit der Frage befasst, wie sehr Eltern leiden, wenn sich ihre Kinder scheiden lassen. (USA)
286 Illustration zu einem Veranstaltungskalender für Kinder in der *New York Times*. (USA)
287 Aus der *New York Times*. Das Thema: Zensur der karibischen Presse. (USA)
288, 289 Illustrationen aus der *New York Times* zu kulinarischen Themen. Abb. 288 gehört zu einem Führer für Restaurants, deren Spezialität Fisch und Meeresfrüchte sind; Abb. 289 illustriert eine Rubrik mit Kochrezepten, hier die Zubereitung von Seeigeln. (USA)

283–285 Illustrations du quotidien *Boston Globe*. La fig. 283 a trait au compte rendu d'un livre de Joseph Alsop sur Franklin D. Roosevelt, la fig. 284 se rapporte à un ouvrage de Philip Roth. La fig. 285 illustre un article qui expose les souffrances des parents dont les enfants divorcent. (USA)
286 Illustration du *New York Times* pour un calendrier de spectacles pour les petits. (USA)
287 Illustration du *New York Times*: la censure qui muselle la presse aux Caraïbes. (USA)
288, 289 Illustrations du *New York Times* pour des sujets culinaires. La fig. 288 fait partie d'un guide des restaurants spécialisés dans les poissons et dans les fruits de mer, la fig. 289 d'une rubrique de recettes, ici pour la préparation de l'oursin. (USA)

283

286

284

285

287

288

ARTIST / KÜNSTLER / ARTISTE:

283–285 Jamie Hogan
286, 289 Randall Enos
287 Marguerita
288 Ed Koren

DESIGNER / GESTALTER:

283, 284 Lucy Bartholomay
285 Sara Giovanitti
286, 288 Nicki Kalish

ART DIRECTOR:

283, 284 Lucy Bartholomay
285 Sara Giovanitti
286, 288 Nicki Kalish
287 John Cayea
289 Nancy Kent

PUBLISHER / VERLEGER / EDITEUR:

283–285 The Boston Globe
286–289 The New York Times

289

115

290

291

292

293a

ARTIST / KÜNSTLER / ARTISTE:

290 Bob Gale
291 Doug Smith
292 James Steinberg
293, 293a Brad Holland

DESIGNER / GESTALTER:

291 Gwendolyn Wong
292 Sara Giovanitti
293, 293a Jerelle Kraus

ART DIRECTOR:

290 John MacLeod
291 Ronn Campisi
292 Sara Giovanitti
293, 293a Jerelle Kraus

AGENCY / AGENTUR / AGENCE:

290 Inx, Inc.

PUBLISHER / VERLEGER:

290 Inx, Inc.
291, 292 The Boston Globe
293, 293a The New York Times

293

290 International terrorism is the subject of this illustration from the *Washington Star* and *Arizona Star* newspapers. (USA)
291 Opening page of *The Boston Globe*'s "Living" section, featuring a Halloween story for children. (USA)
292 Illustration from *The Boston Globe* newspaper, for an article about stealing among children. (USA)
293, 293a Illustration and complete page from *The New York Times*. The feature deals with Ireland's hatred of the English. (USA)

290 Internationaler Terrorismus ist das Thema dieser Illustration aus den Zeitungen *Washington Star* und *Arizona Star*. (USA)
291 Einleitende Seite des Sektors «Leben» im *Boston Globe*, mit einer «Halloween»-Geschichte für Kinder. (USA)
292 Illustration für einen Artikel über das Stehlen unter Kindern. Aus der Zeitung *Boston Globe*. (USA)
293, 293a Illustration und vollständige Seite der *New York Times*. Thema des Beitrags: Der Hass der Irländer auf die Engländer. (USA)

290 Le terrorisme international est le thème traité dans cette illustration des quotidiens *Washington Star, Arizona Star*. (USA)
291 Page initiale de la rubrique «Vivre» du *Boston Globe*, avec une histoire de Halloween pour les petits. (USA)
292 Illustration d'un article du *Boston Globe* consacré aux larcins commis par des enfants au détriment d'enfants. (USA)
293, 293a Illustration et page complète du *New York Times*, où il est question de la haine des Irlandais pour les Anglais. (USA)

294

295

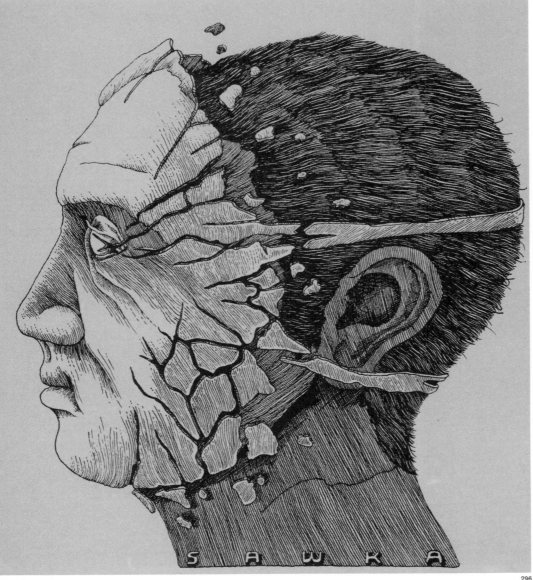

296

297

ARTIST / KÜNSTLER / ARTISTE:

294, 295, 297, 298 Eugène Mihaesco
296 Jan Sawka
299 Frances Jetter

DESIGNER / GESTALTER / MAQUETTISTE:

295, 297 Nicki Kalish

ART DIRECTOR / DIRECTEUR ARTISTIQUE:

294, 298 Jerelle Kraus
295, 297 Nicki Kalish
299 John MacLeod

AGENCY / AGENTUR / AGENCE – STUDIO:

299 Inx, Inc.

PUBLISHER / VERLEGER / EDITEUR:

294, 295, 297, 298 The New York Times
296 Polish Daily
299 Inx, Inc.

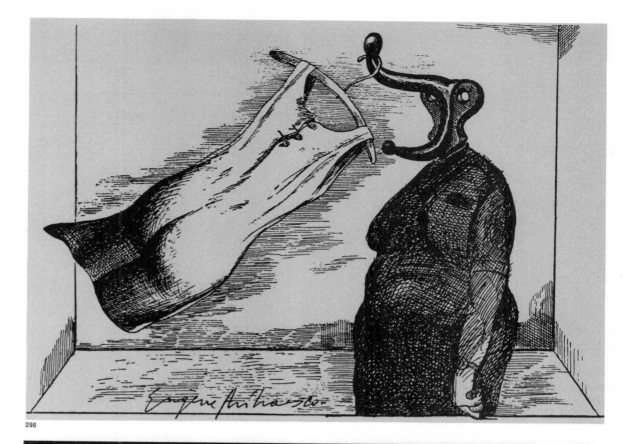

298

299

294 Illustration from the Op-ed page of *The New York Times*: "If you ban a book". (USA)
295 From the "Dining Out Guide" in *The New York Times*, for the Lincoln Center area. (USA)
296 From a New York newspaper that appears in Polish language (issue of 4/11/1981). The subject here is the situation of Polish literature after the events of August 1980. (USA)
297 From the "Dining Out Guide" of *The New York Times*, dealing with Christmas dinner. (USA)
298 Illustration for an article in *The New York Times* about unwarranted and mortifying searches made by the police. (USA)
299 Illustration on the subject of illegal immigrants being sent to detention camps. (USA)

294 «Wenn man ein Buch verbannt.» Illustration aus der *New York Times*. (USA)
295 Aus dem Restaurant-Führer der *New York Times* für das Gebiet des Lincoln-Center. (USA)
296 Aus einer in New York in Polnisch erscheinenden Zeitung (Ausgabe vom 4.11.1981). Es geht um die Situation der polnischen Literatur nach der «Revolution» im August 1980. (USA)
297 Aus dem Restaurant-Führer der *New York Times*, hier mit Weihnachtsangeboten. (USA)
298 Illustration zu einem Artikel, in dem es um ungerechtfertigte Leibesvisitationen durch die Polizei geht. Aus der *New York Times*. (USA)
299 Thema dieser Illustration sind die Lager für illegale Einwanderer in den USA. (USA)

294 «Lorsque vous bannissez un livre.» Illustration en page op-ed du *New York Times*. (USA)
295 Illustration d'un guide des restaurants avoisinant le Lincoln Center publié dans le *New York Times*. (USA)
296 Numéro du 4.11.1981 d'un quotidien polonais paraissant à New York. On y discute de la situation des lettres en Pologne au lendemain de la «révolution» d'août 1980. (USA)
297 Illustration du *New York Times*: guide des restaurants en période de fêtes de Noël. (USA)
298 Illustration d'un article protestant contre les fouilles corporelles injustifiées auxquelles procède la police. Publiée dans le *New York Times*, en noir et blanc. (USA)
299 Illustration se rapportant aux camps où sont internés les immigrants clandestins. (USA)

Newspaper Illustrations
Zeitungs-Illustrationen
Illustrations de journaux

Newspaper Illustrations
Zeitungs-Illustrationen
Illustrations de journaux

300–302 Illustrations for articles in *The New York Times* on the subjects of teenage sexuality, investments in Broadway productions, and the endangered education for Indians. (USA)
303 Illustration for a theatre guide in the Sunday supplement of *The New York Times*. (USA)
304, 305 Illustration for an article, and complete page from *The New York Times*, dealing with the incompetency of the Arms Control and Disarmament Agency. (USA)
306 Illustration for a *Daily News* article entitled: "Pick-up Night at the Met." (USA)

300–302 Illustrationen zu Artikeln in der *New York Times*. Themen: Sexuelle Aufklärung für Teenager, Investitionen in Broadway-Produktionen und die gefährdete Ausbildung der Indianer. (USA)
303 Illustration zu einem Theater-Führer in der *New York Times*. (USA)
304, 305 Illustration für einen Artikel und vollständige Seite aus der *New York Times*. Das Thema ist die Untätigkeit der amerikanischen Behörde für Rüstungskontrolle und Abrüstung. (USA)
306 Für einen Artikel in den *Daily News*: Museumsbesuch als Anbändelgelegenheit. (USA)

300–302 Illustrations du *New York Times* d'articles traitant de l'éducation sexuelle des adolescents, des investissements à Broadway et de l'éducation imparfaite des Peaux-Rouges. (USA)
303 Illustration d'un guide des théâtres publié dans le *New York Times*. (USA)
304, 305 Illustration d'un article et page complète où elle figure dans le *New York Times*. On y dénonce l'inertie de l'Agence américaine pour le contrôle des armes et le désarmement. (USA)
306 Pour un article des *Daily News*: le musée est propice aux rencontres sentimentales. (USA)

300

301

302

303

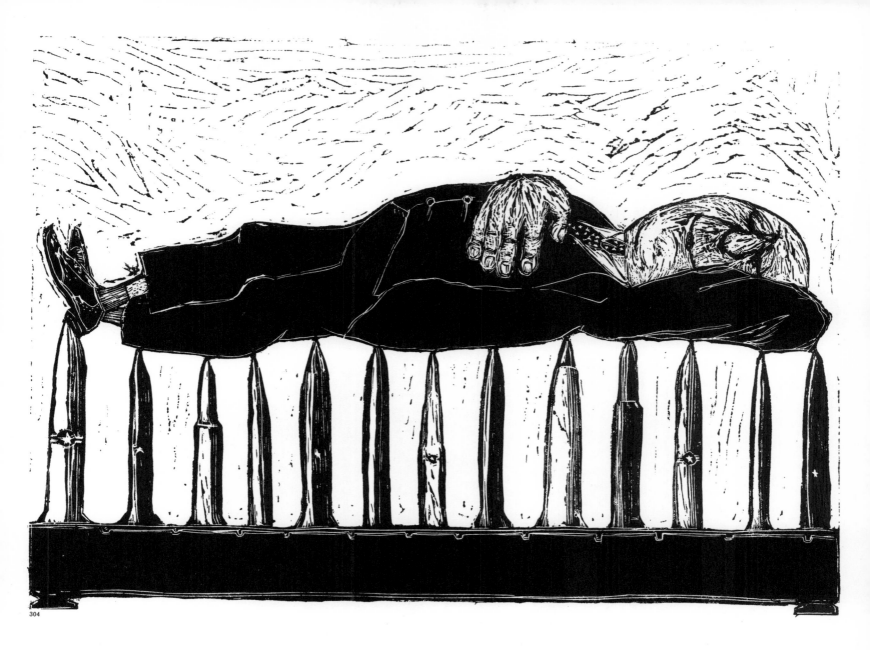

304

305

ARTIST / KÜNSTLER / ARTISTE:

300, 302, 306 Cathy Hull
301 Randall Enos
303 Paul Meisel
304, 305 Frances Jetter

ART DIRECTOR / DIRECTEUR ARTISTIQUE:

300, 302, 304, 305 Jerelle Kraus
301 Nicki Kalish/Mike Todd
303 Nicki Kalish
306 Nancy Meagen

PUBLISHER / VERLEGER / EDITEUR:

300–305 The New York Times
306 The Daily News

306

307

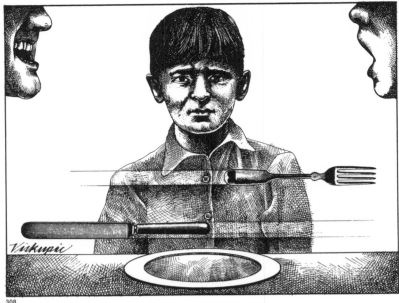

308

ARTIST / KÜNSTLER / ARTISTE:

307–311 Gary Viskupic
312 Jan Sawka

DESIGNER / GESTALTER / MAQUETTISTE:

307–311 Gary Viskupic

ART DIRECTOR / DIRECTEUR ARTISTIQUE:

309 Warren Weilbacher
311 Paul Back
312 Jerelle Kraus

AGENCY / AGENTUR / AGENCE – STUDIO:

307–311 Newsday Edit. Art Dept.

PUBLISHER / VERLEGER / EDITEUR:

307–311 Newsday Inc.
312 The New York Times

310

311

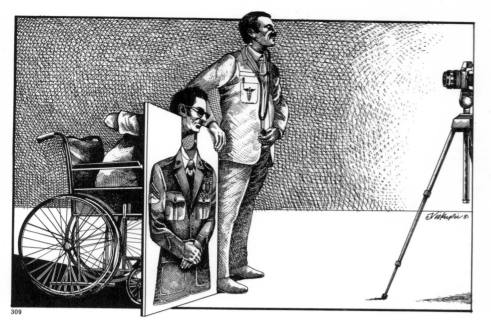

309

307–309 Illustrations from *Newsday*. The articles deal with the dissolving of identity into numbers by use of credit cards (Fig. 307); the emotional effects of children listening to their parents arguing at the dinner table (Fig. 308); and the problems and conditions of war veterans in hospitals (Fig. 309). (USA)
310, 311 More illustrations from *Newsday*. Fig. 310 deals with the "real" Howard Hughes as opposed to his inflated image and ego; Fig. 311 criticises certain behavioural patterns of married men. (USA)
312 For an article on the subject of economic development in Caribbean countries and illegal immigrants from this area, in *The New York Times*. (USA)

307–309 Illustrationen aus *Newsday*. In den Artikeln geht es um die Identifizierung von Menschen durch Nummern, z.B. bei Kreditkarten (307); um die Gefühle von Kindern beim Streit der Eltern (308) und um die Behandlung von Kriegsversehrten (309). (USA)
310, 311 Weitere Illustrationen aus *Newsday*. Abb. 310 bezieht sich auf einen Artikel über das «wahre Gesicht» von Howard Hughes; im Artikel zu Abb. 311 wird das Verhalten von Ehemännern kritisiert. (USA)
312 Für einen Artikel in der *New York Times*. Thema: Die wirtschaftliche Entwicklung der karibischen Länder und die illegalen Einwanderer aus diesem Gebiet. (USA)

307–309 Illustrations de *Newsday*. Les articles en question traitent de la déshumanisation du consommateur qu'apportent p.ex. les cartes de crédit (307), des sentiments des enfants assistant aux querelles de leurs parents (308) et de la maigre attention portée aux besoins et problèmes des mutilés de guerre (309). (USA)
310, 311 Autres illustrations figurant dans *Newsday*. La fig. 310 a trait à un article sur le vrai visage de Howard Hughes; l'article illustré par la fig. 311 critique le comportement de l'homme marié, véritable coq de la famille. (USA)
312 Illustration pour un article du *New York Times* qui discute de l'évolution économique des pays de la Caraïbe et de l'immigration clandestine, aux Etats-Unis, des habitants de cette région. (USA)

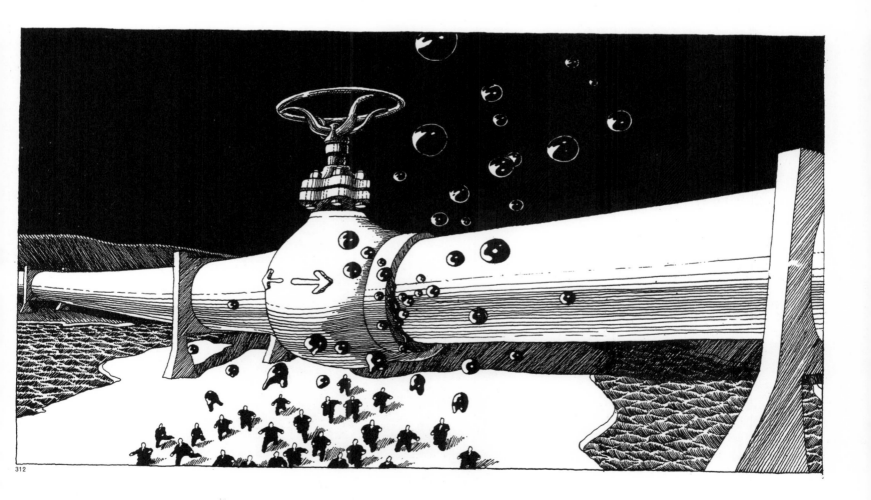

312

313

Newspaper Illustrations
Zeitungs-Illustrationen
Illustrations de journaux

313 Illustration for an article in the *Sydsvenska Dagbladet* about the survival of non-aligned nations after Tito's death. (SWE)
314 Double spread from a student newspaper. (USA)
315 Illustration for a Christmas story by O. Henry that appeared in the *Kölnische Rundschau*: a girl sells her hair in order to buy a watch for her boyfriend; he sells the watch to buy a comb for her hair. (GER)
316 From the *Basler Magazin*. Illustration on eroticism. (SWI)

313 Illustration für einen Artikel im *Sydsvenska Dagbladet* zu der Überlebenschance der Blockfreien nach dem Tod Titos. (SWE)
314 Doppelseite aus einer Studentenzeitung. Thema: Die Gefahr rechtsradikaler Gruppierungen und die versuchte Einflussnahme auf die Bereiche der Erziehung und Ausbildung. (USA)
315 Illustration für eine Weihnachtsgeschichte von O. Henry in der *Kölnischen Rundschau*: «Das teuer erkaufte Geschenk.» (GER)
316 Aus dem *Basler Magazin*. Illustration zum Thema Erotik. (SWI)

313 Illustration pour un article du *Sydsvenska Dagbladet*: les chances de survie du bloc des non-alignés après Tito. (SWE)
314 Double page d'un journal estudiantin consacrée au danger que font peser sur l'enseignement et la formation professionnelle les groupements activistes d'extrême-droite. (USA)
315 Illustration pour un conte de Noël d'O. Henry paru dans la *Kölnische Rundschau*, «Le cadeau chèrement payé». (GER)
316 Illustration d'un texte sur l'érotisme. *Basler Magazin*. (SWI)

314

315

ARTIST / KÜNSTLER / ARTISTE:

313 Karen Engelmann
314 Michael David Brown
315 Eduard Prüssen
316 Walter Grieder

DESIGNER / GESTALTER / MAQUETTISTE:

314 Michael David Brown

ART DIRECTOR / DIRECTEUR ARTISTIQUE:

314 Michael David Brown
316 Hans-Peter Platz / Gérard Wirtz

AGENCY / AGENTUR / AGENCE – STUDIO:

314 Michael David Brown, Inc.

PUBLISHER / VERLEGER / EDITEUR:

313 Sydsvenska Dagbladet
314 Student National Education Assoc.
315 Kölnische Rundschau
316 Basler Zeitung

316

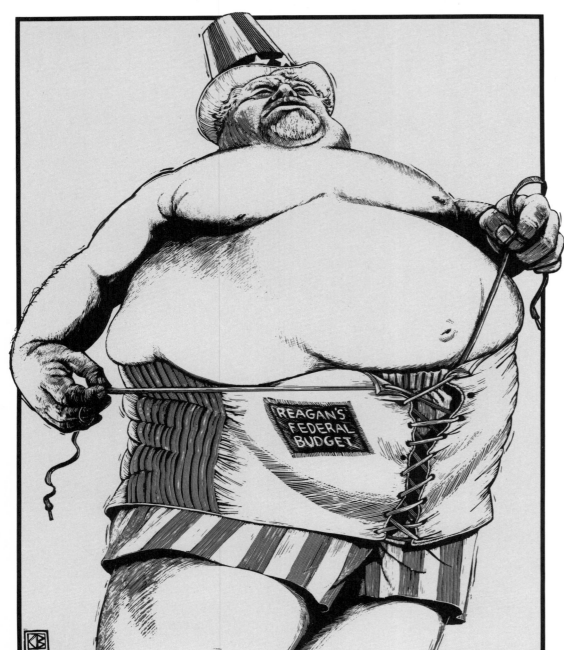

317

ARTIST / KÜNSTLER / ARTISTE:

317, 319, 320 Kent Barton
318 Eugène Mihaesco

ART DIRECTOR / DIRECTEUR ARTISTIQUE:

317, 319, 320 Kent Barton
318 Jerelle Kraus

PUBLISHER / VERLEGER / EDITEUR:

317, 319, 320 The Miami Herald
318 The New York Times

317 Illustration from the "Viewpoint" column of *The Miami Herald* dealing with the subject of President Reagan's economics. (USA)
318 Illustration from an article published in *The New York Times*. The author is the widow of a former C.I.A. agent. (USA)
319, 320 Complete page and illustration, both of which appeared in *The Miami Herald,* for an article about Ronald Reagan likening him to a Republican Franklin D. Roosevelt. (USA)

317 Illustration aus dem *Miami Herald* unter der Rubrik «Blickwinkel», hier zu Präsident Reagans Wirtschaftspolitik. (USA)
318 «Eine CIA-Familie.» Illustration für einen Artikel in der *New York Times.* Die Autorin ist die Witwe eines Agenten. (USA)
319, 320 Vollständige Seite und Illustration für einen Artikel über Ronald Reagan, der hier ein republikanischer Franklin D. Roosevelt genannt wird. Aus *Miami Herald.* (USA)

317 Illustration pour la rubrique Point de vue du *Miami Herald,* critique pour la politique économique du président Reagan. (USA)
318 «Une famille de la C.I.A.» Illustration pour un article du *New York Times* écrit par la veuve d'un agent de la C.I.A. (USA)
319, 320 Page complète et illustration d'un article du *Miami Herald* où Ronald Reagan est taxé de FDR (Franklin D. Roosevelt) républicain. (USA)

318

319

320

321

ARTIST / KÜNSTLER / ARTISTE:

321 Pascal Gachet
322 John Breakey
323–326 Francisco Graells (Pancho)

DESIGNER / GESTALTER / MAQUETTISTE:

322 John Breakey

ART DIRECTOR / DIRECTEUR ARTISTIQUE:

321 Etienne Delessert
322 Jere Warren

AGENCY / AGENTUR / AGENCE – STUDIO:

321 Carabosse
322 Whole Hog Studios

PUBLISHER / VERLEGER / EDITEUR:

321 La Suisse
322 Atlanta Journal
323–326 El Nacional

321 The actor Lino Ventura on the title page of the week-end edition of *La Suisse.* Illustration in brown shades. (SWI)
322 Illustration for a book review in the *Atlanta Journal.* (USA)
323–326 Illustration and a page from *El Nacional.* The subjects dealt with are: the USA–Iran relationship, George Bush, and Haiti "An Island in Conflict"— "The End of a Farce" with a caricature of Duvalier. (VEN)

321 Der Schauspieler Lino Ventura auf der Titelseite der Wochenendausgabe von *La Suisse.* Illustration in Brauntönen. (SWI)
322 Illustration für eine Buchbesprechung im *Atlanta Journal.* (USA)
323–326 Illustrationen und eine Seite aus *El Nacional.* Themen: Die Beziehungen USA–Iran, George Bush, und «Haiti: eine Insel im Konflikt» – «Das Ende einer Farce», mit einer Karikatur von Jean-Claude Duvalier. (VEN)

321 L'acteur Lino Ventura en page de titre de l'édition de fin de semaine de *La Suisse.* Illustration exécutée en divers bruns. (SWI)
322 Illustration pour un compte rendu de livre. *Atlanta Journal.* (USA)
323–326 Illustrations et une page d'*El Nacional.* Thèmes traités: les relations Etats-Unis–Iran; George Bush; «Haïti; une île plongée dans le conflit» – «La fin d'une farce» (Jean-Claude Duvalier). (VEN)

322

324

Newspaper Illustrations
Zeitungs-Illustrationen
Illustrations de journaux

323

325

326

327

328

327, 328 "Multinationals": double spread and illustration in actual size from *Folhetim*. (BRA)
329 Sadat's assassination. The illustration was published in various newspapers. (USA)
330 Illustration for a *Time* report about books which deal with historical crimes such as Lincoln's assassination or the theft of Edward VII's Irish Crown Jewels. (USA)
331 From *The New York Times*, about a fictitious abandonment of New York. (USA)

327, 328 «Multinationale.» Doppelseite und Illustration in Originalgrösse aus *Folhetim*. (BRA)
329 Die Ermordung Sadats. Die Illustration wurde in verschiedenen Zeitungen verwendet. (USA)
330 Illustration für einen *Time*-Bericht über Bücher, die sich mit historischen Verbrechen (die Ermordung Lincolns, der Diebstahl der irischen Kronjuwelen Eduards VII.) befassen. (USA)
331 Aus der *New York Times*. Es geht hier um einen fiktiven Exodus aus New York. (USA)

327, 328 «Multinationales.» Double page de *Folhetim* et illustration au format original. (BRA)
329 L'assassinat de Sadate; illustration publiée dans divers journaux. (USA)
330 Illustration pour un compte rendu, dans *Time*, d'ouvrages traitant de crimes célèbres (l'assassinat de Lincoln, le vol des bijoux irlandais de la Couronne d'Edouard VII). (USA)
331 Illustration publiée dans le *New York Times* pour accompagner un texte proposant l'abandon pur et simple de New York: l'exode fictif. (USA)

329

Newspaper Illustrations
Zeitungs-Illustrationen
Illustrations de journaux

ARTIST / KÜNSTLER / ARTISTE:

327, 328 Rubem Campos Grilo
329 Frances Jetter
330, 331 James Grashow

ART DIRECTOR / DIRECTEUR ARTISTIQUE:

329 John MacLeod
330 Lenny Levine
331 Steve Heller

AGENCY / AGENTUR / AGENCE – STUDIO:

329 Inx, Inc.

PUBLISHER / VERLEGER / EDITEUR:

327, 328 Folha de São Paulo
329 Inx, Inc.
330 Time, Inc.
331 The New York Times

330

331

332

333

Newspaper Illustrations
Zeitungs-Illustrationen
Illustrations de journaux

ARTIST / KÜNSTLER / ARTISTE:
332–334 Rubem Campos Grilo

PUBLISHER / VERLEGER / EDITEUR:
332–334 Folha de São Paulo

332–334 Woodcut illustrations from the Brazilian newspaper *Folhetim*. Fig. 332 refers to the influence of unions; Fig. 333 alludes to the lack of meaningful leisure-time activities; Fig. 334 is a comment on new social legislation in Brazil. (BRA)

332–334 Holzschnitt-Illustrationen aus der brasilianischen Zeitung *Folhetim*. In Abb. 332 geht es um den Einfluss der Gewerkschaften, in Abb. 333 um Freizeitgestaltung, und Abb. 334 bezieht sich auf eine neue Sozialgesetzgebung in Brasilien. (BRA)

332–334 Gravures sur bois illustrant le quotidien brésilien *Folhetim*. La fig. 332 a trait au pouvoir des syndicats; la fig. 333 se rapporte à l'aménagement des loisirs; la fig. 334 concerne une nouvelle législation sociale au Brésil. (BRA)

ARTIST / KÜNSTLER / ARTISTE:

335 Pietro Bestetti
336–339 Tullio Pericoli
340–342 Dora Wespi

ART DIRECTOR / DIRECTEUR ARTISTIQUE:

340–342 Dora Wespi

PUBLISHER / VERLEGER / EDITEUR:

335 Corriere della Sera
336–339 L´Espresso
340–342 Conzett & Huber

336

335

337

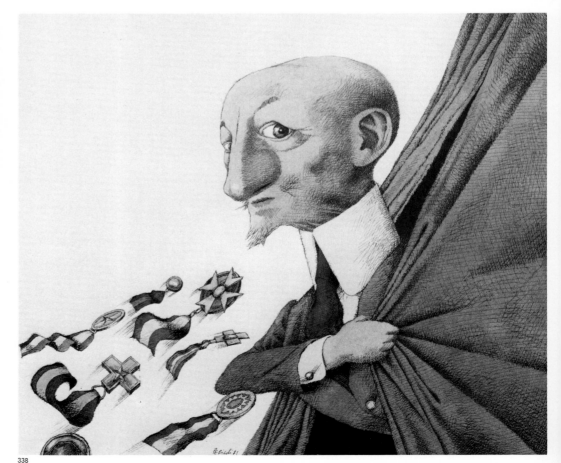

338

Magazine Illustrations
Zeitschriften-Illustrationen
Illustrations de périodiques

CUISINE LITTÉRAIRE

340

341

342

339

335 Full-colour illustration from the *Corriere della Sera* magazine, for an article about "auto-didactic" students. (ITA)
336 "The Anti-Italian." Illustration in brown and yellow for an article in *L'Espresso* magazine in memory of Piero Gobetti, anti-Fascist, student and journalist, who emigrated from Italy and died in Paris before he was twenty-five years old. (ITA)
337, 338 Complete double spread and illustration from *L'Espresso*. The article covers a musical about the life of Gabriele d'Annunzio, Italy's most famous contemporary author, who not only became a national myth but was also known as a dandy. (ITA)
339 "The third Life." Full-colour illustration from *L'Espresso* magazine for a discussion on this subject. (ITA)
340–342 Full-page illustrations from a culinary series in the women's magazine *Femina*, entitled "Cuisine Littéraire". (SWI)

335 Mehrfarbige Illustration aus der Zeitschrift *Corriere della Sera*, für einen Artikel über «Autodidakten» unter den Studenten. (ITA)
336 «Der Anti-Italiener.» Illustration in Braun und Gelb für einen Artikel in dem Magazin *L'Espresso*, zum Gedenken an Piero Gobetti, Antifaschist, Student und Journalist, der aus Italien emigrierte und noch nicht fünfundzwanzigjährig in Paris starb. (ITA)
337, 338 Vollständige Doppelseite und Illustration aus *L'Espresso*. In dem Artikel geht es um ein Musical über das Leben des berühmtesten zeitgenössischen Schriftstellers Italiens, Gabriele d'Annunzio, der nicht nur zum nationalen Mythos wurde, sondern auch als Dandy bekannt war. (ITA)
339 «Das dritte Leben.» Mehrfarbige Illustration aus dem Magazin *L'Espresso* für eine Diskussion über dieses Thema. (ITA)
340–342 Ganzseitige, einleitende Illustrationen zu einer kulinarischen Reihe in der Frauenzeitschrift *Femina*. Unter dem Titel «Cuisine Littéraire» werden hier kulinarische Geschichten, Anekdoten und Rezepte zu jeweils einem speziellen Thema veröffentlicht. (SWI)

335 Illustration polychrome du quotidien *Corriere della Sera* pour un article traitant des «autodidactes» parmi les étudiants. (ITA)
336 «L'anti-Italien.» Illustration en brun et jaune pour un article du magazine *L'Espresso* publié à la mémoire de Piero Gobetti, étudiant et journaliste antifasciste qui mourut à peine âgé de vingt-cinq ans, en exil, à Paris. (ITA)
337, 338 Double page complète et illustration de *L'Espresso*. Dans l'article, il est question d'une comédie musicale sur la vie du plus célèbre écrivain italien contemporain, Gabriele d'Annunzio, dandy accompli et devenu mythe national de son vivant. (ITA)
339 «La troisième vie.» Illustration polychrome du magazine *L'Espresso* pour une discussion sur ce sujet. (ITA)
340–342 Illustrations pleine page pour une série culinaire du magazine féminin *Femina* parue sous le titre de «Cuisine littéraire». (SWI)

343

344

345

346

Magazine Illustrations

ARTIST / KÜNSTLER / ARTISTE:

343, 344 Ken Laidlaw
345 Marvin Mattelson
346 Teresa Fasolino
347, 348 Gilbert Stone

ART DIRECTOR / DIRECTEUR ARTISTIQUE:

343 Denise Barnes
344 Graeme Murdoch
345 Carveth Kramer
346 Robert Priest
347, 348 Bob Cato

343 The positive power of the word "no". From *Cosmopolitan* magazine. (GBR)
344 Illustration for recipes published in the *Observer Magazine*. (GBR)
345 Full-page illustration from *Psychology Today* on the subject of jealousy. (USA)
346 For a critical article in *Esquire* about the trouble with Harvard University. (USA)
347, 348 Opening an excerpt from an unfinished novel published in *McCall's*. (USA)

343 Aus der Zeitschrift *Cosmopolitan*. Es geht um die Kunst des Nein-Sagens. (GBR)
344 «Die Freuden der Milch.» Illustration zu Kochrezepten im *Observer*. (GBR)
345 Ganzseitige Illustration aus *Psychology Today*. Das Thema: Eifersucht. (USA)
346 Für einen kritischen Artikel in *Esquire* über die Harvard-Universität. (USA)
347, 348 Einleitung zu einem in *McCall's* abgedruckten, unvollendeten Roman. (USA)

343 De l'art de dire non: illustration du magazine *Cosmopolitan*. (GBR)
344 «Les plaisirs du lait.» Illustration des recettes de l'*Observer*. (GBR)
345 Illustration pleine page de *Psychology Today*. Sujet: la jalousie. (USA)
346 Pour un article critique d'*Esquire* sur l'Université Harvard. (USA)
347, 348 Page initiale d'un roman inachevé publié dans *McCall's*. (USA)

PUBLISHER / VERLEGER / EDITEUR:

343 Cosmopolitan Magazine
344 Observer Magazine
345 Ziff-Davis Publishing
346 Esquire, Inc.
347, 348 McCall Publishing Co.

347

348

137

349

ARTIST / KÜNSTLER / ARTISTE:

349 Gil Funcius
350 Gary Viskupic
351 Dagmar Frinta
352, 353 Braldt Bralds

ART DIRECTOR / DIRECTEUR ARTISTIQUE:

349 Wolfgang Behnken
350 Miriam Smith
351 Caroline Bowyer
352, 353 Frank Rothman

AGENCY / AGENTUR / AGENCE – STUDIO:

350 Newsday Edit. Art Dept.

PUBLISHER / VERLEGER / EDITEUR:

349 Gruner & Jahr AG & Co.
350 Newsday Inc.
351 Dow Jones & Co.
352, 353 Science Digest

349 Illustration from a story in *Stern* magazine. (GER)
350 From *Long Island Magazine*. The article deals with children's fear of visiting the doctor. (USA)
351 For a collection of short stories in *Book Digest*. (USA)
352, 353 Double spread and illustration from *Science Digest* on the theme of animals predicting earthquakes. (USA)

349 Illustration zu einer Geschichte im Magazin *Stern*. (GER)
350 Aus *Long Island Magazine*. Der Artikel befasst sich mit der Angst der Kinder vor dem Arztbesuch. (USA)
351 Für eine Reihe von Kurzgeschichten in *Book Digest*. (USA)
352, 353 «Wie Tiere Erdbeben voraussagen.» Doppelseite und Illustration aus *Science Digest*. (USA)

349 Illustration d'un récit paru dans le magazine *Stern*. (GER)
350 Illustration d'un article du *Long Island Magazine* sur la peur du docteur chez les petits enfants. (USA)
351 Pour une série de nouvelles dans *Book Digest*. (USA)
352, 353 «Comment les animaux annoncent les tremblements de terre.» Double page et illustration du *Science Digest*. (USA)

352

350

351

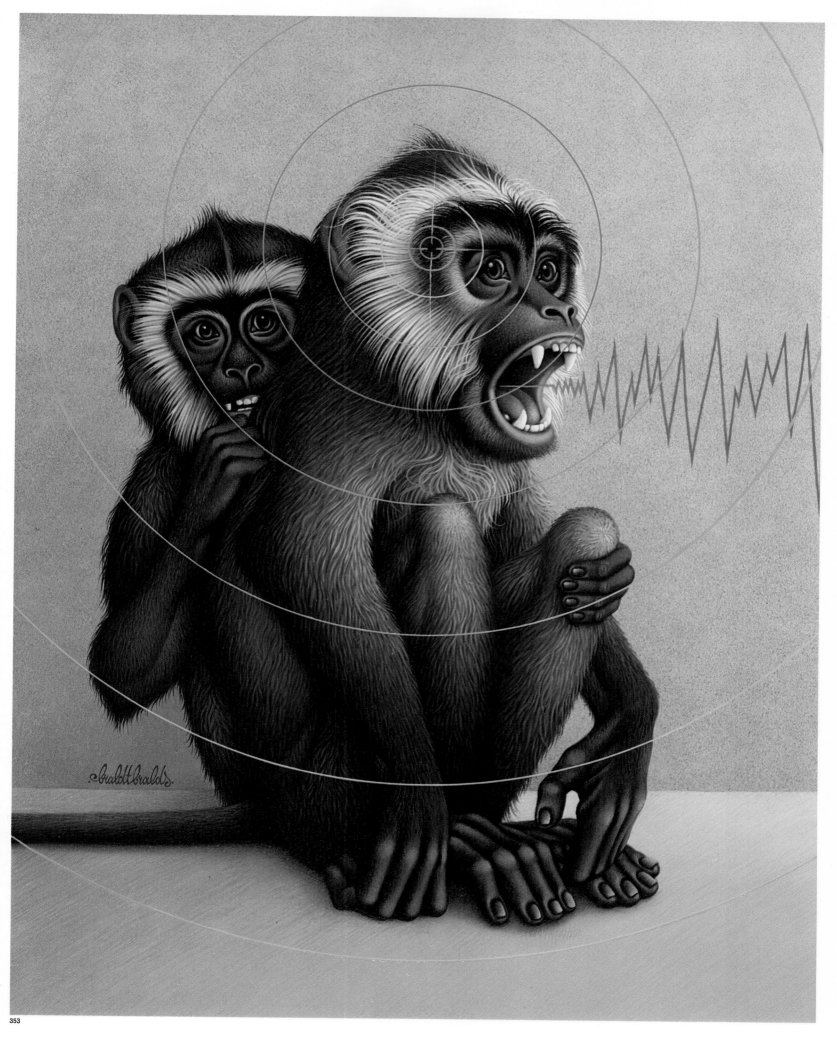

353

ARTIST / KÜNSTLER / ARTISTE:

354 Donald Roller Wilson
355 Mickey Patel
356 Michael Deas

ART DIRECTOR / DIRECTEUR ARTISTIQUE:

354 Frank M. DeVino
355 Mickey Patel
356 Don Duffy/Don Hedin

354 Illustration in actual size for a story in *Omni* magazine about a television show hosting an extraterrestrial guest. (USA)
355 Illustration in black and blue for a collection of tales for children. (IND)
356 Full-colour illustration for a story published in *Reader's Digest*. (USA)

354 Illustration in Originalgrösse für eine Geschichte, die von einer Fernseh-Unterhaltungssendung mit einem ausserirdischen Gast handelt. Aus der Zeitschrift *Omni*. (USA)
355 Illustration in Schwarz und Blau für eine Sammlung von Geschichten für Kinder. (IND)
356 Mehrfarbige Illustration aus einer in *Reader's Digest* abgedruckten Geschichte. (USA)

354 Illustration au format original pour une histoire dans le magazine *Omni* où il est question d'un show télévisé avec un hôte extraterrestre. (USA)
355 Illustration en noir et bleu pour une collection de contes pour enfants. (IND)
356 Illustration polychrome d'un récit paru dans le *Reader's Digest*. (USA)

355

PUBLISHER / VERLEGER / EDITEUR:

354 Omni Publications International Ltd.
355 National Book Trust
356 The Reader's Digest

Magazine Illustrations

356

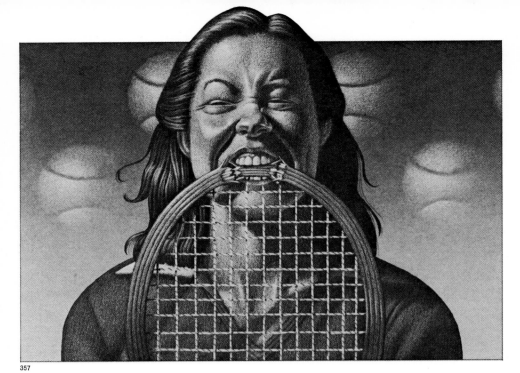

357

Magazine Illustrations
Zeitschriften-Illustrationen
Illustrations de périodiques

357 Illustration in black and white from *Chicago* magazine. The story deals with the other side of the coin in professional tennis. (USA)
358 Introductory double spread for an article dealing with the human side of sporting heroes, published in the magazine *Inside Sports*. Golden "armour" in front of a reddish brown background. (USA)
359 Double spread from a richly illustrated report on sport bars, published in the magazine *Inside Sports*. In full colour. (USA)
360 Useless authority is the theme of this illustration taken from the satirical magazine *Pasquim*. (BRA)
361 "The Pet Rating Game." Illustration in pastel colours for the introductory double spread of an ironical commentary on the problems of keeping pets and how to choose them. From a feature published in the magazine *The Plain Dealer*. (USA)
362 Introductory double spread from an account about the difficulties of a certain university and its baseball trainer to form and maintain a team. From the magazine *Inside Sports*. (USA)

357 Illustration in Schwarzweiss aus dem Magazin *Chicago*. Die Geschichte handelt von der Kehrseite des Profi-Tennis. (USA)
358 Einleitende Doppelseite zu einem Artikel, der sich mit der menschlichen Seite der Sportler befasst. Aus der Zeitschrift *Inside Sports*. Goldene «Rüstung» vor rotbraunem Hintergrund. (USA)
359 Doppelseite aus einem reich illustrierten Bericht über Sport-Bars, aus dem Magazin *Inside Sports*. Mehrfarbig. (USA)
360 Fruchtlose Autorität ist das Thema dieser Illustration aus der satirischen Zeitschrift *Pasquim*. (BRA)
361 Illustration in Pastellfarben für die einleitende Doppelseite zu einer ironischen Betrachtung über das Halten von Haustieren. Die Illustration bezieht sich auf die damit verbundenen Überlegungen. Aus *Plain Dealer*. (USA)
362 Einleitende Doppelseite zu einer Erzählung über die Schwierigkeiten einer bestimmten Universität und deren Baseball-Trainer, eine Mannschaft aufzustellen und zu halten. Aus *Inside Sports*. (USA)

357 Illustration noir-blanc du magazine *Chicago*, pour un rapport sur le revers de la médaille du tennis professionnel. (USA)
358 Double page initiale d'un article discutant du côté humain des sportifs, publié dans le magazine *Inside Sports*. «Cuirasse» dorée sur fond brun rouge. (USA)
359 Double page d'un rapport richement illustré sur les bars sportifs paru dans le magazine *Inside Sports*. En polychromie. (USA)
360 L'autoritarisme inefficace, voilà le sujet de cette illustration publiée dans la revue satirique *Pasquim*. (BRA)
361 Illustration aux tons pastel pour la double page initiale d'un texte ironique sur le besoin qu'éprouvent les humains à s'entourer d'animaux domestiques. L'illustration se rapporte à l'argumentation développée à ce sujet. Extrait du magazine *Plain Dealer*. (USA)
362 Double page initiale d'un récit publié par *Inside Sports* sur l'entraîneur d'une équipe universitaire de base-ball aux prises avec quantité de problèmes de recrutement et de direction. (USA)

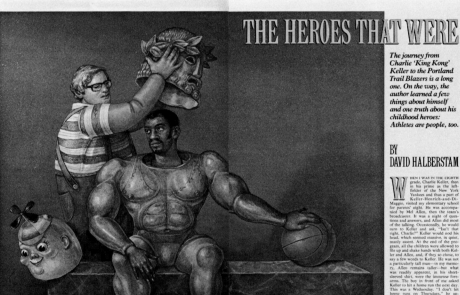

358

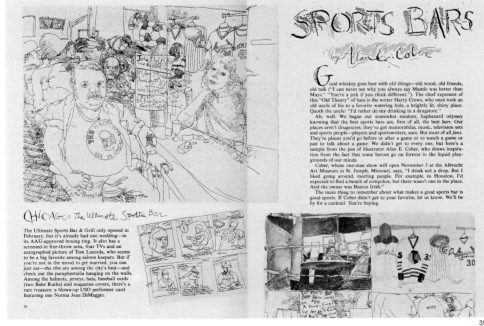

359

360

361

Illustration by Wilson McLean

362

THE ONES THAT GOT AWAY

*First there was
Bill Wennington.
Duke lost out there.
Then Chris Mullin
and Rodney Williams.
Duke lost them, too.
Finally, Uwe Blab
and Jim Miller.
Guess what?*

DUKE HAD A NAME. A REPUTA-tion. It also had a new coach. Mike Krzyzewski, who took the job in March 1980, replacing the popular and successful Bill Foster.

Krzyzewski (pronounced She-shefski) was young enough at 33 to believe in himself totally, but old enough to realize there were compelling reasons for Foster's departure to South Carolina after six seasons at Duke. In his first year, Krzyzewski learned that hard work in recruiting does not necessarily equal success. He didn't have to learn that when Gene Banks and Kenny Dennard graduated in 1981, his life in the Atlantic Coast Conference would be very difficult.

He needed players. Getting them has never been easy at Duke, which has the ACC's toughest admissions standards for athletes. Additionally, Duke is only a few miles from the University of North Carolina. Kids in Carolina grow up dreaming about Chapel Hill, not Durham. In his six

years, Foster successfully recruited one in-state player---Dennard.

One of the players Krzyzewski coveted most last fall was Buzz Peterson, a 6-3 guard from Asheville. Peterson liked Duke but he had always *loved* the Tar Heels and will wear Carolina blue this winter.

So Krzyzewski must recruit nationally at a time when players are being pressured more and more to stay close to home. Last year, with one exception, every top player Duke came close to getting and then lost mentioned distance as a factor. One player, Todd Berkenpas, a guard from Mapleton, Iowa, told assistant coach Bobby Dwyer, "If Duke were in Iowa, I would be going to Duke."

Today, Berkenpas is playing at Iowa, which is in Iowa.

Finally, there were five highly rated players not ruled out by geography or ties to other colleges that Krzyzewski hoped he could get. Four narrowed their decisions last spring to Duke and someone else. The fifth had Duke in his final three. None will play for Krzyzewski this fall.

Having been close, hearing each player say he easily could have gone to Duke and been happy, is no consolation to Krzyzewski. "The problem is, in recruiting, second isn't worth a damn," he said. "If anything, it's just more frustrating."

BILL WENNINGTON, A 6-11 CEN-ter, grew up in Canada but moved to Brookville, Long Island, after his sophomore year of high school when his mother remarried. He is as-wide-as-a-boxcar big, with huge hands and a soft shooting touch.

Wennington liked Krzyzewski the first time he met him. "A lot of people had said he wouldn't know as much as other coaches because he was so young," Wennington said. "But that wasn't true. He was just the kind of

By John Feinstein

65

363

364

ARTIST / KÜNSTLER / ARTISTE:

363, 364 James McMullan
365 Gary Viskupic
366 Tullio Pericoli
367 Paul Dallas
368, 368a John Martin

DESIGNER / GESTALTER / MAQUETTISTE:

367, 368, 368a Bruce Mau

ART DIRECTOR / DIRECTEUR ARTISTIQUE:

363, 364 Walter Bernard
365 Miriam Smith
367, 368, 368a Bruce Mau

AGENCY / AGENTUR / AGENCE – STUDIO:

365 Newsday Edit. Art Dept.
367, 368, 368a Fifty Fingers Inc.

PUBLISHER / VERLEGER / EDITEUR:

363, 364 New York Magazine
365 Newsday Inc.
366 L'Espresso
367, 368, 368a Gulf Canada Ltd.

365

Magazine Illustrations
Zeitschriften-Illustrationen
Illustrations de périodiques

144

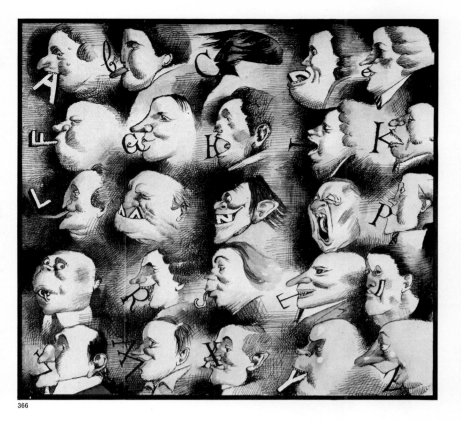

366

363, 364 Illustration from an article in *New York* magazine about the gradual acceptance of marijuana in American society. (USA)
365 Illustration on alcoholism from *Long Island Magazine*. (USA)
366 For an article in *L'Espresso* magazine about whether or not people should be categorized according to their style of expression. In warm shades. (ITA)
367–368a From *Commentator*, house magazine of *Gulf Canada*: two facing pages to illustrate the stagnating deadlock between the Canadian Federal and Provincial Governements over Canada's national energy policy. (CAN)

363, 364 Illustrationen zu einem Artikel in der Zeitschrift *New York* über die allmähliche Billigung von Marihuana in der amerikanischen Gesellschaft. (USA)
365 «Ein Rettungsring für Alkoholiker.» Illustration aus *Long Island Magazine*. (USA)
366 Für einen Artikel über die Frage, ob Personen nach ihrer Ausdrucksweise einzustufen sind. In warmen Tönen, aus der Zeitschrift *L'Espresso*. (ITA)
367–368a Aus *Commentator*, Firmenzeitschrift von *Gulf Canada*. Themen: Zukunftsplanung des Unternehmens und die starren Standpunkte der Bundesregierung einerseits, und der Provinzregierungen andererseits, in der Frage der Energiepolitik. (CAN)

363, 364 Illustrations pour un article du magazine *New York* sur la permissivité croissante de la société américaine face au phénomène de la marijuana. (USA)
365 «Une bouée de sauvetage pour les alcooliques.» *Long Island Magazine*. (USA)
366 Pour un article du magazine *L'Espresso* discutant de la question de savoir si l'on peut classer les gens d'après leur manière de parler. Tons chauds. (ITA)
367–368a Pages de *Commentator*, revue d'entreprise de *Gulf Canada*. Sujets: les prévisions pour l'avenir de l'entreprise; les positions rigides du gouvernement fédéral opposées à celles non moins rigides des provinces en matière d'énergie. (CAN)

Improvements to existing plants will precede residual fuel upgrading, synthetic fuels and petrochemicals ventures.

COMMENTATOR 22

367

368

368 a

369

ARTIST / KÜNSTLER / ARTISTE:

369–372 Bascove
373 Jean Mulatier
374 Frances Jetter
375 Matt Straub
376 Mark Hess

ART DIRECTOR / DIRECTEUR ARTISTIQUE:

369 Roland Schenk
370–372 Robert Ciano
374 John MacLeod
376 Mary Shanahan

AGENCY / AGENTUR / AGENCE – STUDIO:

374 Inx, Inc.

PUBLISHER / VERLEGER / EDITEUR:

369 Mims Magazine
370–372 Esquire, Inc.
373 Dervish International
374 Inx, Inc.
375 City Magazine
376 Rolling Stone

369 Gouache in *Mims Magazine* for an article on children's emotional problems. (USA)
370–372 Black-and-white woodcut sequence illustrating a story in *Esquire* magazine. (USA)
373 A caricature of Jimmy Carter. (FRA)
374 Black-and-white illustration for an article in the magazine *The Progressive*. (USA)
375 For an article in *City* about a well-known baseball player's commitment to children's causes. (USA)
376 Full-page illustration for an article in *Rolling Stone* about ex-Beatle Ringo Starr. (USA)

369 Gouache für einen Artikel über emotionelle Probleme bei Kindern. Aus *Mims Magazine*. (USA)
370–372 Schwarzweisse Holzschnitt-Sequenz für eine Geschichte in der Zeitschrift *Esquire*. (USA)
373 Karikatur von Jimmy Carter. (FRA)
374 Illustration in Schwarzweiss für einen Artikel in der Zeischrift *The Progressive*. (USA)
375 Für einen Artikel in *City* über das Engagement eines bekannten Baseball-Spielers für Kinder. (USA)
376 Ganzseitige Illustration zu einem Artikel über Ex-Beatle Ringo Starr in *Rolling Stone*. (USA)

369 Gouache pour un article sur les problèmes émotionnels des enfants, dans le *Mims Magazine*. (USA)
370–372 Séquence illustrative noir et blanc gravée sur bois pour un récit du magazine *Esquire*. (USA)
373 Caricature de Jimmy Carter. (FRA)
374 Illustration noir-blanc pour un article paru dans le magazine *The Progressive*. (USA)
375 Pour un article de *City* sur l'engagement d'un joueur de base-ball réputé, pour les enfants. (USA)
376 Illustration pleine page pour un article sur l'ancien Beatle Ringo Starr, dans *Rolling Stone*. (USA)

370

371

372

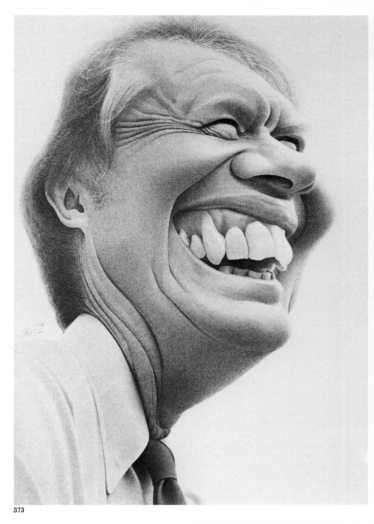

373

374

375

376

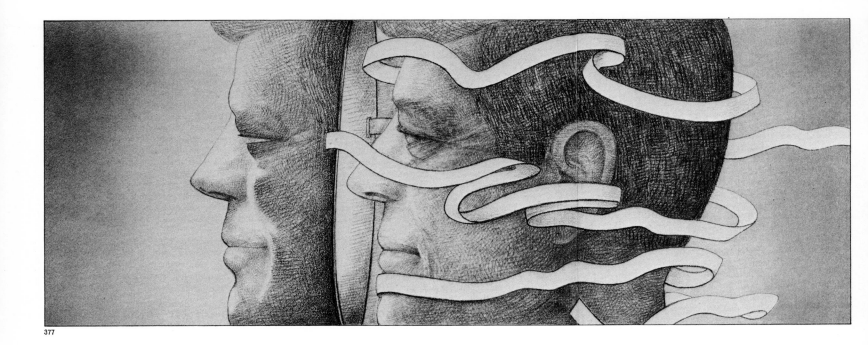

377

ARTIST / KÜNSTLER / ARTISTE:

377 Tom Lulevitch
378, 379 André François
380 Seymour Chwast

377 Example from a series of illustrations in *The Atlantic Monthly* magazine for a critical article about J. F. Kennedy. (USA)
378 Illustration for a feature in the French fashion magazine *Jardin des Modes.* (FRA)
379 Full-colour illustration for a feature on why children don't like reading, published in *The Atlantic Monthly.* (USA)
380 Illustration in actual size for a short story in *The Atlantic Monthly*, entitled "The Overcoat II". (USA)

377 Beispiel aus einer Serie von Illustrationen für einen Artikel über J. F. Kennedy in dem Magazin *Atlantic Monthly.* (USA)
378 Illustration für einen Beitrag in der französischen Modezeitschrift *Jardin des Modes.* (FRA)
379 «Warum Kinder nicht lesen mögen.» Mehrfarbige Illustration zu einem Beitrag in *Atlantic Monthly.* (USA)
380 «Der Übermantel II.» Illustration in Originalgrösse für eine Kurzgeschichte in *Atlantic Monthly.* (USA)

377 Exemple d'une série d'illustrations pour un article de l'*Atlantic Monthly* sur John F. Kennedy. (USA)
378 Illustration pour une contribution au magazine de mode français *Jardin des Modes.* (FRA)
379 «Pourquoi les enfants n'aiment pas lire.» Illustration polychrome pour un article dans l'*Atlantic Monthly.* (USA)
380 «Le pardessus II.» Illustration au format original pour une nouvelle publiée dans le magazine *Atlantic Monthly.* (USA)

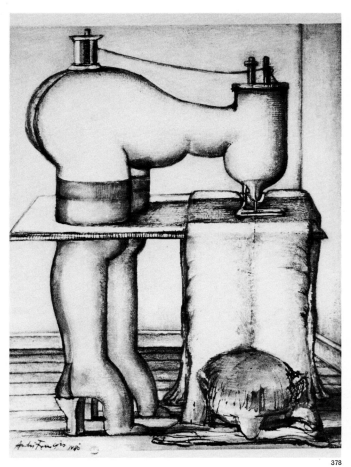

378   379

380

DESIGNER / GESTALTER / MAQUETTISTE:

377, 379, 380 Judy Garlan

ART DIRECTOR / DIRECTEUR ARTISTIQUE:

377, 379, 380 Judy Garlan
378 Bill Butt

PUBLISHER / VERLEGER / EDITEUR:

377, 379, 380 The Atlantic Monthly
378 Jardin des Modes

381 "Sex and The Single Parent." Black-and-white illustration from *New York* magazine. (USA)
382 Illustration for a collection of short stories entitled "The Mind's I" in *Book Digest*. (USA)
383 Full-page illustration for an article in *New York*. In red and yellow shades. (USA)
384 Double spread opening an alphabetical compendium of Christmas ideas from *McCall's* magazine. (USA)
385 For an article about the rise of the crude ethic, published in *Quest* magazine. (CAN)

381 Schwarzweiss-Illustration aus *New York*. Das Liebesleben alleinstehender Elternteile ist das Thema. (USA)
382 Illustration für eine Reihe von Kurzgeschichten über das Ich, in *Book Digest*. (USA)
383 Ganzseitige Illustration für einen Artikel in der Zeitschrift *New York*. In Rot- und Gelbtönen. (USA)
384 Doppelseite aus *McCall's*: Anfang einer alphabetischen Liste mit Geschenkideen für Weihnachten. (USA)
385 «Was ist mit den guten Manieren geschehen?» Für einen Artikel in der Zeitschrift *Quest*. (CAN)

381 Illustration noir-blanc dans *New York*, sur le sujet de la vie amoureuse du parent resté seul. (USA)
382 Illustration pour une série de nouvelles sur le thème du Moi conscient, dans *Book Digest*. (USA)
383 Illustration pleine page pour un article paru dans le magazine *New York*. Tons rouges et jaunes. (USA)
384 Double page initiale d'un répertoire de cadeaux de Noël, dans le magazine *McCall's*. (USA)
385 «Mais où sont restées les bonnes manières?» Pour un article publié dans le magazine *Quest*. (CAN)

381

384

ARTIST / KÜNSTLER

381 Paola Piglia
382 Dagmar Frinta
383 Eugène Mihaesco
385 Blair Drawson

DESIGNER / GESTALTER:

382 Caroline Bowyer
384 Jonson Pederson
    Hinrichs & Shakery
385 Art Niemi

ART DIRECTOR:

381 Robert Best/
    Patricia Bradbury
382 Caroline Bowyer
383 Robert Best
384 Alvin Grossman
385 Stephen Costello

PUBLISHER / VERLEGER:

381, 383 New York Mag.
382 Dow Jones & Co.
384 McCall Publishing Co.
385 Comac Communica-
    tions Ltd.

382

383

385

151

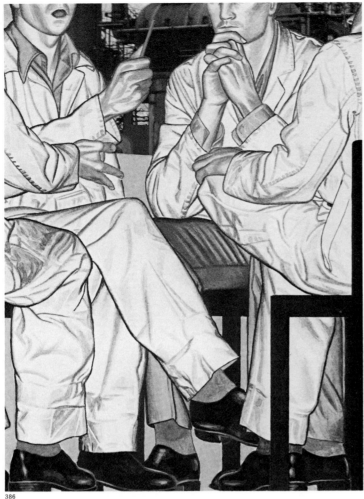

386

387

388

389

ARTIST / KÜNSTLER / ARTISTE:

386 Robin Harris
387, 390 Gottfried Helnwein
388 Phillippe Weisbecker
389 Richard Farrell

DESIGNER / GESTALTER / MAQUETTISTE:

389 Mary Challinor
390 Claire Victor

ART DIRECTOR / DIRECTEUR ARTISTIQUE:

386 Peter Derschka
387 Friedrich Dragon
388 Rostislav Eismont
389 Rodney C. Williams
390 Joe Brooks

AGENCY / AGENTUR / AGENCE – STUDIO:

389 Hellman Design

PUBLISHER / VERLEGER / EDITEUR:

386 Manager Magazin
387 Neue Kronenzeitung
388 Chief Executive Magazine, Inc.
389 American Association for
    the Advancement of Sciene
390 Penthouse International

390

386 Full-page, full-colour illustration from *Manager Magazine* on worker participation. (GER)
387 "The Man who looked like Napoleon." Illustration for a story in *Krone bunt*. (AUT)
388 From an article in *Chief Executive* entitled "Management in Evolution". (USA)
389 Full-colour portrait of Martin Gardner, inventor of mathematical games. From *Science*. (USA)
390 Introductory illustration for a critical report in *Penthouse* about the systematic abuse of civil liberties by the American Internal Revenue Service. (USA)

386 Ganzseitige, farbige Illustration aus *Manager Magazine*. Thema: Mitbestimmung. (GER)
387 «Der Mann, der wie Napoleon aussah.» Illustration für eine Geschichte in *Krone bunt*. (AUT)
388 Aus einem Artikel in *Chief Executive* über neue Wege in der Unternehmensführung. (USA)
389 Mehrfarbiges Porträt von Martin Gardner, Erfinder mathematischer Spiele. Aus *Science*. (USA)
390 «Die neue amerikanische Gestapo.» Einleitende Illustration zu einem kritischen Bericht in dem Magazin *Penthouse* über die amerikanische Steuerbehörde. (USA)

386 Illustration couleur, pleine page, du *Manager Magazine*. Sujet: la participation. (GER)
387 «L'homme qui ressemblait à Napoléon.» Illustration d'un récit paru dans *Krone bunt*. (AUT)
388 Pour un article de *Chief Executive* sur les voies nouvelles de la gestion d'entreprise. (USA)
389 Portrait polychrome de Martin Gardner, inventeur de jeux mathématiques, dans *Science*. (USA)
390 «La nouvelle Gestapo américaine.» Illustration en tête d'une étude critique du magazine *Penthouse* dénonçant les pratiques abusives du fisc américain. (USA)

Magazine Illustrations
Zeitschriften-Illustrationen
Illustrations de périodiques

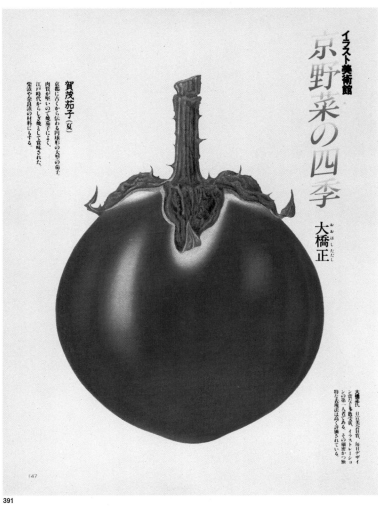

京野菜の四季

大橋 正
（おおはし ただし）

賀茂茄子（夏）

京都に古くから伝わる円球形の大型の茄子。
肉質が堅いので煮くずれしにくく、焼茄子によく、
江戸時代からしぎ焼として賞味された。
茶漬や奈良漬の材料にもする。

大橋正氏、旧王美術資賞、毎日デザ
イン賞などを数々受賞。イラストレーショ
ンの第一人者である。その描写力や細
緻な表現は高く評価されている。

147

391

アメリカの農産物

大橋 正
（おおはし ただし）
（イラストレーター）

Peppers ペッパー

ピーマン アメリカのスーパーの野菜
売り場でもっとも目につくのが、大き
くて赤いピーマンである。緑のピーマ
ンももちろん売られているが、この完
熟して赤くなったもののほうがだんぜ
ん多いようだ。

187

392

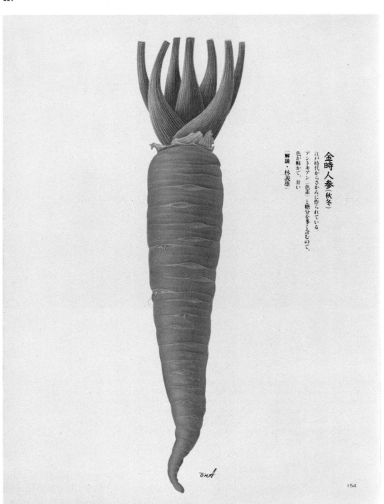

金時人参（秋冬）

江戸時代からさかんに作られている
アントキアン（色素）を多く含むので、
色が鮮やかで、甘い。

〔解説・林義雄〕

154

393

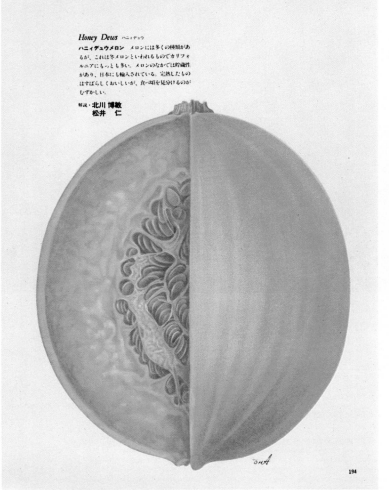

Honey Deus ハニィデュウ

ハニィデュウメロン メロンには多くの種類があ
るが、これは冬メロンといわれるものでカリフォ
ルニアにもっとも多い。メロンのなかでは貯蔵性
があり、日本にも輸入されている。完熟したもの
はすばらしくおいしいが、食べ頃を見分けるのが
むずかしい。

〔解説・北川博敏
松井 仁〕

194

394

154

Magazine Illustrations
Zeitschriften-Illustrationen
Illustrations de périodiques

ARTIST / KÜNSTLER / ARTISTE:
391–395a Tadashi Ohashi
396 Erhard Göttlicher

DESIGNER / GESTALTER / MAQUETTISTE:
391–395a Fumio Shibanaga

ART DIRECTOR / DIRECTEUR ARTISTIQUE:
391–395a Tadashi Ohashi
396 Dick de Moei

PUBLISHER / VERLEGER / EDITEUR:
391–395a Bungei Shunju Co., Ltd.
396 De Geillustreerde Pers

391–394 From a series of full-page illustrations in the Japanese magazine *Climat.* (JPN)
395, 395a Double spreads from *Climat,* a Japanese magazine. Fig. 395: green, violet and white; Fig. 395a: in shades of yellow and orange, green leaf. (JPN)
396 Full-page illustration for a series in *Avenue* magazine about the European woman. (NLD)

391–394 Aus einer Reihe von ganzseitigen Illustrationen in der japanischen Zeitschrift *Climat.* (JPN)
395, 395a Doppelseiten aus der japanischen Zeitschrift *Climat.* Abb. 395 Grün, violett und weiss. Abb. 395a in Gelb- und Orangetönen, grünes Blatt. (JPN)
396 Ganzseitige Illustration für eine Serie in der Zeitschrift *Avenue* über die Frau in Europa. (NLD)

391–394 Exemples d'une série d'illustrations pleine page publiées dans le magazine japonais *Climat.* (JPN)
395, 395a Doubles pages du magazine japonais *Climat.* La fig. 395 est exécutée en vert, violet et blanc, la fig. 395a en tons jaunes et orangés; la feuille est en vert. (JPN)
396 Illustration pleine page pour une série du magazine *Avenue* consacrée aux Européennes. (NLD)

396

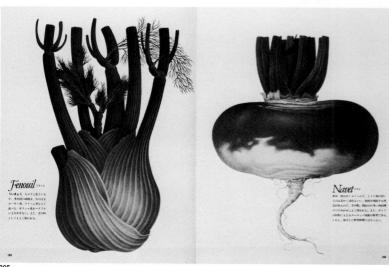

395

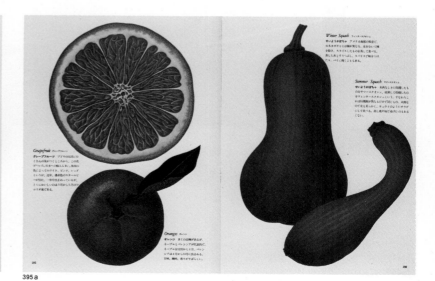

395a

397

ARTIST / KÜNSTLER / ARTISTE:

397 John Martin
398 Monika Hahn
399 Arnhild Johne
400 Harro Maass

DESIGNER / GESTALTER / MAQUETTISTE:

397 Derek Ungless

ART DIRECTOR / DIRECTEUR ARTISTIQUE:

397 Derek Ungless
398–400 Manfred Neussl

AGENCY / AGENTUR / AGENCE – STUDIO:

397 Fifty Fingers Inc.

PUBLISHER / VERLEGER / EDITEUR:

397 Saturday Night Magazine
398–400 Burda-Verlag

397 Illustration for a story in *Saturday Night* magazine on the short affair between two detached people, their isolation, sexual fantasies, relationships and attitudes towards law. (CAN)
398 "Money alone doesn't bring happiness." For a story in *Freundin*. In full colour. (GER)
399 Full-colour illustration for "The Charmed Doll", a story published in *Freundin* magazine. (GER)
400 "She could smile." Full-page illustration from a novel published in *Freundin* magazine. (GER)

397 Illustration in Originalgrösse für eine Kurzgeschichte in der Zeitschrift *Saturday Night*. Thema ist die kurze Affaire zwischen zwei einsamen Menschen, ihre Isolation, sexuellen Phantasien, Beziehungen zu Autoritätspersonen, Gesetz und Todesstrafe. (CAN)
398 «Geld allein macht nicht glücklich.» Für eine Geschichte in der *Freundin*. Mehrfarbig. (GER)
399 Illustration in Farbe für eine Geschichte in der *Freundin*: «Die verzauberte Puppe». (GER)
400 «Lächeln konnte sie.» Ganzseitige Illustration aus einem Roman in der *Freundin*. (GER)

397 Illustration au format original pour une nouvelle parue dans le magazine *Saturday Night*. Le sujet en est une brève liaison entre deux solitaires, leur isolement, leurs fantasmes sexuels, leurs relations avec l'autorité, la loi et la peine de mort. (CAN)
398 «L'argent ne fait pas le bonheur.» Récit publié dans *Freundin*. En polychromie. (GER)
399 Illustration en couleur pour un récit de *Freundin*, «La poupée enchantée». (GER)
400 «Elle savait sourire.» Illustration pleine page pour un roman paru dans *Freundin*. (GER)

398

399

400

401

403

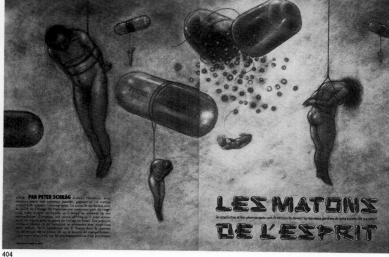

404

405

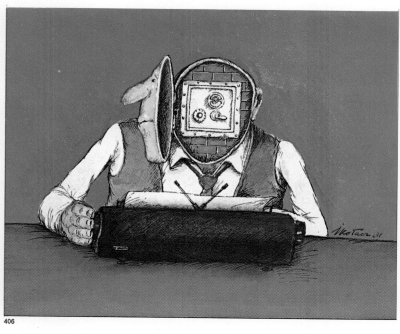

406

ARTIST / KÜNSTLER / ARTISTE:

401, 402 Blair Drawson
403 Tilman Michalski
404 Edgar Clarke
405 Ron Miller
406 Jerzey Kolacz

DESIGNER / GESTALTER / MAQUETTISTE:

403 Maximilian Handschuh
405 Rodney C. Williams
406 Art Niemi

ART DIRECTOR / DIRECTEUR ARTISTIQUE:

401, 402 James Lawrence
403 Manuel Ortiz Juarez
404 Régis Pagniez
405 Rodney C. Williams
406 Stephen Costello

PUBLISHER / VERLEGER / EDITEUR:

401, 402 Camden House Publishing Ltd.
403 Heinrich Bauer Verlag
404 Publications Filipacchi
405 American Association for
the Advancement of Science
406 Comac Communications Ltd.

401, 402 Detail of the illustration and complete double spread from a feature in *Harrowsmith* magazine exploring the emotional pitfalls of the pastoral life. (CAN)
403 Full-colour double spread from the German edition of *Playboy*. The story is about an English rollmops dealer from Paris and his activities at the Munich Oktoberfest. (GER)
404 Double spread from the French edition of *Playboy*, with a report about the misuse of medicaments and drugs in psychiatric clinics. (FRA)
405 For an introductory double spread from a feature published in *Science*. (USA)
406 Illustration in actual size from a feature in *Quest* magazine about media self-censorship. (CAN)

401, 402 Detail der Illustration und vollständige Doppelseite mit einem Beitrag aus *Harrowsmith* über das Leben auf dem Land und die Anforderungen, die es an die Menschen stellt. (CAN)
403 Mehrfarbige Doppelseite aus der deutschen Ausgabe des *Playboy*. In dem Beitrag geht es um einen englischen Rollmops-Händler aus Paris auf dem Münchener Oktoberfest. (GER)
404 Doppelseite aus der französischen Ausgabe des *Playboy* mit einem Bericht über den Missbrauch von Medikamenten und Drogen in psychiatrischen Kliniken. (FRA)
405 «Krieg im Weltall.» Für die einleitende Doppelseite zu einem Beitrag in *Science*. (USA)
406 Illustration in Originalgrösse aus dem Magazin *Quest*. Thema: Selbstzensur der Medien. (CAN)

401, 402 Détail de l'illustration et double page complète d'une étude du «malaise rural» – la vie des campagnards et leurs problèmes émotionnels, dans *Harrowsmith*. (CAN)
403 Double page polychrome de l'édition allemande de *Playboy*. Il y est question d'un marchand anglais de harengs roulés venu de Paris à la Foire d'octobre de Munich. (GER)
404 Double page de l'édition française de *Playboy* se référant à l'abus de drogues et de médicaments dans les cliniques psychiatriques, qu'il convient d'enrayer au plus vite. (FRA)
405 «La guerre dans l'espace.» Pour la double page initiale d'un article de *Science*. (USA)
406 Illustration au format original, dans le magazine *Quest*: l'autocensure des médias. (CAN)

402

Magazine Illustrations
Zeitschriften-Illustrationen
Illustrations de périodiques

ARTIST / KÜNSTLER / ARTISTE:

407 Teresa Fasolino
408 Gene Trindl
409 Randall Enos
410 Tom Herbert
411, 412 Dagmar Frinta

ART DIRECTOR / DIRECTEUR ARTISTIQUE:

407, 408 Jerry Alten
409 Amy Wilentz
410 Paul Richer
411, 412 Nina Scerbo

407

407 Full-page illustration for an article in the *TV Guide* magazine. The feature deals with the husbands of stars who are also their managers. (USA)
408 Almost life-size puppets presenting a TV show. They are manipulated by the men in the background, according to a Japanese method. The latter are invisible as anything coloured blue will be absorbed by the camera through the optical wizardry of a process called chroma key. From *TV Guide*. (USA)
409 Illustration for a book review in *The Nation*. (USA)
410 Illustration from the *Sesame Street Magazine* which is part of a children's TV programme. (USA)
411, 412 Illustration and complete double spread from *McCall's*, for an "anxiety" diet. (USA)

407 Ganzseitige Illustration für einen Artikel in der Fernsehzeitschrift *TV Guide*. Hier geht es um die Ehemänner von Stars, die gleichzeitig Manager ihrer Frauen sind. (USA)
408 «Zauberei in Blau.» Die fast lebensgrossen Puppen präsentieren eine Fernsehshow. Sie werden von den vermummten Männern im Hintergrund nach einer japanischen Methode bewegt, wobei die Männer dank eines Systems, das Blau absorbiert, auf dem Bildschirm unsichtbar sind. Aus *TV Guide*. (USA)
409 Illustration für eine Buchbesprechung: «Die Stunde unseres Todes.» Aus *The Nation*. (USA)
410 Illustration aus dem *Sesame Street Magazine*, das zu der TV-Kindersendung gehört. (USA)
411, 412 Illustration und vollständige Doppelseite aus *McCall's*: Eine «Angst»-Diät. (USA)

407 Illustration pleine page pour un article de la revue *TV Guide*. Il y est question des maris de vedettes qui sont en même temps leurs imprésarios. (USA)
408 «Sortilège en bleu.» Ces deux poupées presque grandeur nature présentent un show télévisé. Elles sont actionnées selon une méthode japonaise traditionnelle par les hommes déguisés que l'on voit au fond, invisibles sur l'écran grâce à l'absorption du bleu. Paru dans *TV Guide*. (USA)
409 Illustration pour le compte rendu du livre «L'heure de notre mort», dans *The Nation*. (USA)
410 Illustration du *Sesame Street Magazine* accompagnant la célèbre émission télévisée. (USA)
411, 412 Illustration et double page complète de *McCall's*: un régime à base d'angoisse. (USA)

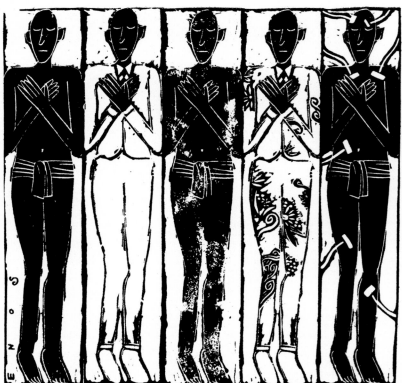

409

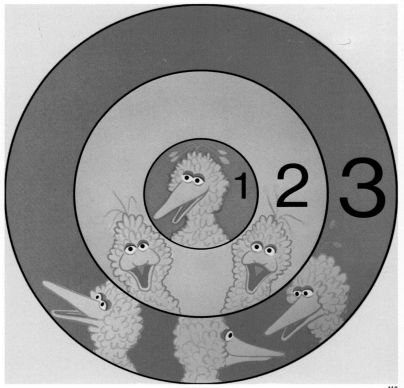

410

408

411

412

PUBLISHER / VERLEGER / EDITEUR:

407, 408 Triangle Publications, Inc.
409 The Nation
410 Children's Television Workshop, Inc.
411, 412 McCall Publishing Co.

413

Magazine Illustrations

ARTIST / KÜNSTLER / ARTISTE:

413 Dieter Ziegenfeuter
414, 417 Tullio Pericoli
415, 416 Franklin McMahon
418 Phillipe Weisbecker

ART DIRECTOR / DIRECTEUR ARTISTIQUE:

413 R. Uhlen
415, 416 Norman S. Hotz
418 Rostislav Eismont

PUBLISHER / VERLEGER / EDITEUR:

413 Cosmopolitan
414, 417 L'Espresso
415, 416 Panorama Magazine
418 Chief Executive Magazine, Inc.

414

415

416

162

417

FINDING

In his autobiography, *My Years with General Motors,* Alfred Sloan said that it is a delusion to expect that your company can have better people. The trick of achieving superior performance is correct placement. There are few placement decisions more critical to a company than the selection of the right chief executive. But

THE RIGHT

when it comes to finding the right person for the job many companies

SUCCESSOR

stumble. Recession pressures, demanding directors and over-eager executive recruiters have contributed to an alarmingly high rate of executive turnover. In this second of a two-part series on chief executive succession, CE asked two management specialists to tell how companies can best reduce the selection gamble. Kenneth Meyers, president and CEO of Golightly & Co. International, a management consulting firm, attributes much succession failure to the inability of candidates to understand the ideology of the organization they intend to lead. Certainly few fail because of a lack of executive ability. Russell Reynolds, chairman and CEO of Russell Reynolds Associates, an executive recruiting firm, argues that companies which define their policy in advance and groom from within are more likely to enlist the support of the organization for a new CEO. Meyers and Reynolds differ on who is best qualified to pick a successor, but they agree that regardless of who decides, the successor will fail if he disregards the shared values of those around him. ▶▶

418

413 "Honey, the fluid that makes you cheerful." Full-page illustration from an article in the German edition of *Cosmopolitan.* (GER)
414, 417 Complete double spread and full-colour illustration for an article in *L'Espresso* magazine. The feature deals with the numerous cultural events and performances during an Italian season. (ITA)
415, 416 An on-the-spot illustrations for an article about the 1980 US presidential campaign and the media reporting of this event, in *Panorama.* The illustrator is also the author of the report. (USA)
418 Double spread with full-colour illustration from *Chief Executive.* (USA)

413 «Honig, der Saft, der munter macht.» Ganzseitige Illustration für einen Artikel in der deutschen Ausgabe von *Cosmopolitan.* (GER)
414, 417 Vollständige Doppelseite und mehrfarbige Illustration für einen Artikel in der Zeitschrift *L'Espresso.* Es wird über die zahlreichen kulturellen Ereignisse und Veranstaltungen einer Saison in Italien berichtet. (ITA)
415, 416 An Ort und Stelle entstandene Illustrationen für einen Artikel über die US-Präsidentschafts-Wahlkampagne 1980 und die Berichterstattung durch die Medien, in *Panorama.* Der Illustrator ist auch der Autor des Berichtes. (USA)
418 «Den richtigen Nachfolger finden.» Doppelseite aus *Chief Executive.* (USA)

413 «Le miel, le suc qui ragaillardit.» Illustration pleine page pour un article publié dans l'édition allemande de *Cosmopolitan.* (GER)
414, 417 Double page complète et illustration polychrome pour un article du magazine *L'Espresso* qui fait état de la diversité des événements et manifestations culturels de la saison en Italie. (ITA)
415, 416 Illustrations réalisées sur place pour un article consacré aux présidentielles américaines de 1980 et à la couverture médias, dans *Panorama.* L'illustrateur est aussi l'auteur de l'article. (USA)
418 «Trouver le successeur parfait.» Double page de *Chief Executive.* (USA)

Magazine Illustrations
Zeitschriften-Illustrationen
Illustrations de périodiques

419

420

421

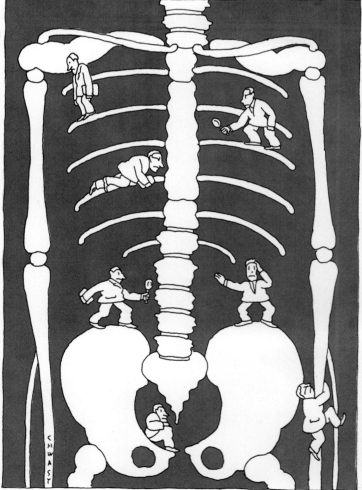

422

423

419 Black-and-white illustration for an article that appeared in *The Plain Dealer*. "Pregnancy by Proxy." (USA)
420 Full-page illustration for an article about economic questions. From *The Atlantic Monthly*. (USA)
421 Illustration for an article published in the graphic-design magazine *Print*. (USA)
422 Black-and-white illustration from the *Harvard Medical* magazine: "On Matters of Doubt." (USA)
423 Illustration from *The Nation*, dealing with the suppression of the media in El Salvador. (USA)

419 Schwarzweiss-Illustration für einen Artikel über künstliche Befruchtung in *The Plain Dealer*. (USA)
420 Ganzseitige Illustration für einen Artikel über Wirtschaftsfragen. Aus *The Atlantic Monthly*. (USA)
421 Illustration für einen Artikel in der Graphik-Zeitschrift *Print*. (USA)
422 Schwarzweiss-Illustration aus *Harvard Medical*, eine Fachzeitschrift, die von der medizinischen Fakultät der Harvard-Universität herausgegeben wird. Thema des Artikels: Zweifelsfälle. (USA)
423 Unterdrückung von Nachrichten in El Salvador ist das Thema dieser Illustration aus *The Nation*. (USA)

419 Illustration noir-blanc pour un article sur l'insémination artificielle, dans *Plain Dealer*. (USA)
420 Illustration pleine page pour un article traitant de l'économie, dans l'*Atlantic Monthly*. (USA)
421 Illustration pour un article de la revue graphique *Print*. (USA)
422 Illustration noir et blanc pour *Harvard Medical*, une revue spécialisée publiée par la Faculté de médecine de l'Université Harvard. Le sujet de l'article: les cas douteux. (USA)
423 Cette illustration dans *The Nation* symbolise la suppression de nouvelles dans les médias du Salvador. (USA)

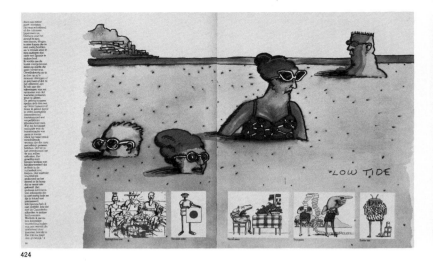

424

425

Magazine Illustrations
Zeitschriften-Illustrationen
Illustrations de périodiques

424 Double spread with full-colour illustrations from a travel report in *Avenue*. (NLD)
425 Introductory double spread for a story in an Italian publication. In full colour. (ITA)
426 Illustration in almost actual size for a story published in *The Atlantic Monthly*. (USA)
427 Full-page illustration for a story in *Omni* on the tricky business of reincarnation. (USA)
428 Black-and-white illustration for an article about a statewide syndicate that gobbles up financially insecure homes and then sells them at a great profit. ((USA)
429 From *The Progressive*. The subject is the Reagan administration's ecology offenders. (USA)
430, 431 From a critical article about John F. Kennedy, published in *The Atlantic Monthly*. (USA)
432 Illustration for a report in the magazine *Amercian Lawyer* about a lawyer who left one of his clients in the lurch. In black and white. (USA)

424 Doppelseite mit mehrfarbigen Illustrationen aus einem Reisebericht in *Avenue*. (NLD)
425 Einleitende Doppelseite zu einer Geschichte in einem italienischen Magazin. (ITA)
426 Illustration, ca. Originalgrösse, für eine Geschichte in *Atlantic Monthly*. (USA)
427 Ganzseitige Illustration für eine Geschichte in *Omni*. Thema: Reinkarnation. (USA)
428 Schwarzweiss-Illustration zu einem Artikel über ein Syndikat, das sich auf Häuser stürzt, wenn die Eigentümer mit den Hypothekarzinsen in Verzug geraten. (USA)
429 Aus *The Progressive*. Thema: Die Umweltsünden der Reagan-Administration. (USA)
430, 431 Aus einem kritischen Artikel über John F. Kennedy in *Atlantic Monthly*. (USA)
432 Illustration für einen Bericht in der Zeitschrift *American Lawyer* über einen Anwalt, der einen Klienten im Stich liess. In Schwarzweiss. (USA)

427

428

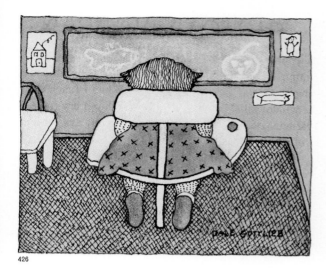

426

430

431

424 Double page d'une relation de voyage illustrée en polychromie, dans *Avenue*. (NLD)
425 Double page initiale d'un récit publié dans un magazine italien. En polychromie. (ITA)
426 Illustration approx. grandeur nature pour un récit de l'*Atlantic Monthly*. (USA)
427 Illustration pleine page pour un récit sur la réincarnation paru dans *Omni*. (USA)
428 Illustration noir et blanc accompagnant un article sur une fédération immobilière qui s'empare des immeubles dont les propriétaires n'arrivent plus à payer les hypothèques. (USA)
429 L'attitude antiécologique de l'administration Reagan illustrée dans *The Progressive*. (USA)
430, 431 Pour un article critique consacré à John F. Kennedy dans l'*Atlantic Monthly*. (USA)
432 Illustration pour un article de la revue *American Lawyer* exposant le cas d'un avocat qui laissa en panne l'un de ses clients. En noir et blanc. (USA)

429

432

ARTIST / KÜNSTLER / ARTISTE:

424 Jim Valentine
425 Adelchi Galloni
426 Dale Gottlieb
427 Piero Fassoni
428, 429, 432 Frances Jetter
430, 431 Tom Lulevitch

DESIGNER / GESTALTER / MAQUETTISTE:

424 Riet Mol
426, 430, 431 Judy Garlan

ART DIRECTOR / DIRECTEUR ARTISTIQUE:

424 Dick de Moei
426, 430, 431 Judy Garlan
427 Frank DeVino
428 Kati Korpijaako
429 Patrick Flynn
432 Pegi Goodman

PUBLISHER / VERLEGER / EDITEUR:

424 De Geillustreerde Pers
426, 430, 431 The Atlantic Monthly
427 Omni Publications International Ltd.
428 New Jersey Monthly
429 The Progressive
432 The American Lawyer

433

434

433 Full-page illustration with greenish and yellowish insects, from an ironical article about lawyers published in *Playboy* magazine. (USA)

434 Full-colour introductory double spread for an article published in *Homemaker's Magazine* about sensible ways of handling difficult situations in life. (CAN)

435, 436 Double spreads from a report on American Football with its equipment and oval ball. In full colour, from the *Frankfurter Allgemeine Magazin*. (GER)

437 Full-page illustration in full colour from *Harrowsmith* magazine, for a report on the new generation of Canadian solar homes drawing the best from past and present designs. (CAN)

438 Illustration for a *Playboy* article about a new, wild and violent breed of sports fan. (USA)

439 Full-colour illustration for an article about the average consumption of ice-cream in Germany. Taken from *P. M. Magazin*. (GER)

437

438

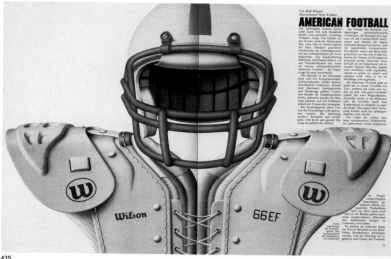

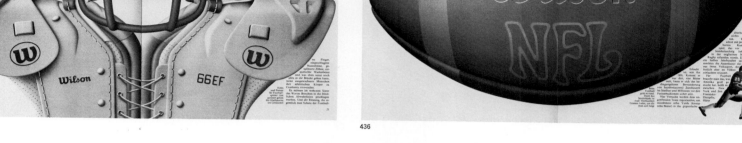

435

436

Magazine Illustrations

439

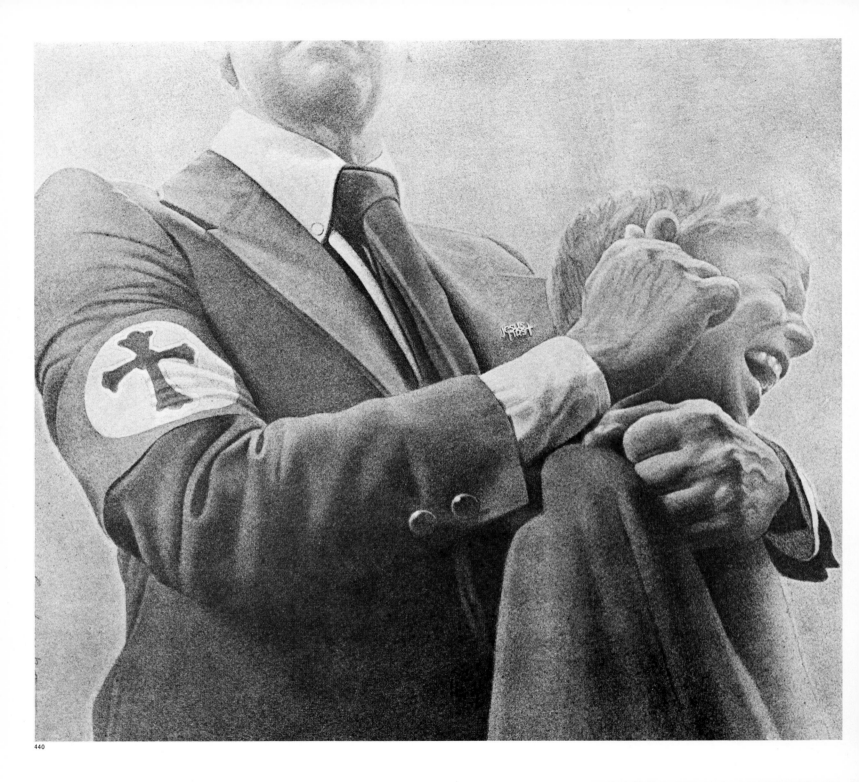

440

441

442

ARTIST / KÜNSTLER / ARTISTE:

440 Alex Gnidziejko
441 Ramon Gonzalez Teja
442 Cervasio Gallardo
443 Wilson McLean
444 Ernst Fuchs

DESIGNER / GESTALTER:

440, 443, 444 Claire Victor
442 George Guther

ART DIRECTOR:

440, 443, 444 Joe Brooks
441 Roman Gonzalez Teja
442 Manuel Ortiz Juarez

PUBLISHER / VERLEGER / EDITEUR:

440, 443, 444 Penthouse
International
441 Playboy
442 Heinrich Bauer Verlag

444

440 Illustration for a critical *Penthouse* article about the ill-treatment of children by new, fanatical, so-called religious groups. (USA)
441 Illustration for a feature in the Spanish edition of *Playboy* about the mistresses of princes and kings at the beginning of the 20th century. (SPA)
442 "Kicker, God and Devil." Double spread with full-colour illustration from *Playboy*. (GER)
443 For a *Penthouse* article about young, rich and miserable people. (USA)
444 Full-page illustration for a *Penthouse* story about the flight of Ukrainian Jews. (USA)

440 Illustration für einen kritischen Artikel über Kindesmisshandlungen durch die neuen fanatischen Gruppen, die sich christlich nennen. Aus *Penthouse*. (USA)
441 Illustration für einen Beitrag in der spanischen Ausgabe des *Playboy*, in dem es um die Mätressen der Fürsten und Könige zu Beginn unseres Jahrhunderts geht. (SPA)
442 Doppelseite mit farbiger Illustration aus der deutschen Ausgabe des *Playboy*. (GER)
443 Für einen Artikel in *Penthouse* über junge, reiche, unglückliche Leute. (USA)
444 Ganzseitige Illustration für eine Geschichte über die Flucht ukrainischer Juden aus dem Ghetto, unter der Führung einer Grossmutter. Aus *Penthouse*. (USA)

440 Illustration d'un article de *Penthouse* qui s'élève contre ces nouveaux bourreaux d'enfants que sont les nouveaux groupements fanatiques sous la bannière du Christ. (USA)
441 Illustration pour un récit historique, dans l'édition espagnole de *Playboy*, sur le rôle des maîtresses des princes et des rois du début du XXe siècle. (SPA)
442 Double page, avec illustration en couleur, de l'édition allemande de *Playboy*. (GER)
443 «Jeune, riche et malheureux»: illustration pour un article de *Penthouse*. (USA)
444 Illustration pleine page pour un récit publié dans *Penthouse* où l'on voit une grandmère organiser la fuite hors du ghetto d'un petit groupe de juifs ukrainiens. (USA)

445

ARTIST / KÜNSTLER / ARTISTE:

445 Brad Holland
446 Anita Kunz
447 Marcia Marx

DESIGNER / GESTALTER / MAQUETTISTE:

445 Bob Post
446 Ursula Kaiser
447 Kerig Pope

ART DIRECTOR / DIRECTEUR ARTISTIQUE:

445, 447 Tom Staebler
446 Georges Haroutiun

PUBLISHER / VERLEGER / ÉDITEUR:

445, 447 Playboy Enterprises, Inc.
446 Comac Communications

446

Magazine Illustrations
Zeitschriften-Illustrationen
Illustrations de périodiques

445 Illustration in actual size for a "lecherous" *Playboy* page. (USA)
446 Full-colour illustration for an introductory double spread belonging to an article about dreams in *Homemaker's Magazine*. (CAN)
447 Detail of the illustration for a double spread in *Playboy* with an excerpt from "Zuckerman Unbound", a new novel by Philip Roth. (USA)

445 Illustration in Originalgrösse für eine Seite im *Playboy*: Wollüstige Poesie. (USA)
446 Mehrfarbige Illustration für die einleitende Doppelseite zu einem Artikel über Träume in *Homemaker's Magazine*. (CAN)
447 Detail der Illustration für eine Doppelseite im *Playboy*, mit einem Auszug aus einem neuen Buch von Philip Roth: «Zuckermans Befreiung». (USA)

445 Illustration au format original pour *Playboy*: poésie de la volupté. (USA)
446 Illustration polychrome figurant sur la double page initiale d'un article du *Homemaker's Magazine* sur les rêves. (CAN)
447 Détail de l'illustration réalisé pour une double page de *Playboy* où figure un extrait d'un nouveau livre de Philip Roth. (USA)

172

449 + 450

ARTIST / KÜNSTLER / ARTISTE:

448 Don Ivan Punchatz
449, 450 Marshall Arisman

DESIGNER / GESTALTER / MAQUETTISTE:

448–450 Claire Victor

ART DIRECTOR / DIRECTEUR ARTISTIQUE:

448–450 Joe Brooks

PUBLISHER / VERLEGER / EDITEUR:

448–450 Penthouse International

448 Illustration in gloomy colours for a double spread in *Penthouse* with an excerpt from a book by William F. Buckley about two CIA agents, a man and a woman. (USA)
449, 450 Double spread and illustration from *Penthouse* covering the Jonestown tragedy. (USA)

448 Illustration in dumpfen Farben für eine Doppelseite in *Penthouse*, mit einem Auszug aus einem Buch, das von zwei CIA-Agenten, einer Frau und einem Mann, handelt. (USA)
449, 450 Vollständige Doppelseite und Illustration aus *Penthouse*. Es handelt sich um einen Auszug aus einem Buch über die Tragödie von Jonestown im Urwald von Guayana. (USA)

448 Illustration aux couleurs étouffées pour une double page de *Penthouse*: extrait d'un livre qui met en scène deux agents de la C.I.A., un homme et une femme. (USA)
449, 450 «Notre Père qui êtes en Enfer.» Double page complète et illustration de *Penthouse*. Il s'agit de la tragédie du suicide collectif de Jonestown, dans la forêt vierge de Guyana. (USA)

448

451

452

451 Illustration in *Penthouse* for an article about foreign investments in America. (USA)
452 For a story in the Australian edition of *Penthouse*. (AUS)
453 For a report by a young girl published in *Penthouse* about how she was completely influenced by a religious sect. (USA)
454 Full-page illustration in shades of blue and grey for a story in *Playboy* about an unusual mistress. (USA)
455 Portrait of Alexander Haig. Australian *Penthouse*. (AUS)
456 Full-page illustration, mainly in black and green, for a *Penthouse* report about a wasteful cancer-fighting agency. (USA)

451 «Der Verkauf von Amerika.» Illustration in *Penthouse* für einen Artikel über ausländische Investitionen in den USA. (USA)
452 Aus *Penthouse*, für eine Geschichte vom Überlebenskampf von Mensch und Tier während der Trockenheit. (AUS)
453 Für den Erlebnisbericht eines Mädchens, das völlig unter den Einfluss einer religiösen Sekte geriet. Aus *Penthouse*. (USA)
454 Illustration in Blau- und Grautönen für eine Geschichte über eine aussergewöhnliche Geliebte, im *Playboy*. (USA)
455 Porträt Alexander Haigs im australischen *Penthouse*. (AUS)
456 Ganzseitige Illustration, vorwiegend in Schwarz und Grün, zu einem Bericht in *Penthouse* über Verschwendung und Erfolglosigkeit eines Krebs-Instituts. (USA)

451 «On brade l'Amérique.» Illustration de *Penthouse* pour un article sur les investissements étrangers aux Etats-Unis. (USA)
452 Dans le *Penthouse* australien: un récit sur la sécheresse et la lutte pour la survie chez l'homme et les bêtes. (AUS)
453 Illustration du récit d'une jeune fille échappée à l'asservissement mental par une secte religieuse. *Penthouse*. (USA)
454 Illustration pleine page aux tons bleus et gris pour une histoire centrée sur une maîtresse insolite. *Playboy*. (USA)
455 Alexander Haig: portrait. *Penthouse* australien. (AUS)
456 Illustration pleine page, tons noirs et verts prédominants, pour un rapport critique de *Penthouse* sur l'inefficacité de la recherche publique sur le cancer aux Etats-Unis. (USA)

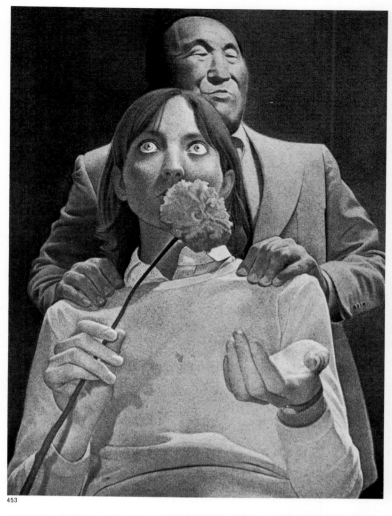

453

454

455

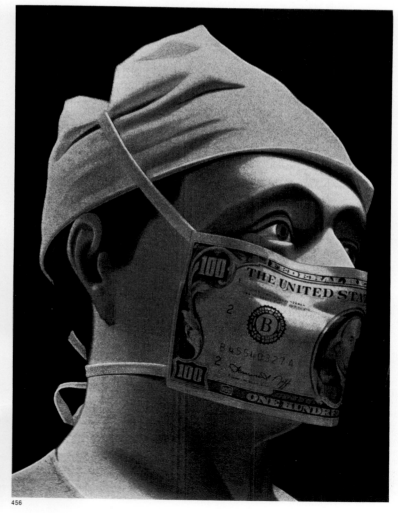

456

177

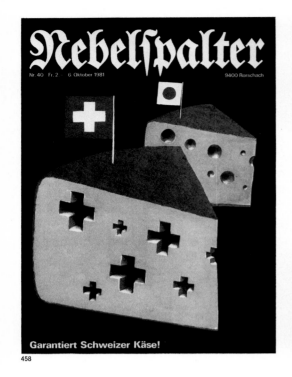

458

459

460

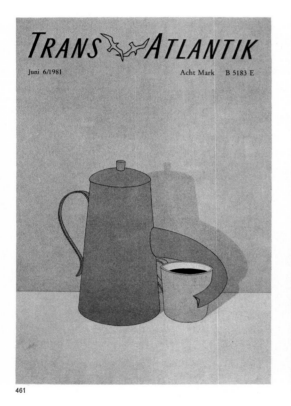

461

462

463

458–460 Cover illustrations of *Nebelspalter*, a satirical weekly magazine. In full colour. (SWI)
461, 462 Covers of *Transatlantik*, a monthly magazine. Fig. 461 in light shades of grey and beige, blue lettering; Fig. 462 in blue and grey shades, magenta lettering. (GER)
463 Cover of a marketing magazine. Illustration in soft colours, the little man in black and white. (BRA)
464 Illustration on the subject of hypnosis for the cover of a Polish magazine. In blue. (POL)
465, 466 Illustrations and complete cover of *New York* magazine. The issue contains a feature on the "Tribal Rites of the New Saturday Night" in New York. (USA)

458–460 Umschlagillustrationen für die satirische Wochenzeitschrift *Nebelspalter*. In Farbe. (SWI)
461, 462 Umschläge des Monatsmagazins *Transatlantik*. Abb. 461 in hellen Grau- und Beigetönen, Schrift blau; Abb. 462 in Blau- und Grautönen, Schrift magenta. (GER)
463 Umschlag für eine Marketing-Zeitschrift. Illustration in sanften Farben, das Männchen schwarzweiss. (BRA)
464 Illustration zum Thema Hypnose für den Umschlag einer polnischen Zeitschrift. In Blau. (POL)
465, 466 Illustration und vollständiger Umschlag für das Magazin *New York*. Die Ausgabe enthält einen Artikel über die «Stammesriten der Samstagnacht» in New York. (USA)

458–460 Illustrations de couverture pour l'hebdomadaire satirique *Nebelspalter*. En couleurs. (SWI)
461, 462 Couverture du magazine mensuel *Transatlantik*. Fig. 461 exécutée en tons gris et beige clair, texte bleu; fig. 462 en tons bleus et gris, texte magenta. (GER)
463 Couverture pour une revue de marketing. Illustration aux couleurs douces; le petit bonhomme en noir et blanc. (BRA)
464 Illustration sur le sujet de l'hypnose, pour la couverture d'un magazine polonais. En bleu. (POL)
465, 466 Illustration et couverture complète pour le magazine *New York*. Le numéro en question contient un article sur les «rites tribaux du samedi soir» à New York. (USA)

ARTIST / KÜNSTLER / ARTISTE:

458–460 Barth
461 Jeroen Henneman
462 Frieder Zimmermann
463 Zélio Alves Pinto
464 Leszek Wisniewski
465, 466 James McMullen

ART DIRECTOR / DIRECTEUR ARTISTIQUE:

458–460 Franz Mächler
461, 462 Bernd Bexte
465, 466 Walter Bernard

PUBLISHER / VERLEGER / EDITEUR:

458–460 Nebelspalter-Verlag
461, 462 NewMag Verlag
463 Meio & Mensagem
464 Przeglad Techniczny
465, 466 New York Magazine

466

464

465

179

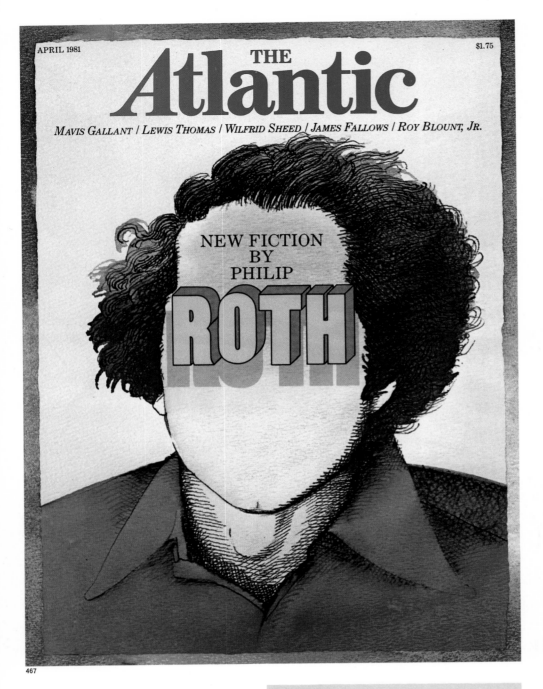

467-470 Four covers from *The Atlantic* magazine. The issue in Fig. 467 contains new fiction by Philip Roth; Fig. 468 refers to an article about the selling of diamonds; Fig. 469: the reasons why children do not like to read; Fig. 470 concerns an article about high-technology weaponry. (USA)
471 Cover for an issue of *Newsweek* containing an article about the KGB in America. (USA)
472 Cover of *Quest* magazine with a portrait of Canada's leader of the opposition, who is said to be a not very powerful man. (CAN)
473 Portrait of Louise Nevelson with one of her sculptures for an issue of *Time* magazine containing a feature on the artist. (USA)

467

468

ARTIST / KÜNSTLER / ARTISTE:

467 Milton Glaser
468 Shigeo Okamoto
469 André François
470 André Thijssen
471, 473 Marvin Mattelson
472 Blair Drawson

DESIGNER / GESTALTER / MAQUETTISTE:

467 Walter Bernard/Milton Glaser
468, 469 Judy Garlan
470 Walter Bernard
472 Art Niemi
473 Rudolph Hoglund

ART DIRECTOR / DIRECTEUR ARTISTIQUE:

467, 470 Walter Bernard
468, 469 Judy Garlan
471 Ron Meyerson/Bob Engel
472 Stephen Costello
473 Rudolph Hoglund

PUBLISHER / VERLEGER / EDITEUR:

467–470 The Atlantic Monthly
471 Newsweek
472 Comac Communications Ltd.
473 Time, Inc.

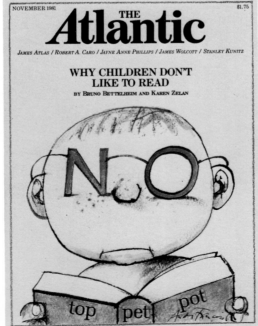

469

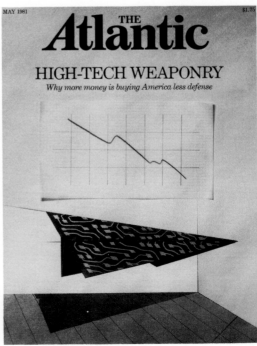

470

467–470 Vier Umschläge der Zeitschrift *The Atlantic*. Die Ausgabe in Abb. 467 enthält Neues von dem Autor Philip Roth; Abb. 468 bezieht sich auf einen Artikel, in dem es um den Verkauf von Diamanten geht; Abb. 469: «Warum Kinder nicht lesen mögen»; Abb. 470 betrifft einen Artikel über hochtechnisierte Waffen. (USA)
471 Für eine Ausgabe von *Newsweek* mit einem Artikel über den sowjetischen Geheimdienst in Amerika. (USA)
472 Porträt des Oppositionsführers in Kanada, der nicht gerade als harter Mann bekannt ist. Umschlag der Zeitschrift *Quest*. (CAN)
473 Vorschlag für einen Umschlag des Magazins *Time* mit einem Porträt von Louise Nevelson vor einer ihrer Skulpturen. (USA)

467–470 Quatre couvertures du magazine *The Atlantic*. Dans le numéro de la fig. 467, on trouve un extrait d'une nouvelle publication de Philip Roth; la fig. 468 traite de la vente de diamants; fig. 469: «Pourquoi les enfants n'aiment pas la lecture»; la fig. 470 traite des armes sophistiquées. (USA)
471 Pour un numéro de *Newsweek* contenant un article sur les menées des services secrets soviétiques aux Etats-Unis. (USA)
472 Portrait du chef de l'opposition au Canada, qui ne passe pas pour être un dur. Couverture du magazine *Quest*. (CAN)
473 Projet de couverture pour le magazine *Time* avec un portrait de Louise Nevelson devant l'une de ses sculptures. (USA)

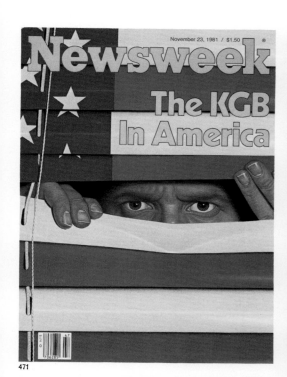

471

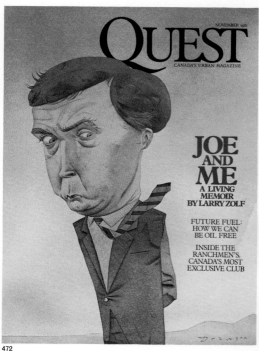

472

473

475

474, 475 Illustration and cover of an issue of *Forbes* magazine. (USA)
476 Cover for *Forbes* business magazine. In greenish grey, lettering and quotation of shares in yellow. (USA)
477 Cover for the magazine *Public Management*. The leading article deals with the salaries of city managers. (USA)
478 For *The New Yorker* magazine. Illustration mainly in light shades of green and yellow, lettering in bright blue. (USA)
479 Cover of *Scope*, a publication of the Japanese *Upjohn* company. Mainly in green shades with violet umbrellas, orange lettering. (JPN)

474, 475 Illustration und vollständiger Umschlag des Wirtschaftsmagazins *Forbes*, in dem es um die führende Rolle der Japaner auf dem Automarkt geht. (USA)
476 «Wo die Zufalls-Anleger fehlgingen.» Umschlag für das Wirtschaftsmagazin *Forbes*. In Grüngrau, Schrift und Aktienkurse gelb. (USA)
477 Umschlag für die Zeitschrift *Public Management*. Im Leitartikel geht es um die

Gehälter der Stadtverwaltungsbeamten. (USA)
478 Für die Zeitschrift *The New Yorker*. Illustration vorwiegend in hellen Grün- und Gelbtönen, Schrift leuchtend blau. (USA)
479 Umschlag von *Scope*, Publikation der japanischen *Upjohn*. Vorwiegend in Grüntönen, mit violetten Schirmen, Schrift orangefarben. (JPN)

474, 475 Illustration et couverture du magazine économique *Forbes*: la position dominante des Japonais sur le marché de l'automobile. (USA)
476 Couverture du magazine économique *Forbes*: gris vert, texte et cours de bourse en jaune. On y critique l'investissement sauvage. (USA)
477 Couverture du magazine *Public Management*: la politique salariale. (USA)
478 Pour le magazine *The New Yorker*. Illustration où prédominent les tons vert et jaune clair; le texte apparaît dans un bleu lumineux. (USA)
479 Couverture de *Scope*, une publication d'*Upjohn*-Japon. Tons verts prédominants, parapluies violets, texte orange. (JPN)

476

477

478

479

ARTIST / KÜNSTLER / ARTISTE:

474, 475 Kinuko Craft
476 Charles B. Slackman
477 Michael David Brown
478 Eugène Mihaesco
479 Yoji Kuri

DESIGNER / GESTALTER:

474, 475 Ronda Kass
476 Everett Halvorsen
477 Michael David Brown
479 Yoji Kuri

ART DIRECTOR:

474–476 Everett Halvorsen
477 Michael David Brown
479 Sumio Yamashita

AGENCY / AGENTUR / AGENCE:

477 Michael David Brown, Inc.

PUBLISHER / VERLEGER / EDITEUR:

474–476 Forbes Inc.
477 International City Management
478 The New Yorker Magazine, Inc.
479 Nippon Upjohn Ltd.

Magazine Covers

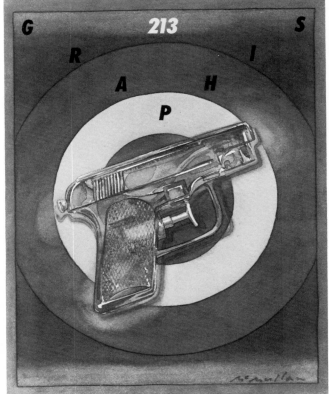

480

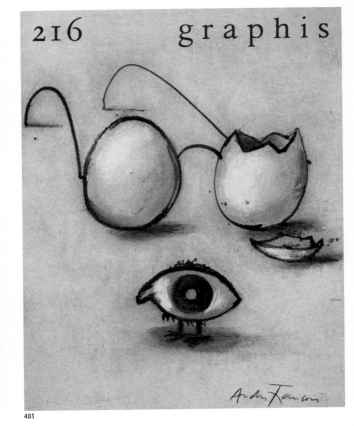

481

482

483

Magazine Covers
Zeitschriftenumschläge
Couvertures de périodiques

ART DIRECTOR:

480, 481 Walter Herdeg
482 Richard Coyne
483 Jeffrey Saks

PUBLISHER/VERLEGER/EDITEUR:

480, 481 Graphis Press Corp.
482 Coyne & Blanchard, Inc.
483 Advertising Trade Publications, Inc.
484–487 Japan Industrial Design
Promotion Organization

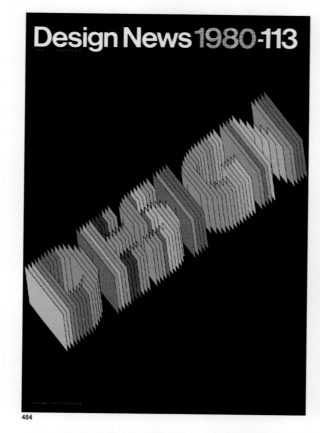

484

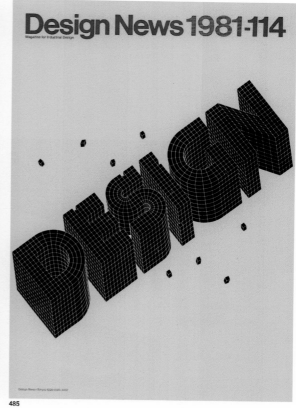

485

486

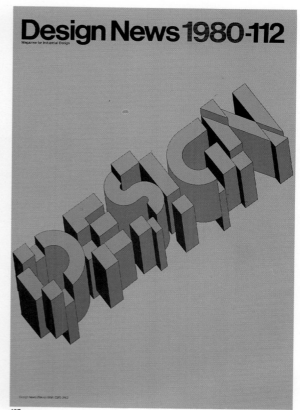

487

480, 481 Covers for *Graphis*. Pistol (Fig. 480) in yellow and green, target in raspberry-red with blue; Fig. 481 sandy with a blue eye. (SWI)
482 Illustration for a cover of *Communication Arts*. This issue contains an article about the illustrator. In full colour. (USA)
483 Cover of *Art Direction*. Full-colour leaves on a grey ground. (USA)
484–487 Covers of four issues of *Design News*, a trade magazine for industrial design. (JPN)

480, 481 Umschläge für *Graphis*. Pistole (480) gelb und grün, Zielscheibe himbeerrot mit Blau; Abb. 481 sandfarben mit blauem Auge. (SWI)
482 Illustration für den Umschlag von *Communication Arts*. Die Ausgabe enthält einen Artikel über die Illustratorin. In Farbe. (USA)
483 Umschlag von *Art Direction*. Bunte Blätter auf grauem Grund. (USA)
484–487 Umschläge für vier Ausgaben von *Design News*, eine Fachzeitschrift für Produktgestaltung. (JPN)

480, 481 Couvertures de *Graphis*. Pistolet (480) jaune et vert, cible framboise et bleu; fig. 481 sable, avec œil bleu. (SWI)
482 Illustration de couverture de *Communication Arts*. Ce numéro contient un article consacré à l'illustratrice. En couleurs. (USA)
483 Couverture d'*Art Direction*. Feuilles colorées, fond gris. (USA)
484–487 Couvertures de quatre numéros de *Design News*, revue spécialisée en esthétique industrielle. (JPN)

Trade Magazines
Fachzeitschriften
Revues professionnelles

488

ARTIST / KÜNSTLER / ARTISTE:

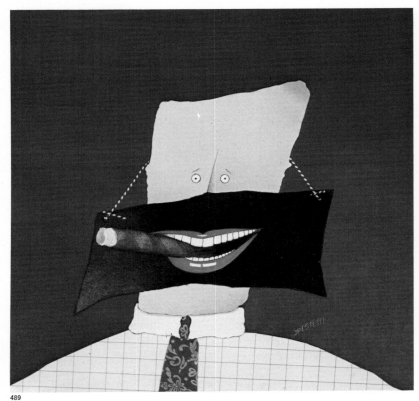

489

490

491

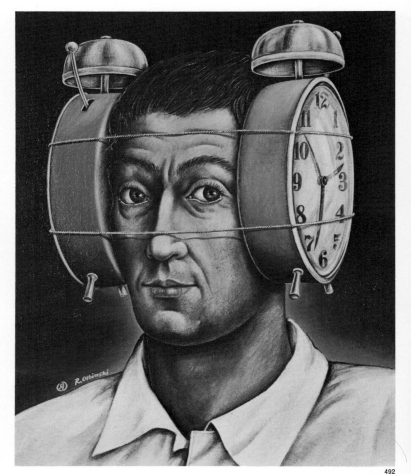

492

PL ISSN 0208-7391

POLSKA

Céna zł 40   Nr 2 (318) 1981

HISTORIA

493

SIN

How to Lie   Sin City, USA   Sleazy Side of New Zealand   Road to Hell

FEB. 1981

NATIONAL LAMPOON

$2.00

THE HUMOR MAGAZINE FOR ADULTS

494

DESIGNER / GESTALTER / MAQUETTISTE:

491 Ed Schneider
492 Carveth Cramer

ART DIRECTOR / DIRECTEUR ARTISTIQUE:

492 Carveth Cramer
493 Lech Zahorski
494 Skip Johnston

PUBLISHER / VERLEGER / EDITEUR:

488–490 Corriere della Sera
491 The Washington Post
492 Ziff-Davis Publishing
493 Polish Interpress Agency
494 National Lampoon

488, 489 Complete cover of the magazine *Il Mondo* and illustration referring to a poll conducted on the most popular professions in Italy. (ITA)
490 "Trade-unionist, missionary or bureaucrat?" Full-colour cover for *Il Mondo*. (ITA)
491 Cover of the *Washington Post Magazine* on the 1980 US presidential campaign. (USA)
492 For a cover of the magazine *Psychology Today*. (USA)
493 Complete cover of the magazine *Poland* which appears in several languages. (POL)
494 Full-colour cover of *National Lampoon*, the humor magazine for adults. (USA)

488, 489 Vollständiger Umschlag der Zeitschrift *Il Mondo* und Illustration, die sich auf eine Umfrage über die beliebtesten Berufe in Italien bezieht. (ITA)
490 «Gewerkschaftler, Missionar oder Bürokrat?» Mehrfarbiger Umschlag für *Il Mondo*. (ITA)
491 Umschlag des *Washington Post Magazine* zum Thema der US-Präsidentschafts-Wahlkampagne '80, mit Anspielung auf Ted Kennedys Rolle. (USA)
492 Für einen Umschlag von *Psychology Today*: «Mit wie wenig Schlaf kommt man aus?» (USA)
493 Vollständiger Umschlag der Zeitschrift *Polen*, die in mehreren Sprachen erscheint. (POL)
494 Mehrfarbiger Umschlag für das humoristische Magazin *National Lampoon*: «Sünde.» (USA)

488, 489 Couverture complète du magazine *Il Mondo* et illustration y figurant. On s'y réfère à un sondage sur les métiers les plus populaires en Italie. (ITA)
490 «Syndicaliste, missionnaire ou bureaucrate?» Couverture polychrome pour *Il Mondo*. (ITA)
491 Couverture du *Washington Post Magazine* sur le sujet des présidentielles de 1980. (USA)
492 «Quel est le minimum de sommeil indispensable?» Couverture de *Psychology Today*. (USA)
493 Couverture complète du magazine *Pologne* publié en plusieurs langues. (POL)
494 Couverture polychrome pour le magazine d'humour *National Lampoon*. Sujet: «le péché.» (USA)

495–498 Complete covers of the magazine *Art* and the *Zeitmagazin* and the illustrations, a portrait of Salvador Dalí and a self-portrait of Gottfried Helnwein. Pictures such as this self-portrait of the Viennese artist, with suture clips, bandages, scars, operation tubes, etc., led to numerous controversies. Helnwein's hyper-realistic pictures are formed by means of coloured crayons, pencils, chalk and watercolour, and thousands of strokes of the brush and pen. The "fastest water-colour painter in the world", as he calls himself, has in the meantime become one of the most sought-after illustrators. (USA)

495–498 Vollständige Umschläge des Kunstmagazins *Art* und des *Zeitmagazins*, und die Illustrationen: ein Porträt von Salvador Dalí und Selbstporträt von Gottfried Helnwein. Bilder wie das Selbstporträt des Wiener Künstlers, mit Wundklammern, Bandagen, Narben, Operationsschläuchen, führten zu zahlreichen Kontroversen. Mit Farb- und Bleistift, Kreide und Tusche und Tausenden von Pinsel- und Federstrichen entstehen Helnweins hyperrealistische Bilder. Der «schnellste Aquarellmaler der Welt», wie er sich selbst nennt, wurde inzwischen zu einem der gefragtesten Illustratoren. Seine Vorbilder: Walt Disney und Norman Rockwell. (USA)

495–498 Couvertures complètes des magazines *Art* et *Zeitmagazin*, portrait de Salvador Dalí et autoportrait de Gottfried Helnwein. Dans ce dernier et dans d'autres illustrations de l'artiste viennois, les agrafes chirurgicales, pansements, tuyaux et cicatrices ont fait frémir le public. Ce «plus rapide aquarelliste du monde» réalise ses tableaux hyperréalistes en juxtaposant des milliers de coups de pinceau et de plume et en utilisant indifféremment le crayon, le crayon couleur, la craie et l'encre de Chine. Il s'inspire de Walt Disney et de Norman Rockwell. (USA)

Magazine Covers

495

497

ARTIST / KÜNSTLER / ARTISTE:

495–498 Gottfried Helnwein

ART DIRECTOR / DIRECTEUR ARTISTIQUE:

495, 496 Axel Hecht
497, 498 Manfred Manke

PUBLISHER / VERLEGER / EDITEUR:

495, 496 Gruner & Jahr AG & Co.
497, 498 Zeitverlag Gerd Bucerius KG

496

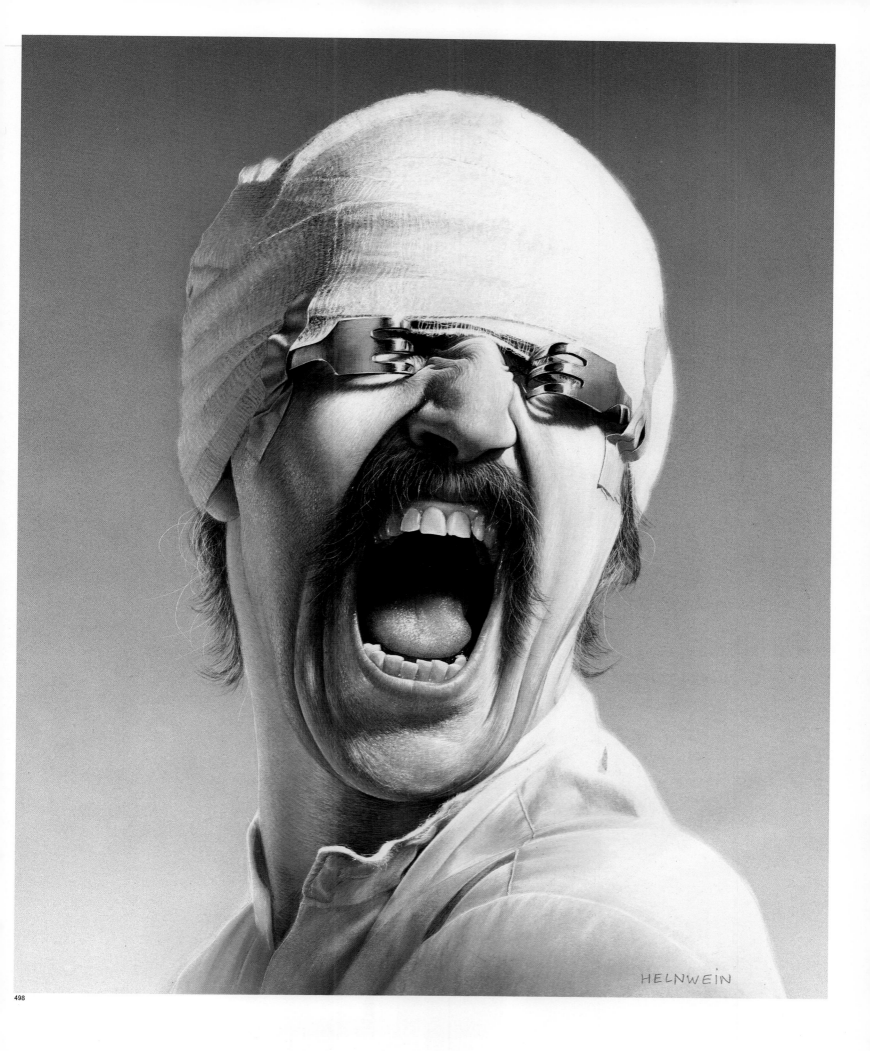

MAGAZINE

MARIO

A refugee here after three years in a Chilean prison

499

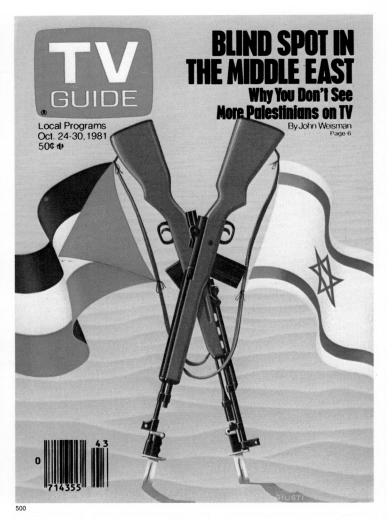

TV GUIDE

Local Programs
Oct. 24-30, 1981
50¢

BLIND SPOT IN THE MIDDLE EAST

Why You Don't See More Palestinians on TV

By John Weisman
Page 6

714355 43

500

MAGAZINE

The Perils of the Good Ship Blossom

502

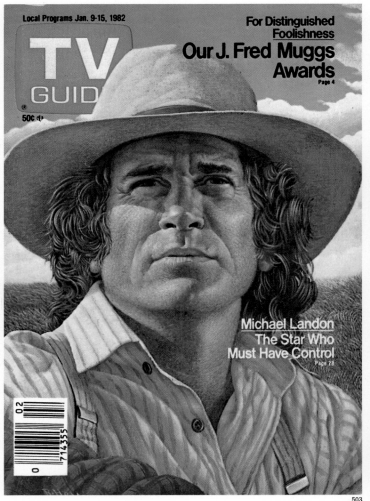

Local Programs Jan. 9-15, 1982

TV GUIDE

50¢

For Distinguished Foolishness
Our J. Fred Muggs Awards
Page 4

Michael Landon
The Star Who Must Have Control
Page 28

714355

503

501a

501

ARTIST / KÜNSTLER / ARTISTE:

499 Daniel Maffia
500 Robert Giusti
501, 501a Tullio Pericoli
502 Elaine Wozniak
503 Richard Hess
504 Michael Manwaring

DESIGNER / GESTALTER / MAQUETTISTE:

499 Greg Paul
502 Sam Capuano
504 Michael Manwaring

ART DIRECTOR / DIRECTEUR ARTISTIQUE:

499 Greg Paul
500, 503 Jerry Alten
502 Sam Capuano
504 Thomas Ingalls/Michael Manwaring

AGENCY / AGENTUR / AGENCE – STUDIO:

504 The Office of Michael Manwaring

PUBLISHER / VERLEGER / EDITEUR:

499, 502 Plain Dealer Publishing Co.
500, 503 Triangle Publications Inc.
501, 501a L'Espresso
504 Metro Magazine

499 Cover of the *Plain Dealer Magazine*. In dark colours. (USA)
500 Cover of the magazine *TV Guide*, with an article about the TV coverage of the situation in the Middle East. (USA)
501, 501a Illustration and complete cover of the magazine *L'Espresso*. The question asked is whether Italy's socialist party can manœuvre its way to power through the economic crisis. Here the leader of the PSI, Bettino Craxi. (ITA)
502 For an issue of the *Plain Dealer Magazine*. In full colour. (USA)
503 For *TV Guide*, with an article about Michael Landon. (USA)
504 Cover of *Metro* magazine on the subject of autumn. (USA)

499 Umschlag des *Plain Dealer Magazine* mit einem Bericht über einen Flüchtling, der drei Jahre in einem chilenischen Gefängnis verbrachte. In dunklen Farben. (USA)
500 Umschlag von *TV Guide* mit einem Artikel über die Situation im Nahen Osten und die Frage, warum nicht mehr Palästinenser im Fernsehen zu sehen sind. (USA)
501, 501a Illustration und vollständiger Umschlag des Magazins *L'Espresso*. Es geht um die Frage, ob es den Sozialisten Italiens gelingt, durch die Wirtschaftskrise an die Macht zu kommen. Hier der Führer der PSI, Bettino Craxi. (ITA)
502 Für eine Ausgabe des *Plain Dealer Magazine* mit einem Beitrag über die Gefahren von Weltumseglungen. In Farbe. (USA)
503 Für *TV Guide*, mit einem Artikel über einen TV-Star. (USA)
504 Umschlag des Magazins *Metro* zum Thema Herbst. (USA)

499 Couverture du *Plain Dealer Magazine*, avec un article sur un réfugié chilien évadé d'une prison de son pays où il avait passé trois longues années. Couleurs sombres. (USA)
500 Couverture de *TV Guide*. On y pose la question de savoir pourquoi l'on voit si peu de Palestiniens à la TV. (USA)
501, 501a Illustration et couverture complète du magazine *L'Espresso* où elle figure. On y voit le chef du PSI, Bettino Craxi, en relation avec la question de savoir si la crise économique italienne pourrait favoriser l'accession des socialistes au pouvoir. (ITA)
502 Pour un numéro du *Plain Dealer Magazine* où l'on discute des dangers des courses de voiliers autour du monde. (USA)
503 Pour *TV Guide*: article sur une vedette de TV. (USA)
504 Couverture du magazine *Metro*. Sujet: l'automne. (USA)

504

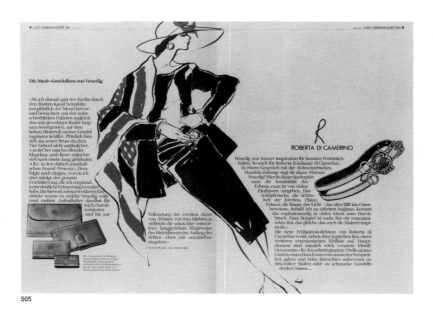

505

House Organs / Hauszeitschriften
Journaux d'entreprise

505 Double spread from the customer magazine of the department store *Les Ambassadeurs*, showing *Roberta di Camerino*'s spring collection. (SWI)
506 Recto of *RF Illustrated*, a publication issued by the Rockefeller Foundation, with a preview of the subjects dealt with in this edition. In three colours. (USA)
507 Double spread from the *Centex Corporation* annual report, a multi-industry company involved in real estate, home building, construction, cement and related products, oil and gas. (USA)
508, 509 Double spreads from a company publication of the paper manufacturer Pappersgruppen AB. Light grey on a black ground. (SWE)
510 Illustration on the cover of an annual report of *Centex Corporation*, a vertically organized multi-industry holding company. (USA)
511 "Better the worm in the apple?" Cover of a *Ciba-Geigy Magazin*. (SWI)
512 Cover of *Pharmascan*, customer magazine of the *Geigy* company. In full colour. (USA)

505 Doppelseite aus der Kundenzeitschrift des Kaufhauses *Les Ambassadeurs*. Hier geht es um die Frühjahrskollektion von *Roberta di Camerino*. (SWI)
506 Vorderseite einer Publikation der Rockefeller-Stiftung mit Übersicht über die in dieser Ausgabe behandelten Themen. Dreifarbig. (USA)
507 Doppelseite aus einem Jahresbericht der *Centex Corporation*, ein diversifiziertes Unternehmen, das in der Baubranche, auf dem Immobilienmarkt und in der Energieversorgung tätig ist. (USA)
508, 509 Doppelseiten aus einer Firmenpublikation des Papierherstellers Pappersgruppen AB. Hellgrau auf schwarzem Grund. (SWE)
510 Illustration des Umschlags eines Jahresberichtes der *Centex Corporation*, ein vertikal ausgerichtetes Unternehmen, das im Bau- und Immobiliensektor sowie in der Energieversorgung tätig ist. (USA)
511 Umschlag des *Ciba-Geigy Magazins*, das einen Beitrag über Pflanzenschutzmittel enthält. (SWI)
512 «Gift aus dem Meer.» Umschlag der Kundenzeitschrift *Pharmascan* von *Geigy*. In Farbe. (USA)

505 Double page de la revue destinée à la clientèle du grand magasin *Les Ambassadeurs*. Il s'agit ici de la collection de printemps de *Roberta di Camerino*. (SWI)
506 Recto d'une publication de la Fondation Rockefeller, avec le sommaire des sujets traités dans ce numéro. Trois couleurs. (USA)
507 Double page d'un rapport annuel de la *Centex Corporation*, un groupe diversifié dans la construction, le marché immobilier et la distribution d'énergie. (USA)
508, 509 Doubles pages d'une revue d'entreprise d'un papetier. Gris clair sur fond noir. (SWE)
510 Illustration de couverture pour un rapport annuel de la *Centex Corporation*, un groupe à intégration verticale se partageant entre la construction, l'immobilier et l'énergie. (USA)
511 Couverture du *Ciba-Geigy Magazin*. Ce numéro contient, sous le titre de «Vous préférez le ver dans le fruit?», un article sur les produits phytosanitaires. (SWI)
512 «Le poison venu de la mer.» Couverture de *Pharmascan* de *Geigy*. En couleurs. (USA)

506

507

508

509

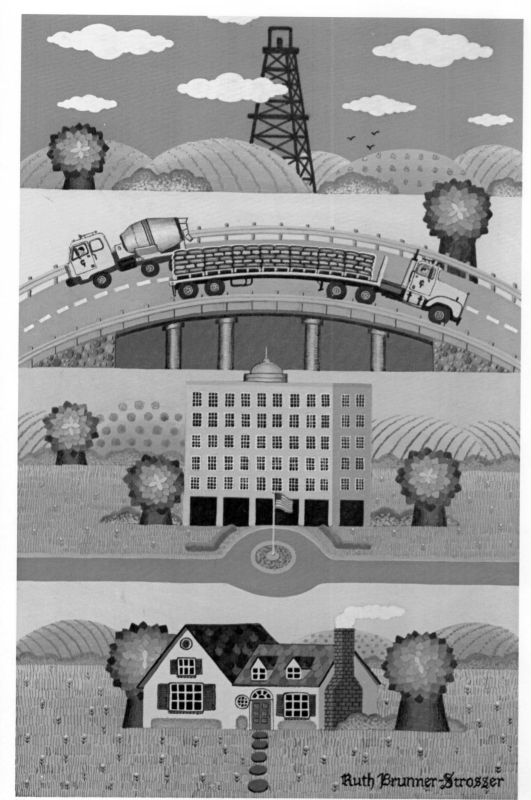

Ruth Brunner-Strosser

510

AGENCY / AGENTUR / AGENCE – STUDIO:

507, 510 Richards, Sullivan, Brock & Associates
508, 509 Artmen AB
511 Ciba-Geigy/Zentrale Werbung
512 Ciba-Geigy/Corporate Art Service

PUBLISHER / VERLEGER / EDITEUR:

505 Les Ambassadeurs
506 The Rockefeller Foundation
508, 509 Pappersgruppen
511 Ciba-Geigy AG
512 Ciba-Geigy Corp.

511

512

ARTIST / KÜNSTLER / ARTISTE:

505 Walter Niggli
507, 510 Ruth Brunner-Strosser
511 Christian Lang
512 David Montiel

DESIGNER / GESTALTER / MAQUETTISTE:

506 Jack W. Beck
507, 510 Chris Rovillo
508, 509 Bengt Göthberg
512 Larry Stires

ART DIRECTOR / DIRECTEUR ARTISTIQUE:

506 Jack W. Beck
507, 510 Chris Rovillo/Ron Sullivan
508, 509 Bengt Göthberg
511 Rolf Dürst/Jean Buck
512 Larry Stires

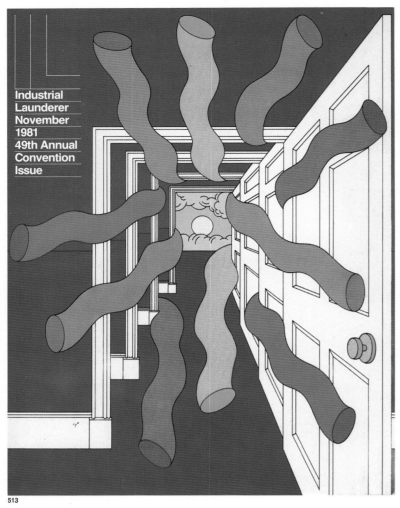

Industrial
Launderer
November
1981
49th Annual
Convention
Issue

513

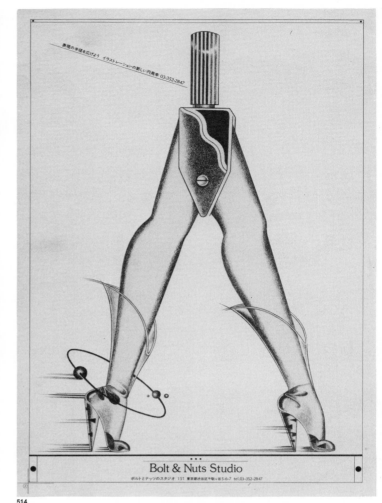

Bolt & Nuts Studio

514

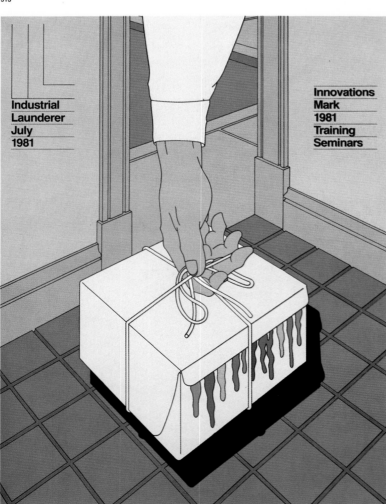

Industrial
Launderer
July
1981

Innovations
Mark
1981
Training
Seminars

515

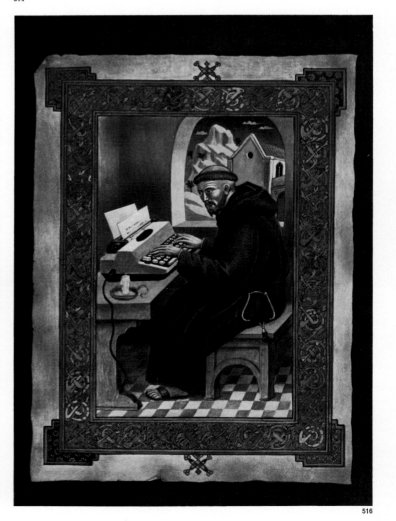

516

Trade Magazines
House Organs

ARTIST / KÜNSTLER / ARTISTE:

513 Pam Lefkowitz
514 Kumiko Nagasaki
515 Jack Lefkowitz
516 Kinuko Craft
517, 518 Miloslav Kolář

DESIGNER / GESTALTER / MAQUETTISTE:

513, 515 Jack Lefkowitz
514 Kenzo Nakagawa
516 James T. Walsh
517, 518 Miloslav Kolář

ART DIRECTOR / DIRECTEUR ARTISTIQUE:

513, 515 Jack Lefkowitz
514 Kenzo Nakagawa
516 Tom Lennon
517, 518 Jaroslav Neubauer

AGENCY / AGENTUR / AGENCE – STUDIO:

513, 515 Jack Lefkowitz Inc.
514 Bolt & Nuts Studio

PUBLISHER / VERLEGER / EDITEUR:

513, 515 Institute of Industrial Launderers
514 Bolt & Nuts Studio
516 Fischer Medical Publications
517, 518 Chemapol

513, 515 Covers for *Industrial Launderer*, trade magazine for laundries. Fig. 513 refers to the annual meeting, whose main theme is the gaining of new markets; Fig. 515: new knowledge gained by seminary participants from large industrial laundries. (USA)
514 Spread from an edition of the house magazine of a graphic-design studio, on the subject of "walking". Green on white. (JPN)
516 Illustration taken from the medical magazine *Emergency Medicine*. (USA)
517, 518 Double spread and illustration taken from the medical magazine *Respharma*. The accompanying article deals with applicability to human beings of experimental results obtained from animals. (CSR)

513, 515 Umschläge für *Industrial Launderer*, Fachzeitschrift für Grosswäschereien. Abb. 513 bezieht sich auf die Jahreskonferenz, deren Thema die Gewinnung neuer Märkte ist; Abb. 515: Neu erworbene Kenntnisse von Seminarteilnehmern der Grosswäschereien. (USA)
514 Seite aus einer Ausgabe der Hauszeitschrift eines Graphik-Studios, deren Thema «Gehen» ist. Grün auf Weiss. (JPN)
516 Illustration aus der medizinischen Fachzeitschrift *Emergency Medicine*. (USA)
517, 518 Doppelseite und ganzseitige Illustration aus der medizinischen Fachzeitschrift *Respharma*. In dem dazugehörigen Artikel geht es um die Anwendbarkeit von Versuchsergebnissen mit Tieren auf den Menschen. (CSR)

513, 515 Couvertures d'*Industrial Launderer* (La Blanchisserie industrielle). 513: conférence annuelle destinée à la conquête de nouveaux marchés; 515: les connaissances nouvelles acquises par les participants à un séminaire spécialisé. (USA)
514 Page d'un numéro de la revue d'entreprise d'un studio graphique, sur le sujet de la marche. Vert sur blanc. (JPN)
516 Illustration tirée de la revue médicale *Emergency Medicine*. (USA)
517, 518 Illustration pleine page et double page complète de la revue médicale *Respharma*. L'article en question discute de la transposition à l'homme de résultats expérimentaux obtenus sur l'animal. (CSR)

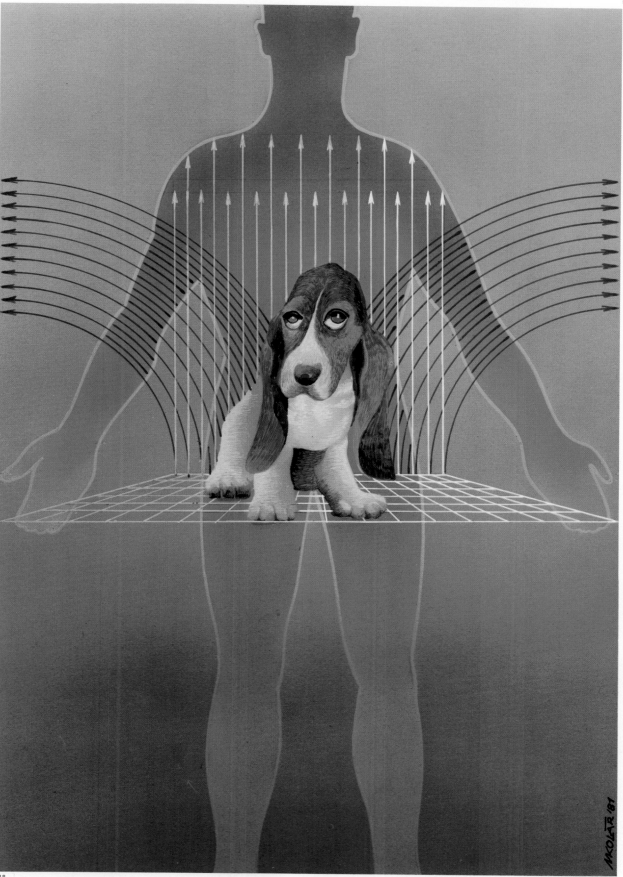

517

518

519–521 Double spreads and illustration from *Dinar*, a publication issued by the Commercial Bank of Kuwait. The subjects dealt with are recent world economic developments and the areas of Arab industrial cooperation. (KUW)
522 From the *Del Monte* house magazine, showing one of the products of a subsidiary company. (USA)
523 Cover of a publication of Switzerland's Federal Office for Industry and Labour. (SWI)
524 Full-page, full-colour illustration from *Pan Am Clipper*, house magazine of *Pan Am*. (USA)
525 From *JD Journal*, house magazine of *John Deere*, manufacturers of agricultural machines. (USA)
526 "Pigeons with Cameras." Cover illustration of *IBM Nachrichten* (IBM News). (GER)

519

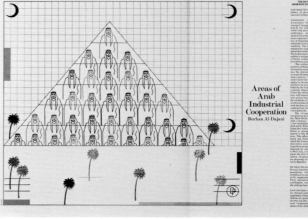

521

House Organs
Hauszeitschriften
Journaux d'entreprise

ARTIST / KÜNSTLER / ARTISTE:

519, 520 Mick Brownfield
521 Dan Fern
522 Jim Ludtke
524 John Rombola
525 Ralph Steadman
526 Dieter Nagel

DESIGNER / GESTALTER:

519–521 David Hillman/Nancy
         Williams/Vicky Gornall
522 David Broom
523 Roland Hirter
525 Tom Sizemore

ART DIRECTOR:

519–521 David Hillman
522 David Broom
523 Roland Hirter
524 G. Woodford Pratt
525 Wayne Burkart

AGENCY / AGENTUR / AGENCE:

519–521 Pentagram
522 Broom & Broom, Inc.

PUBLISHER / VERLEGER / EDITEUR:

519–521 Commercial Bank of Kuwait
522 Del Monte Corporation
523 BIGA Bundesamt für Industrie
     und Arbeit
524 Ziff-Davis Publishing
525 Deere & Company
526 IBM Deutschland GmbH

520

522

524

523

519–521 Doppelseiten und Illustration aus *Dinar*, Wirtschaftspublikation einer Bank. Themen: Kürzliche Entwicklungen in der Weltwirtschaft und industrielle Zusammenarbeit der Araber. (KUW)
522 Aus der Hauszeitschrift der Firma *Del Monte*; hier *Camel*-Zigaretten, eines ihrer Produkte. (USA)
523 Umschlag einer Publikation des Schweizerischen Bundesamtes für Industrie und Arbeit. (SWI)
524 Ganzseitige, farbige Illustration zum Thema Italien, aus der Hauszeitschrift der *Pan Am*. (USA)
525 Aus der Hauszeitschrift von *John Deere*, Hersteller von landwirtschaftlichen Maschinen. (USA)
526 «Tauben mit Kameras.» Umschlagillustration der *IBM-Nachrichten*. (GER)

519–521 Doubles pages et illustrations de *Dinar*, publication économique de la Banque commerciale du Koweït. Les sujets sont les suivants: les derniers développements de l'économie mondiale; la coopération industrielle arabe. (KUW)
522 Pour les cigarettes *Camel*, un produit de *Del Monte*, dans une revue d'entreprise. (USA)
523 Couverture d'une publication de l'Office fédéral suisse de l'industrie et du travail. (SWI)
524 Illustration couleur pleine page dans la revue d'entreprise de *Pan Am*: L'Italie. (USA)
525 Pour la revue d'entreprise de *John Deere*, le fabricant de machines agricoles. (USA)
526 «Pigeons à appareils photo.» Illustration de couverture d'*IBM-Nachrichten*. (GER)

525

526

197

527

528

529

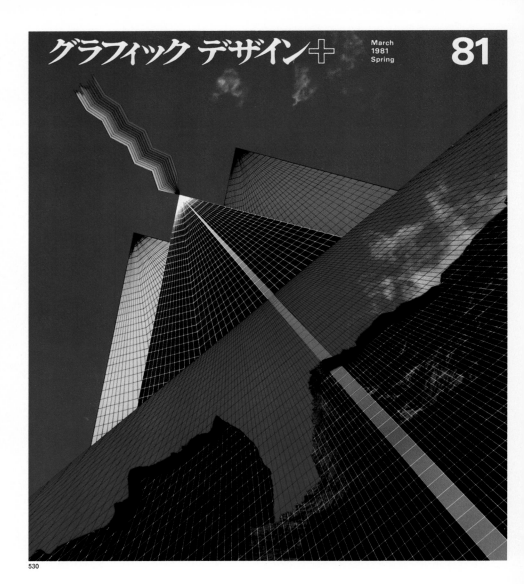

530

531

ARTIST / KÜNSTLER / ARTISTE:

527–529 Oswaldo Miranda (Miran)
530 Kazumasa Nagai
531 Peter Brookes
532–534 Randall Enos

DESIGNER / GESTALTER / MAQUETTISTE:

527–529 Oswaldo Miranda
530 Kazumasa Nagai
531 David Driver
534 Verner Jurgeleit

ART DIRECTOR / DIRECTEUR ARTISTIQUE:

527–529 Oswaldo Miranda
530 Kazumasa Nagai
531 David Driver
532, 533 Pete Libby
534 Verner Jurgeleit

AGENCY / AGENTUR / AGENCE – STUDIO:

527–529 Miran Estudio
530 Nippon Design Center

Trade Magazines
Fachzeitschriften
Revues professionnelles

532

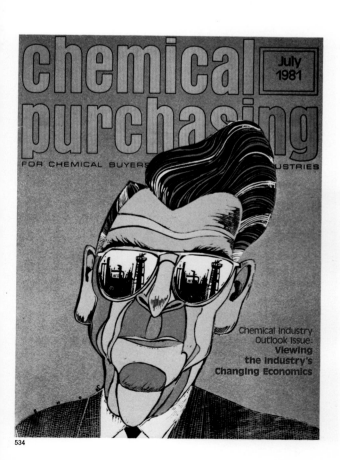

534

533

PUBLISHER / VERLEGER / EDITEUR:

527–529 Raposa Magazine
530 Graphic Design Associates
531 BBC Publications
532, 533 Golf Digest Magazine
534 Chemical Purchasing Magazine

527–529 Spreads from *Raposa*, a humorous graphic-design magazine. Fig. 527: satirical feature on fear; Fig. 528: column for women; Fig. 529: a satirical feature on prayer. (BRA)
530 Cover of a Japanese trade magazine for graphic design. (JPN)
531 Cover of *The Listener*, referring to an article on the rhetoric of medicine (Reith Lectures). (GBR)
532, 533 Illustration and double spread from *Golf Digest*. The article is about the exodus of American golf stars during the off-season to take part in foreign golf tournaments. (USA)
534 Cover of *Chemical Purchasing*, a trade magazine for chemical products. This issue deals with the economic outlook of the chemical industry. (USA)

527–529 Seiten aus *Raposa*, humoristische Graphikerzeitschrift. Abb. 527: satirischer Beitrag über Angst; Abb. 528: Spalte für die Frau; Abb. 529: satirischer Beitrag zum Thema Gebet: (BRA)
530 Umschlag einer japanischen Fachzeitschrift für Graphik-Design. (JPN)
531 Umschlag von *The Listener*: «Die Rhetorik der Medizin» (Die Reith-Vorträge). (GBR)
532, 533 Illustration und vollständige Doppelseite aus *Golf Digest*. In dem dazugehörigen Artikel geht es um die Teilnahme prominenter Golfspieler der USA an Tournieren im Ausland. (USA)
534 Umschlag einer Fachzeitschrift für die Einkäufer chemischer Produkte. In dieser Ausgabe geht es um die wirtschaftlichen Aussichten der chemischen Industrie. (USA)

527–529 Pages de la revue graphique satirique *Raposa*. 527: une contribution satirique au sujet de l'angoisse; 528: la colonne des femmes; 529: satire sur le thème de la prière. (BRA)
530 Couverture d'une revue japonaise spécialisée dans l'art graphique. (JPN)
531 Couverture du *Listener*: «La rhétorique de la médecine» (Conférences Reith). (GBR)
532, 533 Illustration et double page complète du *Golf Digest*. On y discute de la participation des meilleurs golfeurs américains aux tournois rémunérateurs organisés à l'étranger. (USA)
534 Couverture d'une revue professionnelle pour les acheteurs de produits chimiques. Un article de ce numéro traite des perspectives économiques de l'industrie chimique. (USA)

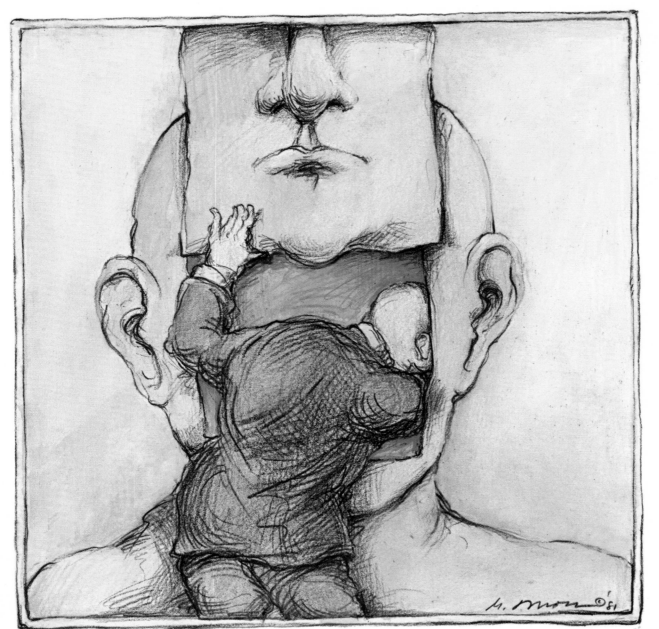

535

ARTIST / KÜNSTLER / ARTISTE:

535 Geoffrey Moss
536 Werner Kappes
537 Jeffrey J. Smith
538 Lonni Sue Johnson
539 Alan Cober
540 Carlo Basile
541 Terry Boles

DESIGNER / GESTALTER / MAQUETTISTE:

536, 537 Tom Lennon

ART DIRECTOR:

535, 538–541 Tina Adamek
536, 537 Tom Lennon

PUBLISHER / VERLEGER / EDITEUR:

535, 538–541 McGraw-Hill, Inc.
536, 537 Fischer Medical Publications

Trade Magazines
Fachzeitschriften
Revues professionnelles

536

537

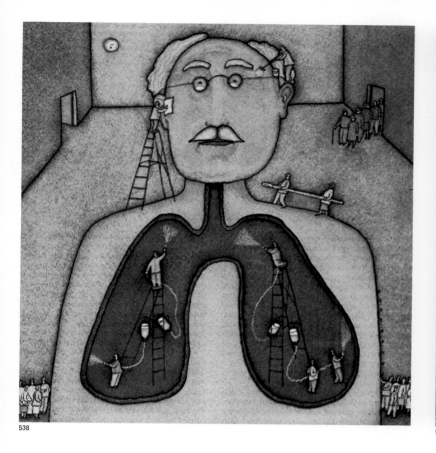

538

539

540

535 Illustration taken from *Postgraduate Medicine*, a magazine for young doctors. (USA)
536, 537 Double spreads from *Emergency Medicine* magazine. Fig. 536: bone fractures caused by skiing accidents; Fig. 537: the management of diving accidents. (USA)
538–540 Full-page, full-colour illustrations from the medical magazine *Postgraduate Medicine*. Fig. 538 deals with the susceptibility of the elderly to catch pneumonia; Fig. 539: the problems of muscular dystrophy; Fig. 540: dietary consideration in cases of hypertension. (USA)
541 Illustration for a feature in the magazine *Physician and Sportsmedicine*. (USA)

535 Illustration aus der medizinischen Fachzeitschrift *Postgraduate Medicine*. In dem Artikel geht es um die Haut als Spiegel versteckter Krankheiten des Organismus. (USA)
536, 537 Doppelseiten aus *Emergency Medicine*, medizinische Fachzeitschrift. Themen: Durch Skiunfälle verursachte Knochenbrüche (Abb. 536) und Behandlung von Tauchunfällen (Abb. 537). (USA)
538–540 Ganzseitige, farbige Illustrationen aus der medizinischen Fachzeitschrift *Postgraduate Medicine*. In Abb. 538 geht es um die Anfälligkeit älterer Patienten für Lungenentzündungen, in Abb. 539 um Muskelschwund, und in Abb. 540 um die Ernährung bei zu hohem Blutdruck. (USA)
541 Aus *Physician and Sportsmedicine* zum Thema der Gewichtskontrolle bei Ringern. (USA)

535 Illustration pour la revue médicale *Postgraduate Medicine*. L'article auquel elle se rapporte étudie le rôle révélateur de la peau dans le dermatodiagnostic des maladies systémiques. (USA)
536, 537 Doubles pages d'*Emergency Medicine*, une revue médicale où l'on discute des fractures des skieurs (fig. 536) et du traitement des accidents de plongée (fig. 537). (USA)
538–540 Illustrations couleur pleine page dans la revue médicale *Postgraduate Medicine*. 538: la fragilité des patients âgés face aux infections pulmonaires; 539: la myopathie primitive progressive; 540: les régimes à mettre en œuvre en cas d'hypertension. (USA)
541 Pour *Physician and Sportsmedicine*. Sujet: comment les lutteurs perdent du poids. (USA)

541

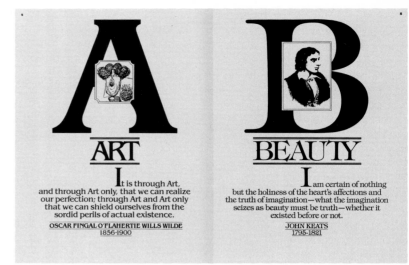

542

543

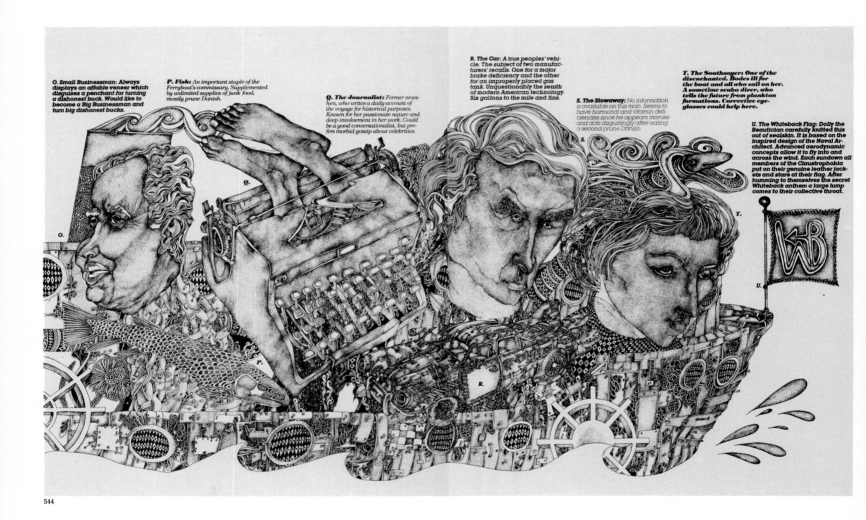

544

542, 543 Cover of *U&lc*, publication of the International Typeface Corporation, and spread from an alphabet in another issue. (USA)
544 Double spread in *U&lc* taken from a parable about prejudice, with a reverse twist (see also Figs. 542, 543). (USA)
545, 546 More double spreads from *U&lc*. The subjects dealt with here are long foreign words, and Benjamin Franklin. (USA)
547, 548 Illustrations from *Planning Review*, a magazine for corporate planners. Fig. 547 refers to a model for identifying political risks involved when establishing foreign production facilities; Fig. 548 illustrates a parable entitled "Collective Wisdom" and adapted from the *Dervish Tales* of Idries Shah. The story is about blind people eager to know what an elephant looks like and their very incomplete impressions. (USA)

542, 543 Umschlag und Doppelseite aus einem in *U&lc*, Fachzeitschrift für Typographie, veröffentlichten Alphabet. (USA)
544 «Die kaukasische Fähre.» Doppelseite aus einer Parabel über Vorurteile, in *U&lc* (s. Abb. 542, 543). (USA)
545, 546 Weitere Doppelseiten aus *U&lc*. Die Themen sind hier lange Fremdwörter und Benjamin Franklin. (USA)
547, 548 Illustrationen aus *Planning Review*, Fachzeitschrift für Unternehmensplaner. Abb. 547 bezieht sich auf einen Artikel, in dem Anhaltspunkte für das Abschätzen politischer Risiken bei Auslandsfabrikationen gegeben werden; Abb. 548 illustriert eine Parabel mit dem Titel «Kollektive Weisheit», in der es um die Vorstellung verschiedener Menschen von einem Elefanten geht, von dem sie nur Teile ertasten, ihn aber nicht sehen konnten. (USA)

542, 543 Couverture et page double d'un alphabet publié dans *U&lc*, revue professionnelle de typographie. (USA)
544 «Le ferry du Caucase»: double page d'un conte pour adultes sur les préjugés, publié dans *U&lc* (cf. 542, 543). (USA)
545, 546 Autres pages doubles d'*U&lc*. Les sujets évoqués sont les longs mots étrangers et Benjamin Franklin. (USA)
547, 548 Illustrations pour *Planning Review*, une revue professionnelle pour la planification d'entreprise. La fig. 547 se rapporte à l'évaluation des risques qu'encourt le déplacement de la production dans des pays politiquement instables. La fig. 548 illustre un conte pour adultes intitulé «Sagesse collective», où des humains tentent de décrire les yeux bandés un éléphant dont ils tâtent différentes parties du corps. (USA)

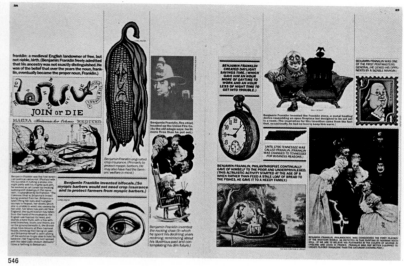

547

ARTIST / KÜNSTLER / ARTISTE:

542 Murray Tinkelman
543 Jason Calfo
544 Jim Spanfeller
546 Lionel Kalish/Wally Neibart
547, 548 Ner Beck

DESIGNER / GESTALTER / MAQUETTISTE:

542–546 Herb Lubalin

ART DIRECTOR / DIRECTEUR ARTISTIQUE:

542–546 Herb Lubalin
547, 548 Robert Randall

AGENCY / AGENTUR / AGENCE – STUDIO:

542–546 Lubalin Peckolick Assoc. Inc.
547, 548 Beck Graphics

PUBLISHER / VERLEGER / EDITEUR:

542–546 International Typeface Corp.
547, 548 Robert J. Allio & Associates

548

203

549–551 Illustrations from a publication for *Xerox* employees. Fig.549 deals with dialogue; Fig.550: ethics; Fig.551: employee benefits. (USA)
552 Cover from an issue of the Bulletin of the Rhode Island School of Design. (USA)
553 Full-colour illustration for an article in *Psychology Today* about patients who form their own ideas about illness. (USA)
554 For the cover of The Newsletter of the Adelaide Art Directors Club. Scraper board illustration. (AUS)
555 Cover of *Adweek* referring to the currently "hottest" product: the Walkman. (USA)

**Trade Magazines
House Organs**

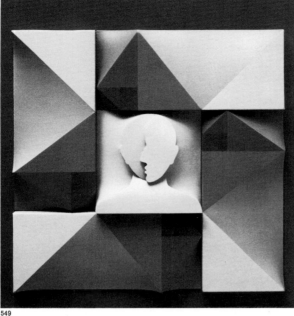

549

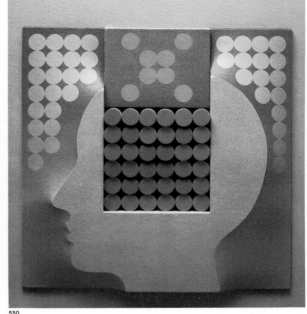

550

551

ARTIST / KÜNSTLER / ARTISTE:

549–551 Stephan Tarantal
553 J. Rafal Olbinski
554 Robert Marshall
555 Robert & David Grossman

DESIGNER / GESTALTER:

549–551 Ford, Byrne & Associates
552 Malcolm Grear Designers
553 Carveth Cramer
554 Robert Marshall

ART DIRECTOR:

553 Carveth Cramer
554 Barrie Tucker
555 Walter Bernard

AGENCY / AGENTUR / AGENCE:

549–551 Ford, Byrne & Associates
554 Barrie Tucker Design

PUBLISHER / VERLEGER / EDITEUR:

549–551 Xerox Corp.
552 Rhode Island School of Design
553 Ziff-Davis Publishing
554 The Adelaide Art Directors Club
555 Adweek

552

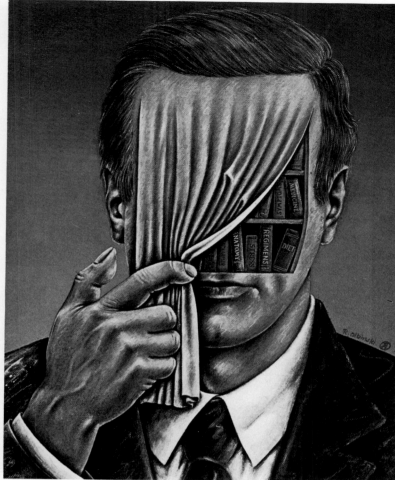

553

554

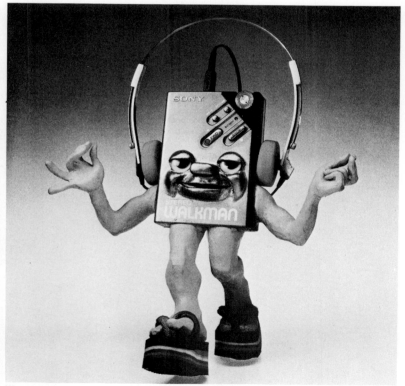

555

549–551 Illustrationen aus einer Publikation für die Angestellten von *Xerox*. Abb. 549 gehört zum Kapitel «Dialog», Abb. 550: «Berufsethos», und Abb. 551: «Fürsorge- und Sozialeinrichtungen». (USA)
552 Umschlag des zweimonatlich erscheinenden Bulletins der Rhode Island School of Design. (USA)
553 Mehrfarbige Illustration für einen Artikel über Patienten, die ihre eigenen Theorien über Krankheiten entwickeln, statt den Anordnungen der Ärzte zu folgen. Aus *Psychology Today*. (USA)
554 Für den Umschlag des Mitteilungsblattes des Art Directors Club, Adelaide. Schabkarton. (AUS)
555 Umschlag von *Adweek*. Hier einer der gegenwärtigen Verkaufsschlager, ein «Walkman». (USA)

549–551 Illustrations pour une publication destinée au personnel de *Xerox*: 549 pour le chapitre «Dialogue», 550 «Ethique professionnelle», 551 «Prévoyance sociale». (USA)
552 Couverture du Bulletin bimestriel de la Rhode Island School of Design. (USA)
553 Illustration polychrome d'un article sur les malades qui ont leur théorie personnelle de la maladie au lieu de s'en remettre aux médecins. Extrait de *Psychology Today*. (USA)
554 Pour la couverture du bulletin de l'Art Directors Club d'Adélaïde. Scraper board. (AUS)
555 Couverture d'*Adweek*, avec un produit-vedette, le walkman. (USA)

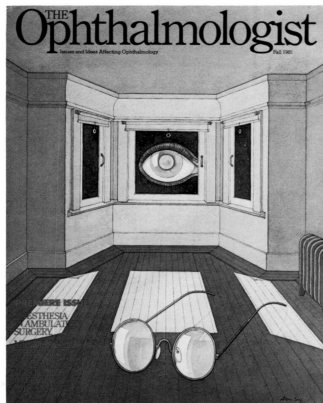

556

557

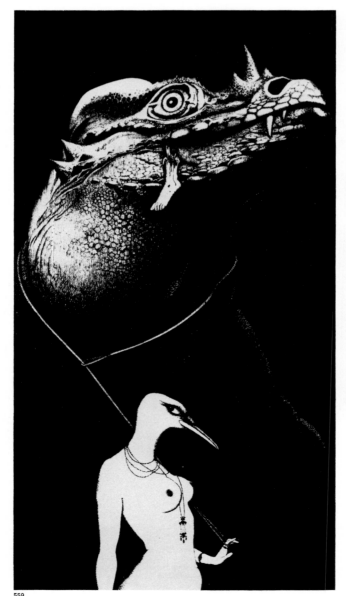

559

560

**Trade Magazines
Annual Reports**

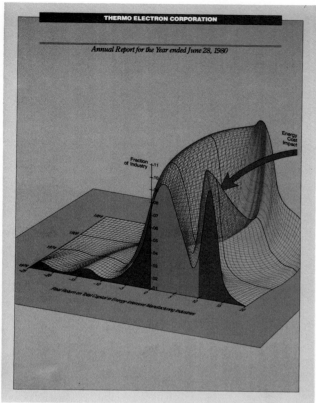

558

561

562

556 Cover of *The Ophthalmologist*. In soft colours, lettering in green. (USA)
557 A special magazine report announced on an *Adweek* cover. Shades of blue and red. (USA)
558 Cover of a *Thermo Electron Corporation* annual report, with a presentation of energy cost impact. (USA)
559 For an article in *Psychologie* about man's reaction to feminism. (FRA)
560 Full-colour cover of an issue of *Adweek*, announcing a special newspaper report. (USA)
561 Cover in full colour for the annual report of Geers Gross Ltd., an advertising agency operating in London and New York. (USA)
562, 563 Detail of the cover illustration and double spread from the annual report of *Foremost-McKesson*, a diversified company. The subjects: Strategy for the 80s and choice of options in pursuing their goal. (USA)

556 Umschlag einer Fachzeitschrift für Augenärzte. In zarten Farbtönen, Schrift grün. (USA)
557 «Turbulente Zeiten im Zeitschriftengeschäft.» Umschlag von *Adweek*, Blau- und Rottöne. (USA)
558 Umschlag eines Jahresberichtes mit Darstellung der Auswirkungen gestiegener Energiekosten. (USA)
559 Für einen Artikel in *Psychologie* über die Reaktionen des Mannes auf den Feminismus. (FRA)
560 Mehrfarbiger Umschlag einer Ausgabe von *Adweek*, die der Lage der Zeitungen gewidmet ist. (USA)
561 Für den Jahresbericht einer Werbeagentur, die in New York und in London zu Hause ist. (USA)
562, 563 Detail der Umschlagillustration und Doppelseite aus dem Jahresbericht eines diversifizierten Unternehmens. Themen: Zielsetzung für die 80er Jahre und Vielzahl der Möglichkeiten. (USA)

556 Couverture d'une revue ophtalmologique. Tons délicats, texte en vert. (USA)
557 Couverture d'*Adweek*, tons rouges et bleus. «La tempête souffle dans la presse.» (USA)
558 Couverture d'un rapport annuel. Le graphique montre le coût croissant de l'énergie. (USA)
559 Pour un article de *Psychologie* détaillant les réactions masculines au féminisme. (FRA)
560 Couverture polychrome d'un numéro d'*Adweek* sur la situation prévalant dans la presse. (USA)
561 Pour le rapport annuel d'une agence de publicité implantée à New York et à Londres. (USA)
562, 563 Détail de l'illustration de couverture et double page du rapport annuel d'un groupe diversifié. Sujets: les objectifs des années 80; une gamme élargie d'options pour les réaliser. (USA)

563

564

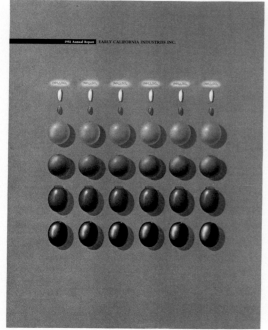

566

567

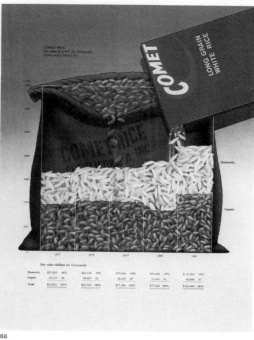

568

ARTIST / KÜNSTLER / ARTISTE:

564, 565 Fred Otnes/Frank Moscotti
566–568 Warren Hile

DESIGNER / GESTALTER / MAQUETTISTE:

564, 565 Alan Peckolick
566–568 Dennis Tani/Playa del Rey

ART DIRECTOR / DIRECTEUR ARTISTIQUE:

564, 565 Alan Peckolick
565–568 Robert Miles Runyan

AGENCY / AGENTUR / AGENCE – STUDIO:

564, 565 Lubalin Peckolick Assoc. Inc./
Corpcom Services, Inc.
566–568 Robert Miles Runyan & Associates

564, 565 Cover in original size of an information brochure about modern Mexico and a view of the opened folder which also contains the annual report and financial report of the *Grupo Industrial Alfa*. The folder is also used to induce foreign investors into Mexico and to interest them in *Alfa*'s diversified concern, and thus serves as a sales kit. (MEX)
566–568 Cover and two spreads with full-colour illustrations from the annual report of *Early California Industries* which, amongst other things, deals with olive, wine and rice products. (USA)

564, 565 Umschlag einer Informationsbroschüre über das moderne Mexiko und Ansicht der geöffneten Faltmappe, welche ausserdem den Jahres- und den Finanzbericht der *Grupo Industrial Alfa*, ein diversifiziertes Industrieunternehmen, enthält. Die Mappe ist auch für ausländische Investoren bestimmt, die von den Möglichkeiten in Mexiko überzeugt werden sollen. (MEX)
566–568 Umschlag und zwei Seiten mit mehrfarbigen Illustrationen aus einem Jahresbericht der *Early California Industries*, die unter anderem mit Produkten aus Oliven, Wein und Reis handeln. (USA)

564, 565 Couverture d'une brochure d'information sur le Mexique moderne et vue du classeur ouvert qui contient en outre les rapports annuel et financier du *Grupo Industrial Alfa*, un conglomérat mexicain. Le classeur est aussi destiné à séduire les investisseurs potentiels à l'étranger. (MEX)
566–568 Couverture et deux pages, illustrées en polychromie, d'un rapport annuel d'*Early California Industries*, un groupe spécialisé entre autres dans la commercialisation de produits contenant des olives, du vin et du riz. (USA)

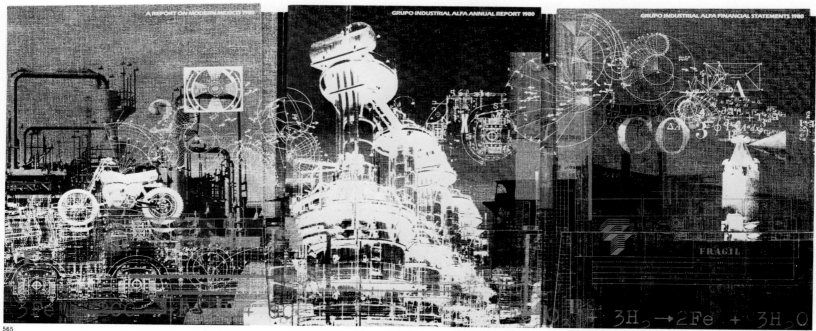

565

572

569 Cover of the *1982 Penrose International Review of the Graphic Arts*, containing an important chapter devoted to typography. Bright red number and pale yellow lettering on a dark blue ground. (GBR)
570 Full-colour dust-jacket of a book on love and suspense entitled "The Roaming Painter". (SWI)
571 Cover illustration for *An Overdose of Death* by Agatha Christie. In full colour. (USA)
572 Cover of a book about pressure groups in Britain between 1720 and 1970 issued by *Penguin Books*. (GBR)
573 Cover illustration for a book of cats' tales issued by Hamlyn Paperbacks. (GBR)
574 For an industrial guide of the companies in the Liège region. (BEL)
575 Cover of a children's book with amusing stories, published by *Nord-Süd*. (GER)
576–578 Cover in blue shades and spreads from a book on biochemistry. (GER)

569

570

571

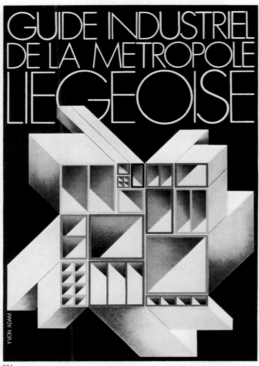

573

574

575

576

PUBLISHER / VERLEGER / EDITEUR:

569 Northwood Publications Ltd.
570 Ex Libris Verlag AG
571 Dell Books
572 Penguin Books
573 Hamlyn Books Ltd.
574 Ville de Liège
575 Nord-Süd Verlag
576–578 Springer-Verlag

569 Umschlag des «Penrose-Jahrbuches der Graphik 1982», in dem ein bedeutendes Kapitel der Typographie gewidmet ist. Leuchtend rote Zahl und blassgelbe Schrift auf dunkelblauem Grund. (GBR)
570 Mehrfarbiger Schutzumschlag eines Buches, in dem es um die Liebe zwischen einem Bauernmädchen und einem Wandermaler und um einen Mord geht. (SWI)
571 Umschlagillustration für einen Kriminalroman von Agatha Christie. In Farbe. (USA)
572 Umschlag für ein Buch über Meinungsmacher in England zwischen 1720 und 1970. (GBR)
573 Umschlagillustration für ein Taschenbuch mit Katzengeschichten. (GBR)
574 Für einen Führer der Industrien und Unternehmen in der Gegend von Lüttich. (BEL)
575 Umschlag eines Kinderbuches mit einer lustigen Geschichte. Vom *Nord-Süd Verlag*. (SWI)
576–578 Umschlag in Blautönen und Doppelseiten eines Lehrbuches über Biochemie. (GER)

569 Couverture de «l'annuel Penrose de l'art graphique 1982», qui renferme un chapitre important consacré à la typographie. Chiffre rouge vif et texte jaune pâle sur fond bleu foncé. (GBR)
570 Jaquette polychrome d'un roman qui met en scène une jeune paysanne éprise d'un peintre itinérant et mêlée à un meurtre. (SWI)
571 Illustration de couverture pour un roman policier d'Agatha Christie. En couleur. (USA)
572 Couverture d'un livre consacré aux groupes de pression en Grande-Bretagne, entre 1720 et 1970, paru aux éditions *Penguin Books*. (GBR)
573 Illustration de couverture pour un recueil d'histoires de chats en édition de poche. (GBR)
574 Pour un guide industriel de Liège et environs. (BEL)
575 Couverture d'un livre d'enfants amusant paru aux *Editions Nord-Süd*. (SWI)
576–578 Couverture aux tons bleutés et doubles pages d'un manuel de biochimie. (GER)

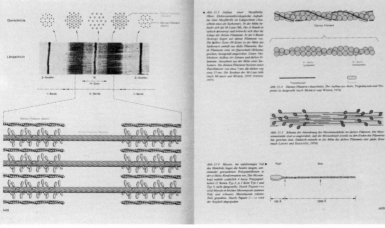

577

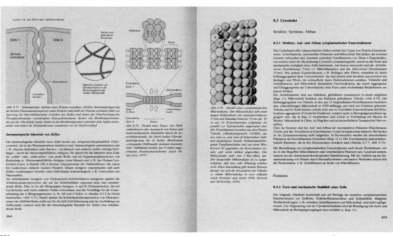

578

579

580

ARTIST / KÜNSTLER / ARTISTE:

579, 580 Mark Hess/Richard Hess/Michele Wilcox
581, 582 Pat Andrea
583 Tadanori Yokoo
586 Rokuro Taniuchi

DESIGNER / GESTALTER / MAQUETTISTE:

579, 580 Richard Hess
581, 582 Hans Versteeg
583, 586 Tadanori Yokoo
584 Celia Wilson
585 Donna Schenkel

579, 580 Cover with an embossed illustration and a double spread from an annual report of the paper manufacturer *Champion International.* (USA)
581, 582 Full-colour cover and a double spread in black and white from an annual report of the Prince Bernhard Foundation. Each year a different artist is commissioned to do the illustrations. (NLD)
583 Cover in actual size for a book from the *Shinshosha* publishing company. (JPN)
584 Dust-jacket for a book about copyright, issued by the *MIT Press.* (USA)
585 Cover of a specialised book published by the *MIT Press.* Red, green and white. (USA)
586 Complete cover with flaps for a Japanese book. (JPN)

579, 580 Umschlag mit geprägter Illustration für einen Jahresbericht des Papierherstellers *Champion International* und eine Doppelseite daraus. (USA)
581, 582 Umschlag in Farbe und Doppelseite in Schwarzweiss aus einem Jahresbericht der Prinz-Bernhard-Stiftung. Jedes Jahr wird ein anderer Künstler mit den Illustrationen beauftragt. (NLD)
583 Umschlag in Originalgrösse für ein Buch des *Shinshosha*-Verlags. (JPN)
584 Schutzumschlag für ein Sachbuch der technischen Hochschule MIT zum Thema «Copyright». (USA)
585 Umschlag für ein Sachbuch der MIT, eine technische Hochschule. Rot, grün und weiss. (USA)
586 Vollständiger Umschlag mit Klappen für ein japanisches Buch. (JPN)

Annual Reports

581

582

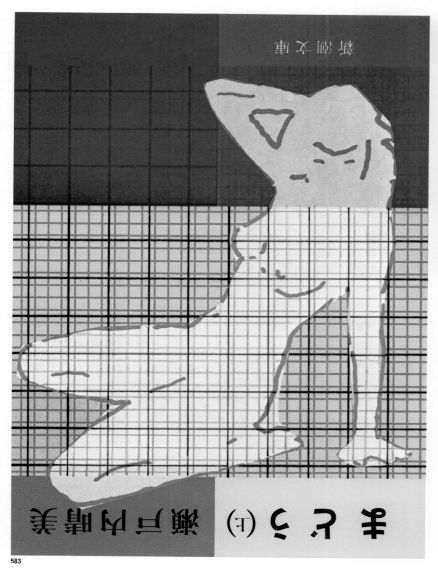

583

The Copyright Book
A Practical Guide

William S. Strong

584

Modeling and
Measuring
Natural Resource
Substitution

edited by
Ernst R. Berndt
and
Barry C. Field

585

ART DIRECTOR / DIRECTEUR ARTISTIQUE:

579, 580 Richard Hess
583, 586 Tadanori Yokoo

AGENCY / AGENTUR / AGENCE – STUDIO:

581, 582 Dots Design
584, 585 MIT Press Design Dept.

PUBLISHER / VERLEGER / EDITEUR:

583 Shinchosha
584, 585 MIT Press
586 Shinshindo, Ltd.

579, 580 Couverture (illustration gaufrée) et double page d'un rapport annuel du papetier *Champion International*. (USA)
581, 582 Couverture couleur et double page noir et blanc d'un rapport annuel de la Fondation du Prince Bernard. Chaque année, un artiste différent s'en voit confier l'illustration. (NLD)
583 Couverture au format original pour un livre publié aux Editions *Shinshosha*. (JPN)
584 Jaquette d'un manuel des droits d'auteur publié par les Editions du M.I.T. (USA)
585 Couverture pour un manuel de l'Université technique M.I.T. Rouge, vert, blanc. (USA)
586 Couverture complète avec ses rabats illustrés, pour un ouvrage japonais. (JPN)

Book Covers

586

587

588

587, 588 Illustration und vollständiger Umschlag für ein Buch von Douglas C. Jones. (USA)
589–591 Doppelseiten und Umschlag eines Buches über «Kultur und Technologie im italienischen Möbel 1950–1980» anlässlich einer Ausstellung im kölnischen Stadtmuseum. (ITA)
592 Mehrfarbiger Umschlag für ein Kinderbuch des *Patmos*-Verlags. Wie häufig bei Kinderbüchern, handelt es sich um eine Co-Produktion mit verschiedenen Ländern. (GER)
593 Illustration für den Umschlag eines Taschenbuches mit dem Titel «Kindergarten». (GBR)
594 Illustration für den Schutzumschlag eines Buches aus der Reihe *Märchen der Welt*, hier *Märchen aus Tibet*, erschienen bei *Ex Libris*. (SWI)

587, 588 Illustration and complete cover of a novel by Douglas C. Jones. (USA)
589–591 Double spreads and cover of a book entitled "Culture and Technology in Italian Furniture 1950–1980" issued on the occasion of an exhibition in the Cologne municipal museum. (ITA)
592 Full-colour cover of a book about Francis of Assisi published by the *Patmos* company. This children's book is a co-production appearing in various countries. (GER)
593 Illustration for the cover of a novel by Peter Rushforth, published by *Avon Books*. (GBR)
594 Illustration for the dust-jacket of a book in the series "The World's Fairy-Tales", published by the *Ex Libris* company. This volume is entitled "Fairy-Tales from Tibet". (SWI)

587, 588 Illustration et couverture complète d'un roman de Douglas C. Jones. (USA)
589–591 Doubles pages et couverture du livre «La Culture et la Technologie dans les meubles italiens 1950–1980» publié à l'occasion d'une exposition au Stadtmuseum de Cologne. (ITA)
592 Couverture polychrome pour un livre d'enfants des Editions *Patmos*. Comme c'est souvent le cas avec les livres d'enfants, il s'agit d'une coproduction multinationale. (GER)
593 Illustration pour la couverture d'un poche intitulé «Jardin d'enfants». (GBR)
594 Illustration pour la jaquette d'un recueil de «Contes du Tibet», publié dans la collection «Contes du monde entier» d' *Ex Libris*. (SWI)

589

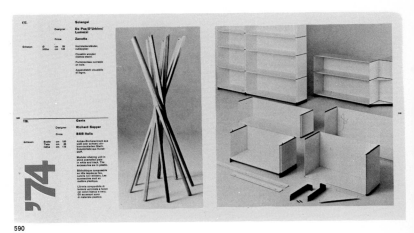

590

592

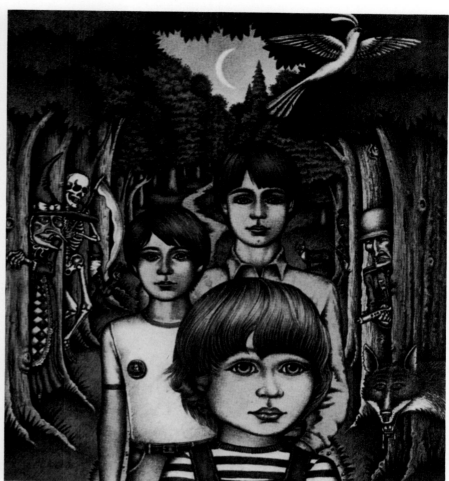

593

ARTIST / KÜNSTLER / ARTISTE:

587, 588 Wendell Minor
592 Antonella Bolliger-Savelli
593 Ken Laidlaw
594 Oskar Weiss

DESIGNER / GESTALTER / MAQUETTISTE:

587, 588 Wendell Minor
589–591 Bruno Monguzzi
592 Antonella Bolliger-Savelli

ART DIRECTOR / DIRECTEUR ARTISTIQUE:

587, 588 Bob Reed
589–591 Roberto Sambonet/Paola Pacca/
Bruno Monguzzi
592 Antonella Bolliger-Savelli
593 Barbara Bertoli
594 Oswald Dubacher

AGENCY / AGENTUR / AGENCE – STUDIO:

589–591 Roberto Sambonet

PUBLISHER / VERLEGER / EDITEUR:

587, 588 Holt, Rinehart, Winston
589–591 ICE Istituto Nazionale
per il Commercio Estero
592 Patmos Verlag
593 Avon Books
594 Ex Libris Verlag AG

591

594

595

596

597

595, 598 Illustration and complete cover for *Venus (Parco View 8)*, a book about the air-brush illustrations of the Japanese Pater Sato between the years 1975 and 1980. (JPN)
596 Cover of a Maigret paperback by the well-known author Georges Simenon. (USA)
597 Woodcut for the cover of a paperback about a myth retold by C. S. Lewis. (USA)
599 Cover of a publication about Armenian classic music. (ITA)

595, 598 Illustration und vollständiger Umschlag für *Venus (Parco View 8)*, ein Buch über Spritztechnik-Illustrationen des Japaners Pater Sato zwischen 1975 und 1980. (JPN)
596 Umschlag eines Maigret-Taschenbuchs von Georges Simenon. (USA)
597 Holzschnitt für den Umschlag eines Taschenbuches mit einer modernisierten Sage. (USA)
599 Umschlag einer Publikation über armenische klassische Musik. (ITA)

595, 598 Illustration et couverture complète de *Venus (Parco View 8)*, un ouvrage consacré aux illustrations à l'aérographe du japonais Pater Sato de 1975 à 1980. (JPN)
596 Couverture d'un Maigret de poche par Georges Simenon. (USA)
597 Gravure sur bois pour la couverture d'un poche: un mythe ancien mis au goût du jour. (USA)
599 Couverture d'une publication consacrée à la musique classique arménienne. (ITA)

Book Covers

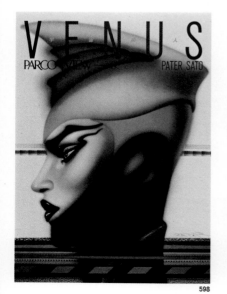

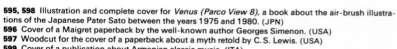

598

ARTIST / KÜNSTLER / ARTISTE:

595, 598 Pater Sato
596, 597 Bascove

DESIGNER / GESTALTER:

599 Herman Vahramian

ART DIRECTOR:

596, 597 Harris Lewine
599 Herman Vahramian

PUBLISHER / VERLEGER:

595, 598 Parco Co. Ltd.
596, 597 Harcourt Brace
 Jovanovich
599 I/COM

599

600

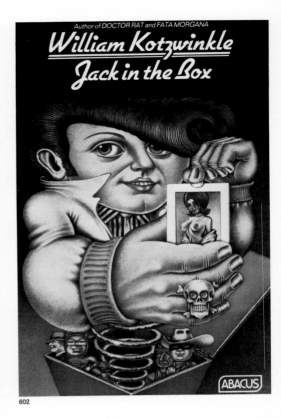

602

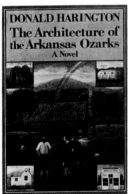

601

ARTIST / KÜNSTLER / ARTISTE:

600, 601 Wendell Minor
602 Ken Laidlaw
603 Winslow Pinney Pels
604 Javad Alizadeh
605 John Alcorn
606 Etienne Delessert
607 Braldt Bralds

DESIGNER / GESTALTER / MAQUETTISTE:

600, 601 Wendell Minor
603 Louise Fili
604 Javad Alizadeh
605 John Alcorn
606 Etienne Delessert
607 Braldt Bralds

ART DIRECTOR / DIRECTEUR ARTISTIQUE:

600, 601 Char Lappan
602 Liz Laczynska
603 Louise Fili
604 Javad Alizadeh
605, 607 Lidia Ferrara
606 Anne van der Essen

AGENCY / AGENTUR / AGENCE – STUDIO:

603 Pantheon Books
606 Carabosse

PUBLISHER / VERLEGER / EDITEUR:

600, 601 Little, Brown & Co.
602 Sphere Books
603 Pantheon Books
604 ATAIY Publications
605, 607 Alfred A. Knopf, Inc.
606 Gallimard/Tournesol

Book Covers
Buchumschläge
Couvertures de livres

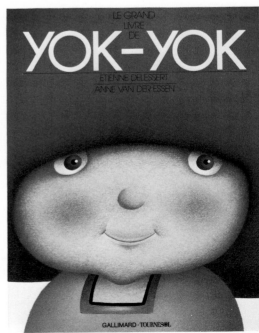

606

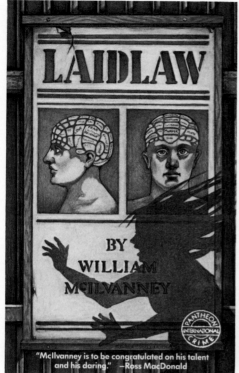

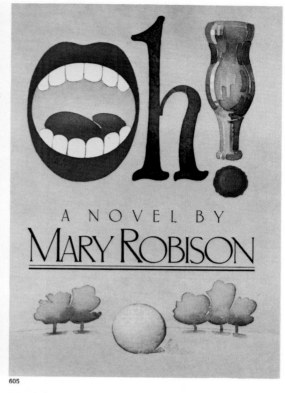

603

604

605

600, 601 Illustration and complete dust-jacket. (USA)
602 Cover for a book, "Jack in the Box", about a young man who lives in the world of comics and supermen. (GBR)
603 Cover illustration for a thriller. (USA)
604 For a book about an Iranian writer. The portrait refers to one of his books, "The Blind Owl". (IRA)
605 Full-colour cover for a book entitled *Oh!* (USA)
606 Cover of a children's book. In warm colours. (FRA)
607 For a book about the Spanish Inquisition in Holland and Belgium entitled *The Sea Beggars*. (USA)

600, 601 Illustration und vollständiger Buchumschlag. (USA)
602 Umschlag für ein Buch über einen jungen Mann, der in der Welt der Comics und Supermänner lebt. (GBR)
603 Umschlagillustration für einen Kriminalroman. (USA)
604 Für ein Buch über einen iranischen Schriftsteller. Sein Porträt ist eine Anspielung auf eines seiner Bücher. (IRA)
605 Mehrfarbiger Umschlag für ein Buch mit dem Titel *Oh!* (USA)
606 Umschlag für ein Kinderbuch. In warmen Farben. (FRA)
607 Für ein Buch über die spanische Inquisition in Holland und Belgien: «Die Geusen des Meeres». (USA)

600, 601 Illustration et couverture de livre complète. (USA)
602 Couverture d'un roman dont le jeune héros vit dans un univers de bandes dessinées et de supermen. (GBR)
603 Illustration de couverture pour un roman policier. (USA)
604 Pour un livre consacré à un écrivain iranien, dont le portrait fait allusion à l'un de ses ouvrages. (IRA)
605 Couverture polychrome d'un livre intitulé *Oh!* (USA)
606 Couverture d'un livre pour enfants. Tons chauds. (FRA)
607 Pour un ouvrage sur l'Inquisition espagnole aux Pays-Bas et en Belgique: «Les Gueux de la mer». (USA)

607

608

ARTIST / KÜNSTLER / ARTISTE:

608 David McKee
609 Tamie Okumura
610 Patrice Ricord
611, 614 Jean-Claude Morchoisne/
Patrice Ricord
612, 613 Jean Mulatier/Patrice Ricord/
Jean-Claude Morchoisne

DESIGNER / GESTALTER / MAQUETTISTE:

608 David McKee
609 Tadanori Yokoo

ART DIRECTOR / DIRECTEUR ARTISTIQUE:

608 David McKee
609 Tadanori Yokoo
610–614 Patrice Ricord

PUBLISHER / VERLEGER / EDITEUR:

608 Anderson Press
609 CBS Sony Shuppan Ltd.
610–614 Dervish International

610

Book Covers

609

611

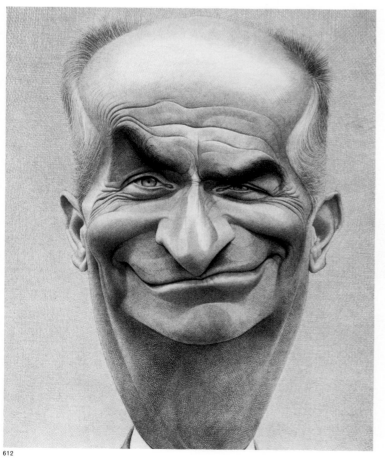

612

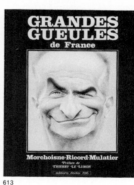

613

614

608 Illustration in actual size for a children's book in the *King Rollo* series. (GBR)
609 Complete cover in full colour for a Japanese book. (JPN)
610 Illustration for the cover of a book with caricatures of the world's superstars. (FRA)
611, 614 Complete full-colour illustration and cover of a book containing caricatures of famous partners, here Adam and Eve. (FRA)
612, 613 The actor Louis de Funès on the cover of a book of caricatures poking fun at famous French people. See also Figs. 610, 611 and 614. (FRA)

608 Illustration in Originalgrösse für ein Kinderbuch aus der Reihe «König Rollo». (GBR)
609 Vollständiger Umschlag in Farbe für ein japanisches Buch. (JPN)
610 Illustration für den Umschlag eines Buches mit Karikaturen der Grossen dieser Welt. (FRA)
611, 614 Vollständige Illustration in Farbe und Umschlag eines Buches mit Karikaturen berühmter Zweiergespanne, hier Adam und Eva. (FRA)
612, 613 Der Schauspieler Louis de Funès auf dem Umschlag eines Buches mit Karikaturen bekannter Grössen in Frankreich. Siehe auch Abb. 610, 611, 614. (FRA)

608 Illustration au format original pour un livre d'enfants, collection «Le Roi Rollo». (GBR)
609 Couverture complète en couleurs pour un livre japonais. (JPN)
610 Illustration de couverture d'un recueil de caricatures des grands de ce monde. (FRA)
611, 614 Illustration couleur complète et couverture d'un recueil de caricatures des couples célèbres de l'Histoire, ici Adam et Eve. (FRA)
612, 613 Le comédien Louis de Funès en couverture d'un recueil de caricatures des personnalités françaises. Cf. les fig. 610, 611, 614. (FRA)

4

Calendars
Trademarks
Letterheads
Record Covers
Packaging

Kalender
Schutzmarken
Briefköpfe
Schallplattenhüllen
Packungen

Calendriers
Marques et emblèmes
En-têtes
Pochettes de disques
Emballages

ARTIST / KÜNSTLER / ARTISTE:
615–619 Flavio Costantini

DESIGNER / GESTALTER / MAQUETTISTE:
615–619 Enzo Mari

ART DIRECTOR / DIRECTEUR ARTISTIQUE:
615–619 Giorgio Soavi

AGENCY / AGENTUR / AGENCE – STUDIO:
615–619 Ufficio Pubblicità Olivetti

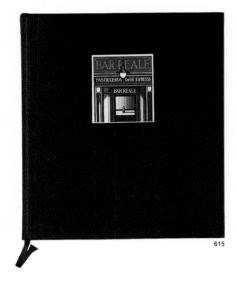

615

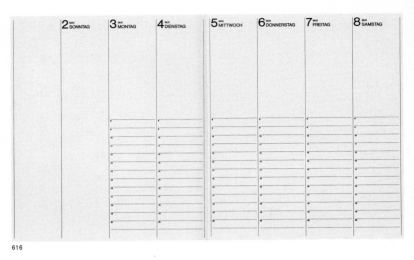

616

615–619 Cover illustration, agenda page, and examples of the full-page illustrations from the 1982 *Olivetti* appointments calender. Each year the illustrations are done by a different artist. Shown here are distemper pictures by the Italian Flavio Costantini. (ITA)

615–619 Umschlagillustration, Agenda-Seite, und Beispiele der ganzseitigen Illustrationen aus dem Terminkalender 1982 von *Olivetti*. Die Illustrationen stammen jedes Jahr von einem anderen Künstler, hier Tempera-Bilder des Italieners Flavio Costantini. (ITA)

615–619 Illustration de couverture, page d'agenda et exemples d'illustrations pleine page du calendrier-planning 1982 d'*Olivetti*. Les illustrations sont réalisées chaque année par un artiste différent, ici à la gouache par l'Italien Flavio Costantini. (ITA)

617

618

FARMACIA

F. Costantini /80

619

Calendars / Kalender / Calendriers

ARTIST / KÜNSTLER / ARTISTE:

620, 621 Tadami Yamada
622, 623 Shindo Yoko
624 Kuwayama Yasaburo
625 Yamashita Hideo
626 Michael Lafortezza
627 John Ireland

ART DIRECTOR / DIRECTEUR ARTISTIQUE:

620, 621 Mogens Sørensen
622–625 Kenzo Nakagawa
627 Gregg Geist

AGENCY / AGENTUR / AGENCE – STUDIO:

620, 621 Bergsøe 1 / Thomas Bergsøe AS
622–625 Bolt & Nuts Studio
627 J. Walter Thompson

620

622

623

620, 621 Complete view and illustration from the wall calendar of the *Scan Dutch* shipping company. Shown here, "The Girl from Mei-Chou", who, according to a Chinese myth, protects sailors and the dwellers by the sea coast, and is accordingly revered. (DEN)
623–625 Interpretations of the months from the Japan Typography Association's calendar. (JPN)
626 Sheet for the month of August from the wall calendar of Herlin Press Inc. Lobsters shed their shells in this month and grow new ones – just like people returning to work after holidays. (USA)
627 Sheet from a calendar with drawings in the style of Heath Robinson, the popular English caricaturist. The subject here is the production and distribution of *Guinness* stout. (GBR)

621

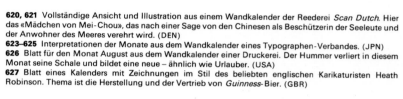

624

625

620, 621 Vollständige Ansicht und Illustration aus einem Wandkalender der Reederei *Scan Dutch*. Hier das «Mädchen von Mei-Chou», das nach einer Sage von den Chinesen als Beschützerin der Seeleute und der Anwohner des Meeres verehrt wird. (DEN)
623–625 Interpretationen der Monate aus dem Wandkalender eines Typographen-Verbandes. (JPN)
626 Blatt für den Monat August aus dem Wandkalender einer Druckerei. Der Hummer verliert in diesem Monat seine Schale und bildet eine neue – ähnlich wie Urlauber. (USA)
627 Blatt eines Kalenders mit Zeichnungen im Stil des beliebten englischen Karikaturisten Heath Robinson. Thema ist die Herstellung und der Vertrieb von *Guinness*-Bier. (GBR)

620, 621 Vue complète et illustration d'un calendrier mural de l'armateur *Scan Dutch*. On voit ici «la jeune fille de Mei-Chou» d'une légende ancienne, adorée par les Chinois comme protectrice des marins et des riverains de la mer. (DEN)
623–625 Interprétation des mois sur le calendrier mural d'une association de typo. (JPN)
626 Feuillet du calendrier mural d'une imprimerie pour le mois d'août. C'est en août que le homard perd sa carapace pour en sécréter une nouvelle, un peu comme les vacanciers. (USA)
627 Feuillet d'un calendrier illustré de dessins dans le style du caricaturiste anglais Heath Robinson, sur le thème de la fabrication et de la distribution des bières *Guinness*. (GBR)

626

627

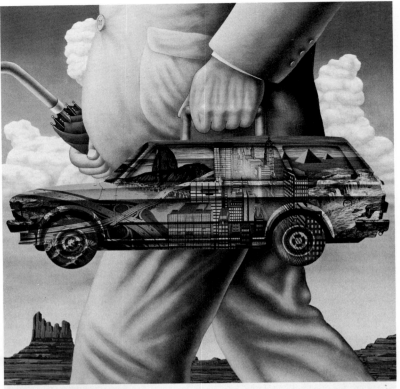

Marzo 1982

Lunedì	Martedì	Mercoledì	Giovedì	Venerdì	Sabato	Domenica	Lunedì	Martedì	Mercoledì	Giovedì	Venerdì	Sabato	Domenica
1	2	3	4	5	6	7	8	9	10	11	12	13	14
15	16	17	18	19	20	21	22	23	24	25	26	27	28
29	30	31											

FIAT

Fantasticamente Fiat - Tiger Tateishi: 127 Panorama

628

Maggio 1982

Lunedì	Martedì	Mercoledì	Giovedì	Venerdì	Sabato	Domenica	Lunedì	Martedì	Mercoledì	Giovedì	Venerdì	Sabato	Domenica
					1	2	3	4	5	6	7	8	9
10	11	12	13	14	15	16	17	18	19	20	21	22	23
24	25	26	27	28	29	30	31						

FIAT

Fantasticamente Fiat - Giovanni Mulazzani: Ritmo 105 TC

629

628, 629, 633 Complete sheets and illustration from a *Fiat* wall calendar. Each month is shown in connection with different *Fiat* models: here "Panorama" in March, "Ritmo" in May and the "Supermirafiori" in July. (ITA)
630–632 Humorous interpretations from a Face Type Ltd. calendar. (GBR)

628, 629, 633 Vollständige Blätter und Illustration aus einem Wandkalender von *Fiat*. Es werden jeweils die verschiedenen *Fiat*-Typen im Zusammenhang mit einem Monat interpretiert; hier «Panorama» im März, «Ritmo» im Mai und «Supermirafiori» im Juli. (ITA)
630–632 Humoristische Interpretationen aus dem Wandkalender einer Schriftsetzerei. (GBR)

628, 629, 633 Feuillets complets et illustration d'un calendrier mural de *Fiat*. Chaque mois est associé à un modèle de voiture déterminé: le mois de mars à la «Panorama», le mois de mai à la «Ritmo», le mois de juillet à la «Supermirafiori.» (ITA)
630–632 Interprétations taquines pour le calendrier mural d'un atelier de composition. (GBR)

630

631

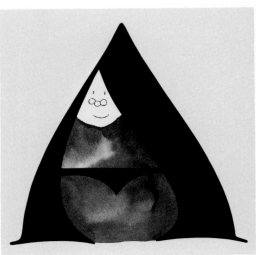

632

ARTIST / KÜNSTLER / ARTISTE:

628 Tiger Tateishi
629 Giovanni Mulazzani
630–632 Michael Foreman
633 Ferenc Pintér

DESIGNER / GESTALTER / MAQUETTISTE:

630–632 John Gorham/Howard Brown

ART DIRECTOR / DIRECTEUR ARTISTIQUE:

630–632 John Gorham

AGENCY / AGENTUR / AGENCE – STUDIO:

628, 629, 633 Fiat Auto/Pubblicità e Immagine

633

634

635

ARTIST / KÜNSTLER / ARTISTE:

634, 635 Karel Havlíček
636 Caiphas Nxumalo
637 Paul Stickland
638 John Ireland
639 Pierre Le-Tan
640 Randall Enos

DESIGNER / GESTALTER / MAQUETTISTE:

634, 635 Hans Ulrich Osterwalder
636 Herbert Wenn
637, 638 Lynn Trickett/Brian Webb/Andrew Thomas
639, 640 Andrew Kner

ART DIRECTOR / DIRECTEUR ARTISTIQUE:

634, 635 Margarethe Hubauer
636 Herbert Wenn
637, 638 Trickett & Webb Ltd.
639, 640 Andrew Kner

AGENCY / AGENTUR / AGENCE – STUDIO:

634, 635 Margarethe Hubauer
637, 638 Trickett & Webb Ltd.

636

637

638

634, 635 Illustration and complete double spread from the 1982 agenda of Margarethe Hubauer, illustrators' agent, who presents some of her clients here. (GER)
636 From a calendar of the International Catholic missionary organization, with linocuts and woodcuts of Biblical subjects fashioned by African artists, here Babylon. (GER)
637, 638 From a calendar which is the result of joint efforts of a design studio, an illustration studio and a printer. The theme is the number three. (GBR)
639, 640 Cover and double spread from a *New York Times* agenda. (USA)

634, 635 Illustration und vollständige Doppelseite aus der Agenda 1982 von Margarethe Hubauer, Agentin für Illustratoren, die hier die von ihr vertretenen Künstler vorstellt. (GER)
636 Aus einem Wandkalender des Internationalen Katholischen Missionswerks mit Linol- und Holzschnitten afrikanischer Künstler zu biblischen Themen; hier «Babylon die Grosse». (GER)
637, 638 Aus einem Wandkalender, der in Zusammenarbeit eines Design-Studios, eines Illustrations-Ateliers und einer Druckerei entstand. Das Thema ist daher die Zahl Drei. (GBR)
639, 640 Umschlag und Doppelseite aus einer Agenda der *New York Times*. (USA)

634, 635 Illustration et double page complète de l'agenda 1982 de Margarethe Hubauer, agence d'illustrateurs, qui présente ainsi les artistes qu'elle représente. (GER)
636 «La Grande Babylone»: pour un calendrier mural de la Mission catholique internationale, illustré de bois et linogravures bibliques par des artistes africains. (GER)
637, 638 Ce calendrier mural est le fruit de la coopération entre un atelier de design, un studio d'illustration et une imprimerie, d'où les variations sur le chiffre trois. (GBR)
639, 640 Couverture et double page d'un agenda du *New York Times*. (USA)

Calendars / Kalender / Calendriers

639

640

641

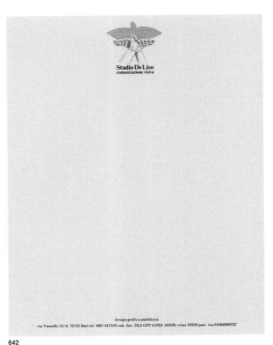

642

643

645

646

647

641 Stationary for a non-profit organization advocating American pre-eminence in space. Blue and white symbol, red letters. (USA)
642 Letterhead of a graphic-design studio, Studio de Liso. Grey with violet shadow on cream-coloured stock. (ITA)
643 For an architect. Black and white with red and green. (GER)
644 Stationery for Otto Kasper, studio for advertising photography. With a cut-out circle. (GER)
645 Letterhead for an import-export firm. Blue and red. (CUB)
646 Stationery for *Music Unlimited*. Brown lettering. (ITA)
647 For the *Follmann* clearing house. Black and white. (GER)
648 Stationery for *Sharpshooter Productions*. Blind embossed logotype with cut-out "O"s. (CAN)
649 Stationery and envelope for Lisney Associates, architects and landscape architects. Cream stock paper, black tree. (GBR)
650 For *The Pep'e Company*. Red logotype. (USA)
651 Stationery with envelope of the small publishing concern *Um die Ecke* (Around the Corner). Red lettering on white. (SWI)

641 Briefbogen einer Vereinigung für amerikanische Überlegenheit im All. Symbol blau und weiss, Schrift rot. (USA)
642 Briefkopf eines Graphik-Design-Studios. Grau mit violettem Schatten auf crèmefarbenen Papier. (ITA)
643 Für einen Architekten. Schwarzweiss mit Rot und Grün. (GER)
644 Briefbogen für Otto Kasper, Studio für Werbefotografie. Mit ausgestanztem Kreis. (GER)
645 Briefkopf für einen Im- und Exporteur. Blau und Rot. (CUB)
646 Briefbogen für *Music Unlimited*. Braune Schrift. (ITA)
647 Für die Abrechnungsstelle *Follmann*. Schwarzweiss. (GER)
648 Briefbogen für *Sharpshooter Productions* (übersetzt: Scharfschützen). Blindgeprägter Schriftzug und ausgestanzte «O»s. (CAN)
649 Briefpapier mit Umschlag für Lisney Assoc., Architekten und Landschaftsplaner. Crèmefarbenes Papier, schwarzer Baum. (GBR)
650 Für *The Pep'e Company*, mit rotem Schriftzug. (USA)
651 Briefbogen mit Umschlag für den Kleinverlag *Um die Ecke*. Rote Schrift auf Weiss. (SWI)

644

648

649

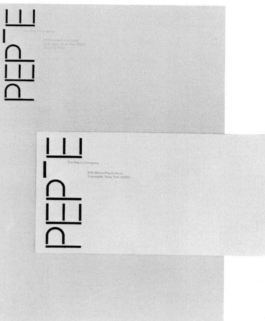

650

651

641 En-tête d'une association pour la suprématie américaine dans l'espace. Symbole bleu, blanc, texte rouge. (USA)
642 En-tête d'un studio d'art publicitaire. Gris, ombre violette sur papier crème. (ITA)
643 Pour un architecte. Noir et blanc, plus rouge et vert. (GER)
644 En-tête pour Otto Kasper, studio de photographie publicitaire. Le cercle est découpé. (GER)
645 En-tête pour une maison d'import-export. Bleu, rouge. (CUB)
646 En-tête pour Music Unlimited. Texte brun. (ITA)
647 Pour le bureau de compensation Follmann. Noir, blanc. (GER)
648 En-tête pour les Sharpshooter Productions (mot qui veut dire Tireurs d'élite). Logo gaufré, O découpés. (CAN)
649 En-tête et enveloppe pour les architectes-paysagistes Lisney Associates. Papier crème, arbre noir. (GBR)
650 Pour la Pep'e Company. Logo rouge. (USA)
651 En-tête et enveloppe pour un petit éditeur, Um die Ecke (Au coin de chez nous). Texte rouge sur blanc. (SWI)

Letterheads
Briefköpfe
En-têtes

DESIGNER / GESTALTER / MAQUETTISTE:

652, 653 Marcello Minale
654 Barrie Tucker/Robert Marshall
655 Ken White/Harold Burch
656 Steven Sieler
657 Roger Cook/Don Shanosky
658 Christian Lang
659, 660 Guido Callews

653

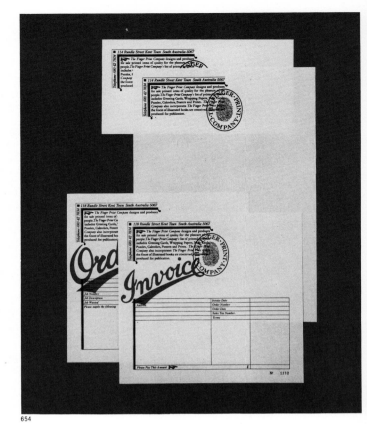

654

652

657

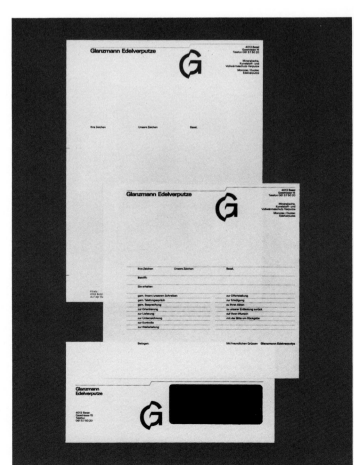

658

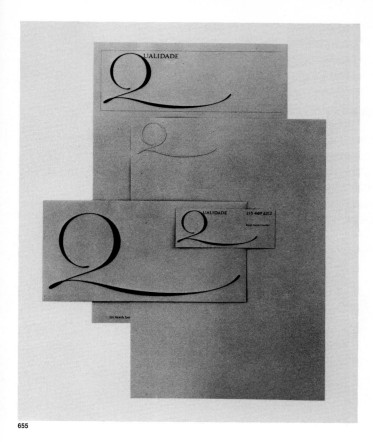

655

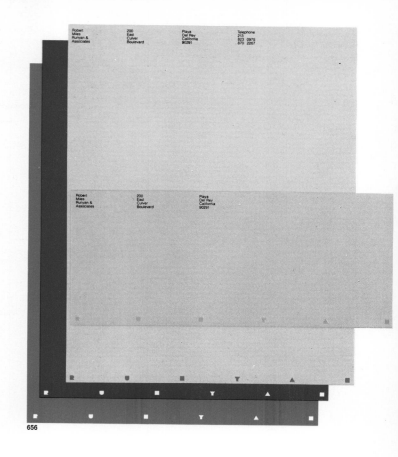

656

ART DIRECTOR / DIRECTEUR ARTISTIQUE:

652, 653 Marcello Minale
654 Barrie Tucker
655 Harold Burch/Ken White
656 Robert Miles Runyan
657 Roger Cook/Don Shanosky
658 Christian Lang
659, 660 Guido Callews

AGENCY / AGENTUR / AGENCE – STUDIO:

652, 653 Minale, Tattersfield & Partners
654 The Finger Print Company
655 Ken White Design Office, Inc.
656 Robert Miles Runyan & Assoc.
657 Cook & Shanosky Assoc.
659, 660 Grafiek Groep

660

659

652, 653 Symbol and stationery of a London furniture company. (GBR)
654 Stationery with envelope, invoice forms and order forms of the *Finger Print Company*; a graphic design studio that above all produces gift wrapping paper, greetings cards and other printed matter. Symbol in blue, marking of forms in red, with black lettering on cream stock. (AUS)
655 Stationery with envelope and visiting card for *Qualide*. The "Q" is embossed except on the envelope. Reddish brown lettering on beige stock. (USA)
656 Stationery with envelope whose interior is yellow, red verso of stationery and green verso of the invoice form. For Robert Miles Runyan & Associates, an advertising agency. (USA)
657 Logotype for a pharmaceutical mail-order company. (USA)
658 Stationery, notepaper and envelope for Glanzmann Edelverputze. Red "G", black lettering on white. (SWI)
659, 660 Envelope and symbol for IVBO (incinerators for the city of Brugge and its environment). (BEL)

652, 653 Signet und Briefpapier für eine Londoner Möbelfirma. (GBR)
654 Briefbogen mit Umschlag, Rechnungs- und Bestellformularen der *Finger Print Company*, ein Graphik-Design-Studio, das vor allem Geschenkpapier, Glückwunsch-karten und andere Drucksachen herstellt. Signet in Blau, Bezeichnung der Formulare in Rot, Schrift schwarz auf crèmefarbenem Papier. (AUS)
655 Briefpapier mit Umschlag und Visitenkarte für *Qualide*. Ausser auf dem Umschlag ist das «Q» geprägt. Schrift rotbraun auf beigefarbenem Papier. (USA)
656 Briefbogen mit Umschlag, dessen Innenseite gelb ist, rote Rückseite des Bogens und grüne Rückseite der Rechnungsformulare. Für Robert Miles Runyan & Associates, eine Werbeagentur. (USA)
657 Schriftzug für ein Versandgeschäft der Pharma-Industrie. (USA)
658 Briefbogen, Kurzbriefformular und Umschlag für Glanzmann Edelverputze. Rotes «G», Schrift schwarz auf Weiss. (SWI)
659, 660 Briefumschlag und Signet für IVBO (Verbrennungsanlagen für die Stadt Brügge und Umgebung). (BEL)

652, 653 Sigle et en-tête pour une maison d'ameublements londonienne. (GBR)
654 En-tête et enveloppe, facture et bulletin de commande de la *Finger Print Company*, un studio publicitaire qui produit surtout du papier-cadeau, des cartes de vœux et autres imprimés. Sigle bleu, caractérisation des formules en rouge, texte noir sur papier crème. (AUS)
655 En-tête, enveloppe et carte de visite pour *Qualide*. Sauf sur l'enveloppe, le «Q» est gaufré. Texte brun rouge sur papier beige. (USA)
656 En-tête, enveloppe jaune à l'intérieur, verso rouge du papier à lettres et verso vert des factures. Pour l'agence de publicité Robert Miles Runyan & Associates. (USA)
657 Logo pour une maison de VPC de produits pharmaceutiques. (USA)
658 En-tête, mémo et enveloppe pour les enduits fins Glanzmann. «G» rouge, texte noir sur blanc. (SWI)
659, 660 Enveloppe et sigle pour la sociète IVBO (incinérateurs pour la ville de Bruges et les environs). (BEL)

Trademarks
Schutzmarken
Marques et emblèmes

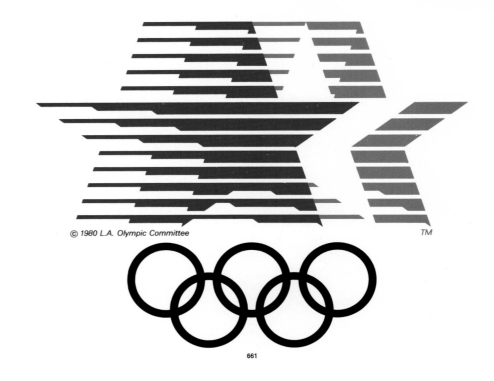

© 1980 L.A. Olympic Committee   TM

661

DESIGNER / GESTALTER / MAQUETTISTE:

661 Robert Miles Runyan & Associates
662, 667 Shigeo Katsuoka
663 John Grant
664 Susan Hochbaum
665 Lilli De Liso
666 Arie J. Geurts
668 Mark & Nevosad
669 Klaus Kuhn
670 Read Viemeister
671 John Emery
672, 673 Ake Lindstrom

665

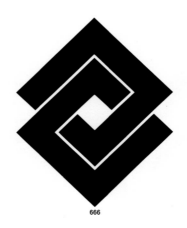

666

667

671

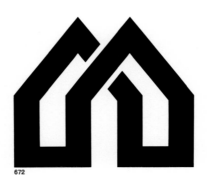

672

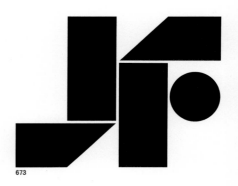

673

ART DIRECTOR / DIRECTEUR ARTISTIQUE:

661 Robert Miles Runyan
663 John Grant
664 Peter Harrison
665 Giuseppe De Liso
666 Arie J. Geurts
668 Mark & Nevosad
669 Klaus Kuhn
670 Read Viemeister
671 John Emery
672, 673 Ake Lindstrom

AGENCY / AGENTUR / AGENCE – STUDIO:

661 Robert Miles Runyan & Associates
663 Grant Design Ltd.
664 Pentagram
665 Studio De Liso
666 Benchmark, Inc.
668 Mark & Nevosad
669 Kuhns Körner
670, 671 Vie Design Studios, Inc.
672, 673 Lindstrom Graphic Design

662

663

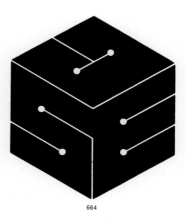

664

668

669

670

661 Emblem of the Los Angeles Olympic Organizing Committee for the 1984 Summer Games. (USA)
662 Symbol for *Itox*, manufacturer of packaging systems. (JPN)
663 Symbol for *Vector*. The arrows stand for the "V", rotating, digging, power and direction. (USA)
664 Symbol of the Science Management Corporation, portraying the interactive nature of its component businesses. (USA)
665 Logotype for VIP, a movie theatre. (ITA)
666 Symbol for the "Bank of the West" in Colombia. (COL)
667 Symbol for *Honda* cars, alluding to their slogan. The streamline stripes suggest the lanes of a highway. (JPN)
668 Logo for *Schneiders*, a vertically organized company that produces and sells textiles and accessories. (AUT)
669 Symbol for gas and oil produced from coal by the Ruhrkohle Öl und Gas GmbH. (GER)
670 Symbol of the Baralin Photography studio. (USA)
671 Symbol for C. B. Boyer, collector and dealer in rare and antiquarian books. (USA)
672 Symbol for manufacturers of coated profile steel sheets. (SWE)
673 Logo for Stockholm's *Jurist Förlag*, law publishers. (SWE)

661 Symbol des olympischen Organisations-Komitees Los Angeles für die Sommerspiele 1984. (USA)
662 Signet für *Itox*, Hersteller von Verpackungssystemen. (JPN)
663 Signet für die Firma *Vector*. Die Pfeile stehen für das «V», Rotieren, Graben, Kraft und Richtung. (USA)
664 Symbol der Science Management Corp. Es soll das Ineinandergreifen der Geschäftsaktivitäten verdeutlicht werden. (USA)
665 Signet für VIP, ein Kino. (ITA)
666 Symbol für die «Bank des Westens» in Kolumbien. (COL)
667 Symbol für *Honda*-Automobile: «Das Auto, das Sie lieben, lieben wir auch.» Die Stromlinien symbolisieren die Strasse. (JPN)
668 Signet für Schneiders, Kaufhaus für Bekleidung und Zubehör mit eigener Fabrikation. (AUT)
669 Symbol für Gas und Öl aus Steinkohle von der Ruhrkohle Öl und Gas GmbH. (GER)
670 Signet für das Photostudio Baralin Photography. (USA)
671 Signet für C. B. Boyer, Händler und Sammler von seltenen und antiquarischen Büchern. (USA)
672 Symbol für einen Hersteller von Stahlverschalungen. (SWE)
673 Signet des *Jurist Förlag* (juristische Publikationen). (SWE)

661 Emblème du comité olympique organisant les jeux d'été de 1984 à Los Angeles. (USA)
662 Sigle pour *Itox*, fabricant de gammes d'emballages. (JPN)
663 Sigle pour *Vector*. Les flèches symbolisent le «V», rotation, forage, force, direction. (USA)
664 Emblème de la Science Management Corporation symbolisant l'interaction des activités du groupe. (USA)
665 Emblème du cinéma VIP. (ITA)
666 Emblème de la *Banco de Occidente* colombienne. (COL)
667 Emblème des voitures *Honda*: «L'auto que vous aimez, nous l'aimons aussi.» Lignes aérodynamiques: symbole de pistes. (JPN)
668 Emblème de *Schneiders*, fabricant et maison de confection et d'accessoires. (AUT)
669 Emblème du gaz et du carburant de houille produits par la Ruhrkohle Öl und Gas Sàrl. (GER)
670 Sigle du studio de photo Baralin Photography. (USA)
671 Sigle pour C. B. Boyer, marchand-collectionneur de livres rares et anciens. (USA)
672 Emblème d'un fabricant de revêtements en acier. (SWE)
673 Sigle du *Jurist Förlag*, publications de droit. (SWE)

PARCO

674

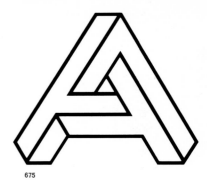

675

679

Trademarks
Schutzmarken
Marques et emblèmes

674 Logo for *Parco*, a chain of shopping centres in Japan. (JPN)
675 Symbol for the *Automata* company. (USA)
676 Symbol of the *Pharmavite* pharmaceutical concern. (USA)
677 Emblem of the American Federation of Arts. (USA)
678 Symbol of Ikola Designs, a graphic design studio. (USA)
679 Symbol for *Union Press*, a Japanese printing firm. (JPN)
680 Symbol for the Banff Centre, a school for advanced studies in the Rocky Mountains. The interwoven peaks symbolize its three divisions. (USA)
681 Human being with tree and leaves as a symbol for the 150th anniversary of the "Garden State" of Victoria in Australia. (AUS)
682 Symbol of an administrative firm for golf-courses and tennis-courts. (ITA)
683 Emblem of the Military Benefit Association. (USA)
684 Symbol for the Métro (Underground) of the city of Lille. (FRA)
685 Environmental protection symbol for the German *Shell*, a prize-winning design from the Alsterdamm art school in Hamburg. (GER)
686 Symbol for a Mexican company. (MEX)
687 Symbol of a small self-promotion booklet, printed on a hand-operated press by the graphic designer Eduard Prüssen. (GER)

674 Schriftzug für *Parco*, Eigner einer Kette von Einkaufszentren in Japan. (JPN)
675 Signet für eine Firma mit dem Namen *Automata*. (USA)
676 Symbol für das pharmazeutische Unternehmen *Pharmavite*. (USA)
677 Signet der American Federation of Arts, ein Kunstverein in den USA. (USA)
678 Signet von Ikola Designs, ein Graphik-Design-Studio. (USA)
679 Signet für *Union Press*, eine japanische Druckerei. (JPN)
680 Symbol für eine Fachschule in den Rocky Mountains. Die Spitzen stehen für die drei Lehrprogramme des Instituts. (USA)
681 «Zusammenwachsen.» Mensch mit Baum und Blättern als Symbol für die 150. Jahresfeier des «Garten-Staates» Victoria in Australien. (AUS)
682 Symbol für eine Verwaltungsgesellschaft von Golf- und Tennisplätzen. (ITA)
683 Symbol einer amerikanischen Fürsorgeorganisation für das Militär. (USA)
684 Symbol für die Métro (Untergrundbahn) der Stadt Lille. (FRA)
685 Umweltschutzsymbol für die *Deutsche Shell*, ein mit dem ersten Preis ausgezeichneter Entwurf der Hamburger Kunstschule Alsterdamm. (GER)
686 Signet eines mexikanischen Unternehmens. (MEX)
687 Symbol für die «Donkey (Esel)-Press», die auf einer Handpresse hergestellte Kundenzeitschrift des Graphikers Eduard Prüssen. (GER)

683

674 Logo pour *Parco*, chaîne de centres commerciaux au Japon. (JPN)
675 Sigle d'une entreprise du nom d'*Automata*. (USA)
676 Emblème de la compagnie pharmaceutique *Pharmavite*. (USA)
677 Emblème de l'American Federation of Arts. (USA)
678 Sigle d'Ikola Designs, un studio d'art publicitaire. (USA)
679 Sigle d'*Union Press*, une imprimerie japonaise. (JPN)
680 Emblème d'une école professionnelle dans les Rocky Mountains. Les sommets symbolisent les trois divisions de cet institut. (USA)
681 «Croître ensemble.» Homme, arbre et feuilles symbolisant les 150 ans de «l'Etat-jardin» de Victoria en Australie. (AUS)
682 Emblème d'une société administrant des links et des courts. (ITA)
683 Emblème d'une organisation de prévoyance de l'armée américaine. (USA)
684 Emblème du métro de Lille. (FRA)
685 Emblème de la protection de l'environnement, premier prix d'un concours organisé par la *Deutsche Shell*, par l'Ecole d'art de Hambourg-Alsterdamm. (GER)
686 Sigle d'une entreprise mexicaine. (MEX)
687 Emblème du «Donkey Press» ou Courrier du Baudet réalisé sur une presse à bras par le graphiste Eduard Prüssen pour ses clients. (GER)

687

676

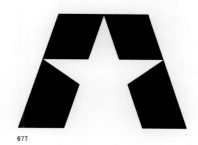

677

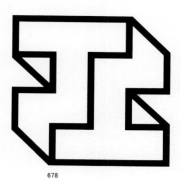

678

680

681

682

684

685

686

DESIGNER / GESTALTER / MAQUETTISTE:

674 Takenobu Igarashi
675 Andrew Radigan
676 Paul Bice/Dennis Tani
677 Philip Gips
678 Gale William Ikola
679 Ivor Kaplin
680 Robert Burns/Yoichi Shimizu
681 Flett Henderson & Arnold
682 Franco Grignani
683 Linda Grimm
684 Marc Piel/Karena Zeheme
685 Bibiana Surma
686 Alfonso Capetillo y Asociados, S. C.
687 Eduard Prüssen

ART DIRECTOR / DIRECTEUR ARTISTIQUE:

674 Takenobu Igarashi
675 Andrew Radigan
676 Robert Miles Runyan
677 Philip Gips/Steve Frankfurt
678 Gale William Ikola
679 Ivor Kaplin
680 Robert Burns
682 Franco Grignani
683 John Waters
684 Marc Piel
685 Gerd F. Setzke

AGENCY / AGENTUR / AGENCE – STUDIO:

674 Takenobu Igarashi Design
676 Robert Miles Runyan & Assoc.
677 Gips & Balkind & Assoc., Inc.
678 Ikola Design
679 Design International
680 Burns, Cooper, Hynes Ltd.
681 Flett Henderson & Arnold
682 Studio Grignani
683 John Waters Associates
684 Enfi Design
685 Kunstschule Alsterdamm, Hamburg
686 Alfonso Capetillo y Asociados, S. C.

688

689

688 Record cover for a production involving various pop-music stars, for the benefit of children. In full colour. (USA)
689 Record cover for recordings of McCoy Tyner, jazz pianist and former member of the John Coltrane Quartet. (USA)
690 Record cover for an album by the Ramones group. (USA)
691 For the dialect radio performance of "Puss in Boots". (SWI)
692 For recordings of music by Jean Michel Jarre, played solely by him on synthesizers. Yellow, red and blue. (FRA)
693 Full-colour cover for a record of film music. (USA)
694 For an album of children's songs. (BRA)
695 Record cover for an album of music by the Toto group. (USA)
696 For an album by the Target group. (USA)
697 Cover of an album of music by the Weatherreport group. (USA)
698 "The gift of life." For an album of popular songs and classical music by famous personalities, for the benefit of cancer research, with the support of the UNESCO. (FRA)

688 Plattenhülle für eine Produktion mit verschiedenen Stars der Pop-Musikszene zugunsten von Kindern. In Farbe. (USA)
689 Schallplattenhülle für Aufnahmen mit McCoy Tyner, Jazz-Pianist und ehemaliges Mitglied des John Coltrane Quartetts. (USA)
690 Plattenhülle für Aufnahmen der Gruppe Ramones. (USA)
691 Für die Dialekt-Hörspielfassung einer Märchenaufführung. (SWI)
692 Für Aufnahmen einer vollständig auf Synthesizern von Jean Michel Jarre hergestellten Musik. Gelb, Rot und Blau. (FRA)
693 Mehrfarbige Hülle für eine Schallplatte mit Filmmusik. (USA)
694 Für eine Schallplatte mit Kinderliedern. (BRA)
695 Plattenhülle für Aufnahmen der Gruppe Toto. (USA)
696 Für eine Platte der Gruppe Target (Zielscheibe). (USA)
697 Hülle für Aufnahmen der Gruppe Weatherreport. (USA)
698 Für eine Schallplatte mit Aufnahmen populärer Chansons und klassischer Musik von berühmten Interpreten, zugunsten der Krebsforschung, mit Unterstützung der UNESCO. (FRA)

688 Pochette de disque pour une production réunissant diverses vedettes pop en faveur des enfants. En couleurs. (USA)
689 Pochette de disque pour des enregistrements de McCoy Tyner, pianiste de jazz, ancien membre du John Coltrane Quartet. (USA)
690 Pochette d'un disque du groupe Ramones. (USA)
691 Pochette de disque: «Le Chat botté» en patois. (SWI)
692 Pochette d'un disque de musique de synthétiseur par Jean-Michel Jarre. Jaune, rouge, bleu. (FRA)
693 Pochette polychrome pour un disque de musique de film. (USA)
694 Pochette d'un disque de chansons enfantines. (BRA)
695 Pochette d'un disque du groupe Toto. (USA)
696 Pochette d'un disque du groupe Target (Cible). (USA)
697 Pochette d'un disque du groupe Weatherreport. (USA)
698 Pochette d'un disque de bienfaisance en faveur de la recherche sur le cancer: chansons populaires et morceaux classiques d'interprètes célèbres; avec le concours de l'UNESCO. (FRA)

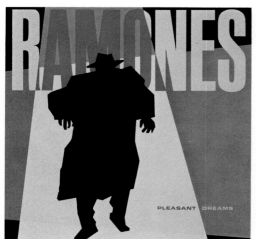

690

691

692

693

ARTIST / KÜNSTLER / ARTISTE:

688 Seymour Chwast
689 James McMullan
690 Carol Bokuniewicz
691 Oskar Weiss
692, 698 Michel Granger
693 David Wilcox
694 Zélio Alves Pinto
695 Tony Lane
696, 697 Lou Beach

694

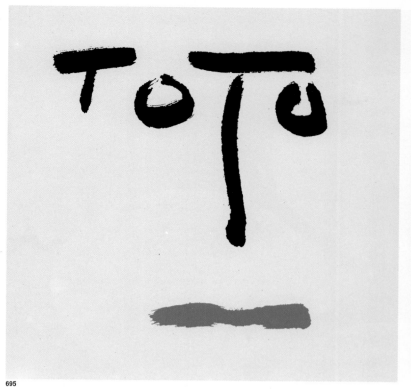

695

696

697

698

DESIGNER / GESTALTER / MAQUETTISTE:

688 Paula Scher
689 Carin Goldberg
690 Carol Bokuniewicz
693 Henrietta Condak
695 Tony Lane

ART DIRECTOR / DIRECTEUR ARTISTIQUE:

688 Paula Scher
689 Carin Goldberg
690 Carol Bokuniewicz/Tibor Kalman/Guy Juke
691 Oswald Dubacher
693 Henrietta Condak
695 Tony Lane
696 Roland Young
697 Nancy Donald

AGENCY / AGENTUR / AGENCE – STUDIO:

688, 689, 693, 695 CBS Records
690 M & Co.

PUBLISHER / VERLEGER / EDITEUR:

688, 689, 693, 695, 697 CBS Records
690 Sire Records Co.
691 Ex Libris
692 Francis Dreyfus Music
694 Continental Discos
696 A & M Records
698 Pathé Marconi/EMI

699

700

ARTIST / KÜNSTLER / ARTISTE:

699 Hans Reisinger/Barend Köhler
701, 702 Hans Reisinger

DESIGNER / GESTALTER / MAQUETTISTE:

699, 701, 702 Joep Bergmans
700 David Broom

ART DIRECTOR / DIRECTEUR ARTISTIQUE:

699, 701, 702 Joep Bergmans
700 David Broom

AGENCY / AGENTUR / AGENCE – STUDIO:

699, 701, 702 Ten Cate Bergmans Design BV
700 Broom & Broom, Inc.

699 Packaging series for curd with fruit. Photograph by Henk van der Heijden, Maarssen. (NLD)
700 Can as packaging for "Tsar Nicholas" caviar. Label and banderol in blue with white and black. (USA)
701, 702 Bottle styling for a vodka and a gin. The photographs were taken in the photo-studio of Henk van der Heijden, Maarssen, Holland (see also Fig. 699). (NLD)

699 Serie von Verpackungen für Speisequark mit Früchten. Aufnahme von Henk van der Heijden, Maarssen. (NLD)
700 Dose als Verpackung für «Zar-Nikolaus»-Kaviar. Etikett und Banderole in Blau mit Weiss und Schwarz. (USA)
701, 702 Flaschengestaltung für einen Wodka und einen Gin. Die Sachaufnahmen stammen von dem Photostudio Henk van der Heijden, Maarssen, Holland (s. auch Abb. 699). (NLD)

699 Gamme d'emballages de fromage blanc aux fruits. Photo Henk van der Heijden, Maarssen. (NLD)
700 Boîte de caviar «Tsar Nicolas». Etiquette et banderole bleue, plus blanc et noir. (USA)
701, 702 Etudes de bouteilles de vodka et de gin. Les photos proviennent du studio de photo Henk van der Heijden, Maarssen, Pays-Bas (cf. la fig. 699). (NLD)

701

702

703

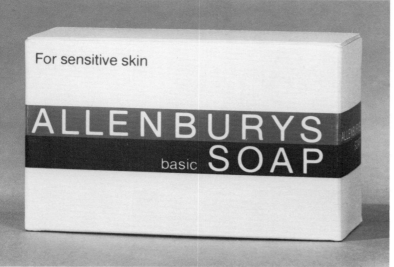

For sensitive skin

ALLENBURYS
basic SOAP

704

703 Gift package with a Japanese noodle soup and seasoning. (JPN)
704 Packaging of a cosmetic soap for sensitive skin. (CAN)
705, 706 Bottle styling and label for an Italian table wine which is bottled in Italy for a London wine-merchant. Fig. 705 shows the utilization of the label on three red wine bottles and two white wine bottles. (GBR)
707 Gift packaging for traditional Japanese pastries made by the Kisoji Shogetsudo Confectionery Company. Warm, dark shades on a beige ground. (JPN)

703 Geschenkpackung mit einer japanischen Nudelsuppe und Gewürz. (JPN)
704 Verpackung einer Kosmetik-Seife für empfindliche Haut. (CAN)
705, 706 Flaschengestaltung und Etikett für einen italienischen Tischwein, der in Italien für einen Londoner Weinhändler abgefüllt wird. Abb. 705 zeigt die Verwendung des Etiketts auf drei Rotwein- und zwei Weissweinflaschen. (GBR)
707 Geschenkverpackung für traditionelles japanisches Gebäck der Kisoji Shogetsudo Confectionery Company. Warme, dunkle Farbtöne auf beigefarbigem Grund. (JPN)

703 Emballage-cadeau pour un potage au vermicelle et des épices japonais. (JPN)
704 Conditionnement d'un savon cosmétique pour peaux sensibles. (CAN)
705, 706 Etudes de bouteilles et étiquette pour un vin de table italien mis en bouteilles en Italie pour un marchand de vins londonien. La fig. 705 montre l'emploi de l'étiquette sur trois bouteilles de vin rouge et deux de vin blanc. (GBR)
707 Emballage-cadeau pour des biscuits japonais traditionnels de la Kisoji Shogetsudo Confectionery Company. Tons sombres chauds sur fond beige. (JPN)

244

Packaging
Packungen
Emballages

DESIGNER / GESTALTER / MAQUETTISTE:

703, 707 Shozo Kakutani
704 Rolf Harder
705, 706 David Hillman

ART DIRECTOR / DIRECTEUR ARTISTIQUE:

703, 707 Shozo Kakutani
704 Rolf Harder
705, 706 David Hillman

AGENCY / AGENTUR / AGENCE – STUDIO:

704 Rolf Harder & Assoc.
705, 706 Pentagram

705

706

707

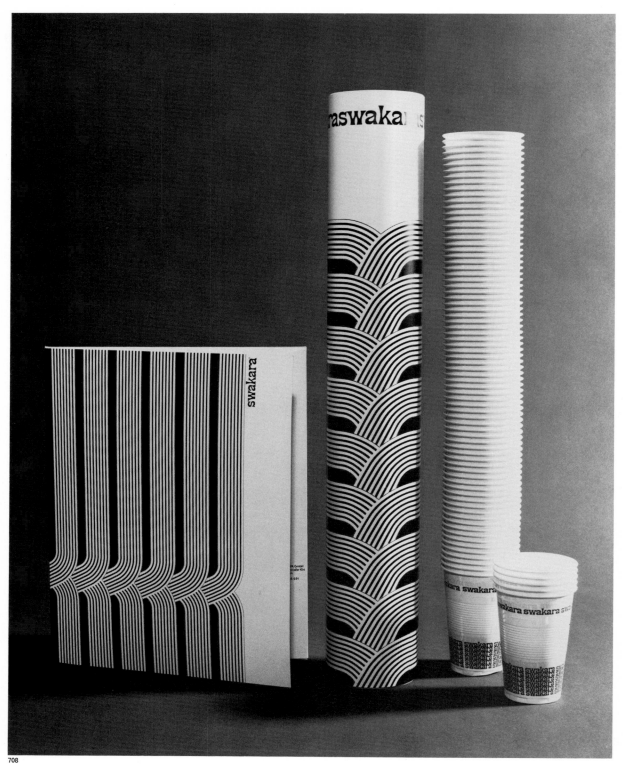

708

ARTIST / KÜNSTLER / ARTISTE:

708 Lutz Reinhardt

DESIGNER / GESTALTER / MAQUETTISTE:

708 Lutz Reinhardt
709 Rolf Harder
710 Bruno Monguzzi
711 Keizo Matsui
712 Ivor Kaplin

ART DIRECTOR / DIRECTEUR ARTISTIQUE:

708 Lutz Reinhardt
709 Rolf Harder/Peter Decker
710 Roberto Sambonet
711 Keizo Matsui
712 Ivor Kaplin

AGENCY / AGENTUR / AGENCE – STUDIO:

708 Swakara Team, J. Walter Thompson GmbH
709 Rolf Harder & Assoc.
710 Sambonet S.p.A.
712 Nippon International Agency

708 Press folder, cups and their packaging. The black-and-white lines run through the whole of the advertising material for *Swarkara* furs, offered to special dealers for various types of presentation. (GER)
709 Packaging for doctors' samples, made by the *Hoffmann-La Roche* pharmaceutical company. (CAN)
710 Packaging series in various green shades for *Sambonet* tableware. (ITA)
711 Point-of-sale display package for *Elene* hairbrushes. (USA)
712 Packaging for an intestinal medicament manufactured by the Teiho Pharmaceutical Co., Ltd. (JPN)

708 Pressemappe, Trinkbecher und deren Verpackung. Die schwarzweisse Lineatur zieht sich durch das gesamte Werbe-material für *Swarkara*-Pelze, das dem Fachhandel für Veranstaltungen angeboten wird. (GER)
709 Packung für Ärzte-Muster des pharmazeutischen Unternehmens *Hoffmann-La Roche*. (CAN)
710 Verpackungslinie in verschiedenen Grüntönen für Geschirr aus dem Hause *Sambonet*. (ITA)
711 Ladentisch-Präsentationspackung für Haarbürsten der Marke *Elene*. (JPN)
712 Verpackung eines Magendarm-Medikaments der Teiho Pharmaceutical Co., Ltd. (JPN)

708 Documentation presse, gobelet et emballage pour ce dernier. Le dessin linéaire caractérise tous les éléments publici-taires des fourrures *Swarkara* mis à la disposition des détaillants. (GER)
709 Emballage d'un échantillon médical de la compagnie pharmaceutique *Hoffmann-La Roche*. (CAN)
710 Gamme d'emballages en verts nuancés pour la vaisselle de la marque *Sambonet*. (ITA)
711 Présentoir P. L. V. pour les brosses à cheveux de la marque *Elene*. (JPN)
712 Emballage d'un médicament gastro-intestinal de la Teiho Pharmaceutical Co., Ltd. (JPN)

709

710

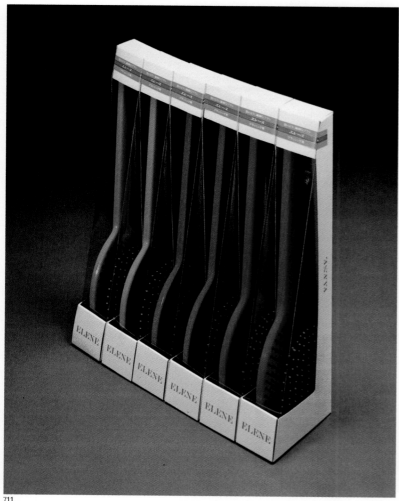

711

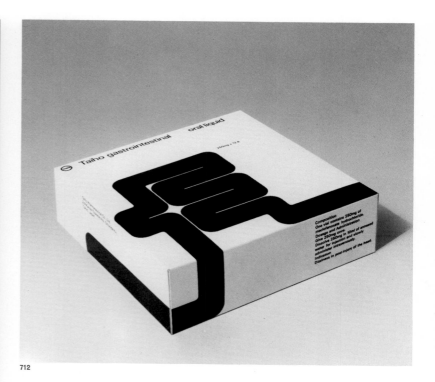

712

713

ARTIST / KÜNSTLER / ARTISTE:

716 Shozo Kakutani
718, 719 Takenobu Igarashi

DESIGNER / GESTALTER / MAQUETTISTE:

713 Nobuhiro Nakazaki
714 John & Yvonne Nowland
715 So Man-yee
716 Shozo Kakutani
717 Helmut Schmid
718, 719 Takenobu Igarashi

ART DIRECTOR / DIRECTEUR ARTISTIQUE:

713 Michio Yamato
714 John Nowland
715 Hon Bing-wah
716 Shozo Kakutani
717 Shota Nishio/Helmut Schmid

AGENCY / AGENTUR / AGENCE – STUDIO:

714 John Nowland Graphic Design
715 Kinggraphic
717 JMS Creative Center
718, 719 Takenobu Igarashi Design

713 Special bottle styling for *Suntory* whisky on the occasion of an exhibition in Kobe. (JPN)
714 Box for six table napkins with flower motifs, available in three varieties. (AUS)
715 Paper carrier-bag for *Bang! Bang!* shoes. (HKG)
716 Carrier-bag for traditional Japanese confectionery from *Kisoji Shogetsudo*. (JPN)
717 Paper bag in grey and white for *Ruban D'Or* confectionery and pastry. (JPN)
718, 719 Carrier-bags in black and white for *Parco*, a chain of shopping centres. (JPN)

714

Packaging
Packungen
Emballages

715

716

717

718

719

713 Spezielle Flaschengestaltung für *Suntory* Whisky anlässlich einer Ausstellung in Kobe. (JPN)
714 Schachtel für sechs Tischservietten mit Blumenmotiven, die in drei Varianten erhältlich sind. (AUS)
715 Papier-Tragtasche für Schuhe der Marke *Bang! Bang!* (HKG)
716 Tragtasche für traditionelles japanisches Gebäck und Konfekt von *Kisoji Shogetsudo*. (JPN)
717 Papiertasche in Grau und Weiss für *Ruban D'Or* Konfekt und Gebäck. (JPN)
718, 719 Tragtaschen in Schwarzweiss von *Parco*, eine japanische Kette von Einkaufszentren. (JPN)

713 Etude d'un flacon spécial pour le whisky *Suntory* pour une exposition à Kôbe, ville portuaire. (JPN)
714 Carton pour six serviettes de table décorées de motifs floraux, en vente en trois variantes. (AUS)
715 Sac en papier pour les chaussures *Bang! Bang!* (HKG)
716 Cabas pour les biscuits et bonbons japonais traditionnels de *Kisoji Shogetsudo*. (JPN)
717 Cabas en papier, gris et blanc, pour les bonbons et biscuits *Ruban d'Or*. (JPN)
718, 719 Cabas noir et blanc de la chaîne japonaise des centres commerciaux *Parco*. (JPN)

720

721

722

723

724

ARTIST / KÜNSTLER / ARTISTE:

723 Robert Marshall
724 Flett Henderson & Arnold

DESIGNER / GESTALTER / MAQUETTISTE:

720 Terry Lesniewicz/Al Navarre
721 Helmut Schmid
722 Satoshi Takahashi/Katsu Kimura
723 Barrie Tucker
724 Flett Henderson & Arnold
725 Barrie Tucker/Robert Marshall
726 Studio CDIP

ART DIRECTOR / DIRECTEUR ARTISTIQUE:

720 Terry Lesniewicz/Al Navarre
721 Shota Nishio/Helmut Schmid
722 Katsu Kimura
723, 725 Barrie Tucker
726 Bernard Rabiller

AGENCY / AGENTUR / AGENCE – STUDIO:

720 Lesniewicz/Navarre
721 JMS Creative Center
722 Packaging Direction Co., Ltd.
723, 725 The Finger Print Company
724 Flett Henderson & Arnold
726 Studio CDIP

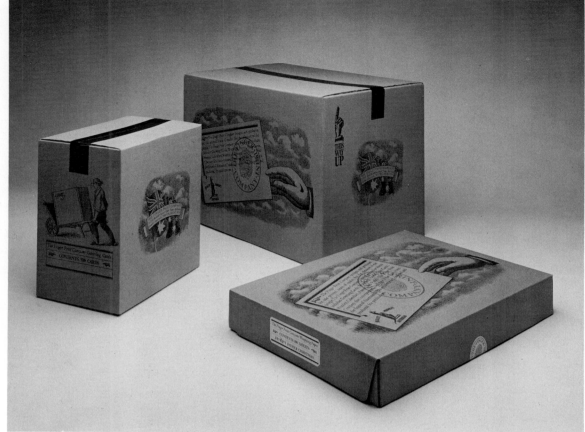

725

720 Computer sales tool for the Roofing Products Operating Division's sales personnel of the *Owens-Corning Fiberglass* company. (USA)
721 *Ruban D'Or* wrapping paper (see Fig. 717) for pastry and confectionery. In grey and white. (JPN)
722 Cardboard box for *Hannae Mori* bed-linen. Trademark in gold on a white lid. (JPN)
723 Gift package for an apron and a set of linen dishcloths, with the pattern and design shown on the outside of the box. (AUS)
724 An aluminium paper-weight with packaging for the launching of the symbol on the occasion of the 150th anniversary of Australia's Victoria State. (AUS)
725 Boxes for the *Finger Print Company*'s wrapping paper and greetings cards. Light brown with black, symbol of the company in blue. (AUS)
726 Packaging for *Gauloise* perfume by *Molyneux*, based on the traditional image of the typical French woman. White with medium blue. (FRA)

720 Verpackung für Demonstrationsmaterial des Aussendienstes von *Owens-Corning Fiberglass*. (USA)
721 Einwickelpapier für *Ruban D'Or* Konfekt und Gebäck (s. Abb. 717). In Grau und Weiss. (JPN)
722 Kartonschachtel für Bettwäsche von *Hannae Mori*. Markenname in Gold auf weissem Deckel. (JPN)
723 Geschenkpackung für eine Schürze und einen Satz Geschirrtücher aus Leinen, mit dem auf der Schachtel gezeigten Design. (AUS)
724 Briefbeschwerer aus Aluminium mit Verpackung für die Lancierung des Symbols zur 150sten Jahresfeier des australischen Staates Victoria. (AUS)
725 Versandschachteln für Einwickelpapier und Grusskarten von der *Finger Print Company*. (AUS)
726 Verpackungslinie für das Parfum *Gauloise* von *Molyneux*, aufgebaut auf dem traditionellen Image der Französin. Weiss mit Mittelblau. (FRA)

720 Emballages pour du matériel de démonstration du service de vente d'*Owens-Corning Fiberglass*. (USA)
721 Papier d'emballage pour les bonbons et biscuits *Ruban d'Or* (cf. fig. 717). Gris, blanc. (JPN)
722 Carton pour le linge de maison de chez *Hannae Mori*. Logo or sur couvercle blanc. (JPN)
723 Emballage-cadeau pour un tablier et un jeu de linges de cuisine en lin au motif indiqué sur le carton. En polychromie. (AUS)
724 Presse-papiers en aluminium, avec son emballage, pour le lancement de l'emblème des 150 ans d'existence de l'Etat australien de Victoria. (AUS)
725 Boîtes d'expédition pour le papier d'emballage et les cartes de vœux de la *Finger Print Company*. (AUS)
726 Gamme de conditionnements pour le parfum *Gauloise* de *Molyneux*, agencée en fonction de l'image traditionnelle de la femme française. Blanc, bleu. (FRA)

726

Paper / Papier: Papierfabrik Biberist–Biber GS SK3, blade coated,
pure white 115 gm² and Biber Offset SK3, pure white, machine-
finished, 140 gm² / Biber GS SK3, hochweiss, satiniert, 115 gm²
und Biber-Offset SK3, hochweiss, maschinenglatt, 140 gm²

Printed by / gedruckt von: J. E. Wolfensberger AG, Zürich (Colour
pages / Farbseiten), Merkur AG, Langenthal (black and white /
schwarzweiss), BDV Basler Druck- und Verlagsanstalt AG, Basel
(dust jacket / Schutzumschlag)

Typesetting / Lichtsatz: Sauerländer AG, Aarau (Univers,
MONOTYPE-Lasercomp)

Cover / Einband: Buchbinderei Schumacher AG, Bern / Schmitten

Glossy lamination / Glanzfoliierung: Durolit AG, Pfäffikon SZ